C000230582

Photograph credits

British Picture Corporation Ltd., 23, 27
hotography, 3
n Archive, London, 24, 25, 26, 27, 28, 30, 31,

wn & Co., 11, 12, 21
Pictorial, 36

Caugh

Associated
Lafayette P
National Fil
32, 34
Norman Bro
The Sunday

Caught in the Act

The Story of My Life

Richard Todd

Hutchinson

London Melbourne Auckland Johannesburg

© Richard Todd 1986

This edition first published in 1986 by Century Hutchinson Ltd
Brookmount House, 62–65 Chandos Place, London WC2N 4NW

Century Hutchinson Publishing Group (Australia) Pty Ltd
PO Box 496, 16–22 Church Street, Hawthorn, Melbourne,
Victoria 3122

Century Hutchinson Group (NZ) Ltd
PO Box 40–086, 32–34 View Road, Glenfield, Auckland 10

Century Hutchinson Group (SA) Pty Ltd
PO Box 337, Bergvlei 2012, South Africa

British Library Cataloguing in Publication Data
Todd, Richard, *1919–*
   Caught in the act: the autobiography of
   Richard Todd.
   1. Todd, Richard, *1919–*   2. Actors –
   Great Britain – Biography
   I. Title
   792′.028′0924   PN2598.T5/

   ISBN 0-09-163800-3

Photoset by Rowland Phototypesetting Ltd
Bury St Edmunds, Suffolk
Printed and bound in Great Britain by
Anchor Brendon Ltd, Tiptree, Essex

To my father and mother who between them made this story possible

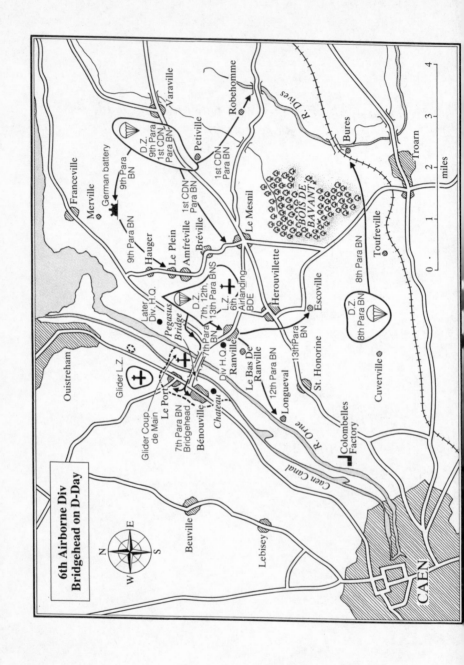

6th Airborne Div Bridgehead on D-Day

1

IN THE BEGINNING

'On 11 June 1919 to Major and Mrs A. W. P. Todd a son, Richard Andrew.'

I did not actually see the announcement at the time, but presumably it followed the traditional format. Certainly, I can vouch for its accuracy.

Mercifully, the details of my birth totally escape my recollection, as I don't suppose I enjoyed the proceedings one bit, and I have to rely on the fragmentary accounts given to me from time to time by my parents, and sundry aunts and uncles. What I chronicle as fact, therefore, may well be pure fiction, or at least wishful thinking.

My headmaster's remarks at the end of my final school report contained this double-edged observation: 'If this boy had the command of facts which his ability to write about them warrants, he would be outstanding.' Captain J. C. Airey, MC, MA, never did spare either the rod or the rules of learning.

But at least I can begin with a fact about which there can be no dispute: I *did* get born.

I understand that I was about a month premature and my Aunts Amy and Dolly, who later became my principal sources of familial information, told me that this was because some dealer had brought a young horse for my mother to look at and she couldn't resist being hoisted into the saddle to try the beast, even at that late stage of my development – whereupon the animal gave her a very testing few minutes of iron-mouthed equine acrobatics, culminating in my mother being rushed off to the nursing home. At least, up to that point she and I were still together, which said a lot for the hardiness of my tiny, frail parent.

I bet that brave little story was not true. My aunts were great admirers of their half-sister and were much given to fanciful and charming tales of their own very Irish invention.

Their version of my early arrival was certainly more attractive than the probable truth – that my mother had eaten something that disagreed with her (or with me) causing me to beat a hasty retreat from my claustrophobic surroundings.

What I do know for sure is that I was born at 89, Lower Baggott Street in Dublin, and that the gynaecologist who was hurriedly called to the nursing home that day was Bethel (Polly) Solomons, Master of the Rotunda, the great Irish teaching centre for obstetrics and gynaecology. He had been one of my father's mentors at Trinity College and was a world authority in his profession.

That I was born in Dublin was due solely to the fact that my mother happened to be there at the time. As a family we had no deeply rooted connection with the grand old city, but my paternal grandparents had a house there in Hatch Street which my father and mother were using after the war pending my father's RAMC posting overseas.

My father's family had lived and farmed in County Tyrone for a very long time and my mother's people hailed from County Kerry. Anybody who knows Ireland will realise that these two areas are separated by a good many miles and nowadays, sadly, by something more divisive than distance. But when I made my entrance Ireland was Ireland and Dublin was the administrative centre of the whole country.

My grandfather Todd was a judge, hence his residence in the capital city, and my mother had stayed there during most of the First World War while my father was on active service with the British Army.

The only previous relation of mine to claim a strong connection with Dublin, so far as I know, was Gore Normanton, Archbishop of Dublin in the early nineteenth century. The nearest I ever came to following his vocation was when I played a Presbyterian minister in a film. Most of my forebears on both sides seem to have been involved either in farming or in the Armed Services.

But the Law, too, seems to have provided gainful employment for a few of the members of my family. These included my grandfather, Judge Todd, my uncle, Justice Fintan Fitz-Patrick, and Viscount Somerton, County Court Judge of Galway nearly a couple of centuries ago.

My parents themselves were not in any way distinguished. I was an only child, which is probably just as well since they were never in a position to pamper one child, let alone a covey of them. This genteel perpetual penury seems to have been a characteristic of all my close relations, and I have maintained the family trait very faithfully, except for a period when I was able to live something like a film star.

My mother was born Marvilla Rose Agar-Daly but, much to her relief, Marvilla (after an ancestral Agar) was habitually shortened to Vill. She was a member of an Anglo-Irish family which had settled in Kerry in 1660, and which, over a period of some two hundred years, had become possessed of a hefty estate of 30,000 acres centred on Ballymalis Castle near Killarney. The head of the Agars had been created Earl of Normanton, and descendants of Alexander Agar, progenitor of the Kerry Agars, had been Hibernianised by marriage to various old Irish families with such euphonious names and titles as The McCarthy More, The Sovereign of Dingle and The O'Donoghue of the Glens.

She was a fragile little person, small-boned, shapely and with a typically Celtic beauty of features and colouring. Her hair was raven-black, her great, sad Irish eyes were forget-me-not blue and her skin had that rose-petal quality that seems to be a product of the Irish climate. I was always immensely proud of my pretty mother, especially as I advanced towards my teens and began to develop a lively appreciation of feminine charms.

I know I was not alone in this, for she had never lacked admirers, and when she married my father, himself an extremely good-looking man, they must have made a devastating pair.

Mother had lived mostly in Northern Ireland, at Brecart, the home of her stepfather, S. R. Hunter, her father having died of pneumonia contracted during a typically damp salmon-fishing expedition somewhere in the west of Ireland. She had gone to school in Sussex, had absolutely no cultural attainments, but did play the piano, albeit rather badly and from a limited repertoire which became more so as her sheets of music got increasingly tattered.

Up to the time of her marriage, her main interests seem

to have centred on dogs and horses. Although she was far
from being one of the tweeds and brogues brigade, she must
have been physically tough, since, for a couple of years after
1914, her contribution to the war effort consisted of breaking
and schooling cavalry remount horses in Phoenix Park. Personally, I approach any strange horse with extreme caution,
and *never* from the rear, and much prefer an elderly, well-
trained and docile nag with no will of its own and a tendency
to breathlessness when urged beyond a canter.

My mother was obviously made of sterner stuff.

Her chief canine enthusiasm was formidable too – bull
terriers. She had contracted this weakness during the few
years she spent in India, where the breed had evidently
established a reputation for being resistant both to heat and
to Indians. We had a collection of these dogs throughout my
childhood and the last one, Bruiser, was with her when she
died.

This, then, was my mother: pretty, headstrong, gay and
hardy, but still totally feminine.

My father, Andrew William Palethorpe Todd, was a complex man. I was always scared stiff by him, even in my teens
and after. I don't think it was entirely his fault: my dithering
feebleness in our relationship was such that even when in
later life we were on comparatively pally terms, I would still
suddenly get all tongue-tied, or giggle shrilly at some faintly
amusing remark of his, and then swallow my drink the wrong
way and come up gasping. He had a knack of nearly always
disparaging anything I did. Once, after having watched me
playing rugger at school, he observed that while I had done
well to score a try, I had merely carried the ball over the line
when somebody else had set up the movement. If I got a
knock he would most probably tell me it was because I had
funked a tackle and hadn't gone in hard enough.

I find it dreadfully hard to be objective about my father
or about his influence over my early life. Certainly it was
very difficult to please him or gain his admiration in anything
I did. To this day my memories of him are confused and full
of contradictions. I was in awe of him mentally and physically
and regarded him almost with hero-worship. But I didn't like
him very much. I was immensely proud of some of his

qualities and achievements, but I detested, even as a child, the selfish and cruel side of him, which was displayed only to my mother and me at infrequent but devastating intervals. I don't think he liked himself very much.

However, he was immensely popular and well-liked by his friends. I have heard it said that he could charm the birds out of the trees. And probably this was the reason for his worst faults: everything had come to him so easily that he had rarely bothered to use his intrinsic abilities to any useful purpose. In his younger days and during the early years of his marriage to my mother his way of living had been gay, feckless, robust and totally carefree. It subsequently became dissolute, fuddled and sour. And that is when I was growing up and knew him best.

But there were other sides to his nature, and other aspects of our relationship, which were happier. He had a lovely, whimsical sense of humour that never dropped far below the surface and perhaps, if his life had had some sense of direction, he could have been an ideal husband and father. Just as I tried too hard to please him, I suspect that he both wanted too much for me and expected too much from me. Just as my mother worshipped him, with all his shortcomings, so he, I believe, adored her and hated himself for failing to be all that he would have liked to be for her sake. Theirs was a tempestuous life together.

As a little boy and then as an adolescent, I floundered along with them, never quite sure whether the next moment would bring something to laugh or cry about.

Once, when I was about eleven, a puny little runt just home from school, I told my father about one particular boy who had bullied me. I told him this not as a complaint but simply as a piece of schoolboy news I thought might interest him. Far from showing any sympathy, my father was furious with me and snorted that I was a bloody little coward, because only cowards let themselves be bullied by anybody. I was no son of his . . . Shaking with injured pride and tearful sense of injustice, I rushed out of the room, and up to my bedroom. There, resolved to show him I was no coward, I plotted how I should restore his respect for me. My decision made, I stalked downstairs shaking and sweaty (but bravely,

I thought), marched into his study where he was sitting reading, and thumped him on the cheek with my fist. I then stood back in a fighting attitude and squeaked, 'I'll show you if I'm a coward. I'll fight *you*!'

My father gave me one of his baleful glares, carefully laid aside his book, stood up, suddenly whipped me round with my hands behind my back, gripped my wrists and carried me up to my room, where he hurled me onto my bed. Then he said, very slowly and distinctly, 'Only a coward hits a man who is sitting down. Remember that.'

The funny thing was, he hadn't sounded at all cross. But here was just one more incident when I simply hadn't got things right.

My father, born in 1890, had been brought up in a severely Victorian atmosphere. The judge, his father, was apparently an extremely strict and rather pompous man, and my grand-mother was typical of her day – totally subservient to her husband, as she had been to her stern old father, and not daring to spoil openly her beloved son – a limitation for which she compensated after the judge's death in 1921. Perhaps this restrictive background accounted for some of my father's behaviour in his adult years: his own roistering escape from parental fetters whilst at the same time expecting from me a level of obedience modelled on his own ex-perience.

So there we were, father and son, both wanting desperately to get to know each other, yet never quite finding a common language. We did finally achieve a bond of affection and respect, but that was only a few months before my father's death, when our new-found warmth had to combat separa-tion by the chill North Atlantic. In fact it was not until they were gone that I fully realised how much I had loved and needed both my parents.

My branch of the Todd clan had been settled in County Tyrone for centuries and by the 1800s they had become fairly prosperous land-owning farmers, county gentry, solid, respectable, but by no means distinguished. Like so many of their kind in Ireland and Scotland they lived simple, unsophisticated lives. They provided their share of JPs and volunteers for the North Irish Horse in times of emergency, and generally did nothing to bring shame on a family which claimed to have come over to Ireland with Robert Bruce in the early fourteenth century.

I believe it was my great-great-grandfather who built the scutch mill that still stood and operated in the grounds of Fyfin, our home, when I was last there in 1942. This mill threshed and separated the linen strands from the flax for the region, and was the precursor of the local linen industry which became a major contributor to Northern Ireland's economy. In the garden of Fyfin there are still the remains of the original earth-floored home, little more than a cottage, where my great-grandfather was born and lived until the present larger, but still modest, house was built, around 1840.

I have not been to Fyfin for many years, and never knew it well. I only know that there was no room for my father in the family vault – my grandmother was the last Todd to be buried there. And perhaps some of my own enjoyment of life stems from the certainty that I shall never have to share a shelf with a row of glowering ancestral cadavers in that now-sealed vault in its bleak and gloomy churchyard near Fyfin.

At the time of my birth my father was already a well-known and popular figure in Ireland. He was, for one thing, a remarkable athlete. He had been Victor Ludorum at Shrewsbury School and for a while held the English Schools high-jump and sprint records. At the same time he was a promising oarsman, and stroked the school eight.

On entering Trinity College, Dublin, to study for a medical degree, he lost no time in stroking the Trinity College boat at Henley, and, even more importantly, became the full-back in the Trinity College Rugby Football fifteen. Since Shrewsbury was a soccer playing school, his conversion to rugger must have been very rapid.

He crowned his rugger career by becoming a full international and was the Irish full-back for a couple of seasons until the outbreak of the First World War, playing with the great Dicky Lloyd, amongst others. In addition to all this, he was a fine horseman, reputedly one of the best game shots in Ireland, and the Irish high-board diving champion (although, like me, a rotten swimmer). He was also a scratch golfer, and later played for the All-India polo team during his army service.

No wonder my father was a hero-figure to me in my schooldays. It is not surprising, either, that he was so lionised in a country where sport, especially in horsey and rugger circles, is followed with such fanaticism.

That, then, was my father's heyday.

By the outbreak of the 1914–1918 War he had qualified as a doctor, but he rushed to join a cavalry regiment, to which he was commissioned. However, when the Royal Army Medical Corps was formed, and it was realised that he was in fact a doctor, he was transferred to the RAMC. I don't think he ever regretted this, though perhaps he missed the dashing image of a cavalry officer! Certainly he became a good and practised surgeon during the war and won the Military Cross for, according to the citation, 'displaying great gallantry under the heavy artillery fire to which the advanced collecting post had been subjected during the day. He attended to large numbers of wounded men with devotion . . . and also went forward under heavy fire with stretcher bearers to the aid posts, and by his able leadership did valuable service in evacuating the wounded.'

Sadly, his extensive collection of cups, medals, rugger caps and other trophies, which he had given to me, together with his Military Cross and his sword, were lost early in 1940 when all my possessions and keepsakes were stored in a furniture repository which was destroyed in a bombing raid. I lost literally everything that day, including furniture and pictures that I had been given, all my school mementoes and records, books of family photographs, bundles of letters, and all the little treasures that a youngster tends to collect. Even my birth certificate was gone, but I obtained a copy years later, so at least I know that I was born officially and respectably . . .

Thus it was in the beginning.

2

BEGINNER'S CALL

As I have said, I made my entrance onto the world stage on 11 June 1919, weighing only five pounds, the result, presumably, of my premature arrival and my mother's small stature. Apparently I too was small but perfectly formed, a proportion which I struggle nowadays to maintain. My prep school nickname, Sausage, was no reflection on my shape but rather derived from my third name Palethorpe, which happened to be also the name of a popular brand of British banger. I was christened Richard Andrew Palethorpe Todd.

When I was six months old I sailed with my mother to India to join my father who was posted there in the British Army. We lived in Secunderabad, and in summertime went up to a hill station called Kotagiri (my spelling is phonetic, as I cannot find the place on a map).

I gather my parents enjoyed their few years in India, as did most of our countrymen during the halcyon days of the British raj. But, although social awareness was probably confined to dinner parties, chota pegs, the Military Club and very well-staffed officers' quarters, and not much attention was paid to conditions prevailing in the country itself, I have heard that my father did do a lot of good work for the local civilian population, and in fact began to specialise in the study of the diseases of women and children.

My own gadding about was necessarily rather more restricted, no doubt, but I expect I quite enjoyed the attentions of a devoted ayah and my first equestrian excursions, strapped into a basket chair, a device which was prevalent in those days and which at least kept me firmly glued to my pony. The only record I have of those early years consists of a few sepia-coloured snaps and two photographs of my mother, one of her mounted on a retired polo pony of my father's, looking very dashing in her long white riding habit and a white pith helmet, the other driving the same pony in the shafts of a smart little buggy attended by her Indian groom.

We left India before I was three. My father had decided to retire from army service and come home because of his own persistent malaria symptoms and my mother's health not being suited to the Indian climate. It was a decision that caused frequent bickering and recriminations between them in later years, but at least for once I was not blamed for it.

It was somewhere during 1922 that my first conscious memories were recorded for I have a hazy picture of being carried down a ship's gangway and of seeing a sea of upturned faces and waving hands clustered on the dockside. Then came my first really happy, jolly memory – my tummy binder.

I should explain that it had evidently been decided that I should at all times be well wrapped up against the rigours of an Irish winter. When I went outside, I was cocooned in a fur coat, woolly hat and leather gaiters and beneath all the usual undergarments were yards of fine creamy light flannel wound round and round my middle and secured with safety pins. This was my tummy binder. The fun came in the evening when I was being prepared for bath, in a metal slipper bath in my bedroom at Brecart.

My two adoring spinster aunts, Amy and Dolly, were always in attendance on these occasions, having seemingly completely taken over my management and care from my mother, who was not considered to be well enough to do much more than sit around looking wan and winsome during those first few months at home.

At the great moment of unveiling before being lowered into the tin bath, I would take up position at one side of the room, while Amy or Dolly unpinned the binder and held on to the free end. Then I would spin as fast as my stubby legs would allow me towards the other side, unwinding the length of flannel as I tottered round and round till I was free of the binder and collapsed, slightly giddy and very giggly. I can still actually *feel* the laughter and the happiness of those evenings in my bedroom.

Just as my memory began to record events and people at that time, so I also became aware of places, and my grandfather's house, Brecart, is the first house in my recollection. The dear, shabby old place was for many years home to me.

Brecart, near the village of Toome in County Antrim, Northern Ireland, was a long, low L-shaped house of Queen Anne origin, the outside rendered over and painted a greyish-white. The L-shape was formed into a square by the extension of courtyard buildings; stables, carriage houses, tack-rooms, laundry, buttery and a couple of other smaller compartments used latterly as hen-houses or kennels. The courtyard was paved with stone sets and cobbles, and had a well in one corner which supplied our drinking water, whilst all the washing water was pumped up daily from the river, so that my bath water always looked pretty dirty before I even got into it.

Backing onto the courtyard was another square, stone-flagged yard enclosed by the home farm buildings; cow byres, cart sheds, bull pens and corn or hay barns. Occasionally a minor crisis would occur as dairy cows got into the garden and grazed contentedly amongst the roses or the vegetables, or when calves scampered about on the tennis court, noisily chased by our motley pack of dogs. Such scenes were nothing out of the ordinary in Ireland, but would never have been tolerated in the better-ordered routine of an English country house.

On the eastern side of the house, opposite the courtyard was the garden, which our solitary gardener, Pat Scullion, who also doubled up as milkman for the house cows, struggled to maintain as a fairly tidy collection of rose beds in a daisy-clad lawn. The east wall of the house was partially obscured by espalier-trained fruit trees, mostly plum and pear, and one of my childhood delights was to lean out of bedroom windows and guzzle quantities of plums, my favourites.

The level site for the house and farm buildings had been carved out of the side of the Hill of Brecart like a wedge of cheese from an Edam. The high end of the wedge was buttressed by a large crenellated wall running behind the rose garden and buildings. This castellated effect was given to other wall-tops round the house and its battlemented cover gave me lovely loop-holes behind which I could crouch and fire catapults and home-made bows and arrows – and, later, my Diana airgun – in all directions when I played solitary games of cowboys and Indians, the unfortunate Rhode Island Red hens being the attacking Redskins. This amusing activity – the birds merely jumped and scuttled away when hit – came to a tearful end when my grandfather bit into a small lead pellet whilst devouring a boiling fowl.

Beyond the drive in front of the house, a bank and steps led down to an area of lawn which included a tennis court. The grass was laboriously kept in some sort of order by the use of push-mowers and shears, the worst of the bumps being levelled out from time to time by a horse-drawn roller, and the family and visitors swiped away happily on the court for hours.

The grounds around the house were wooded, mostly with ash, oak and lime, with various ornamental trees. My favourite was an old weeping willow which formed a perfect canopy and enclosed my den. This was furnished with chairs, tables and a cupboard, all fashioned from orange boxes, the cupboard being the secret repository for all manner of forbidden possessions such as penknives, catapults and evil-smelling jam-jars full of worms for my fishing. I regarded this for years as my summer residence and shared it with Snooks and Major, the two alsatian-red setter cross dogs who were my constant companions and who added their own particular aroma to the stench of rotting worms.

My greatest moments of self-importance were on the occasions when tea was brought to me in the den and I scoffed in silence, attended only by the two drooling dogs who always knew that they would come in for a share of the cake.

Beyond the lawn lay a strip of grassland bordered by a beautiful line of fifty lime trees, and then the river. The river was at this point fairly wide, and appeared to my young eyes to form almost a lagoon. The fishing thereabouts was quite good, with plenty of trout and the odd salmon, but gradually pike and perch (grunts, as we called them) took control. Even so, it was here that I first handled a rod, casting worms and later progressing to the fly, usually tied for me by my grandfather or by Pat Scullion, the gardener-cum-milker and self-appointed water bailiff.

Pat was a tall, bony, lugubrious character, deafeningly silent with most people but quite chatty with me. He had never been to school and had learned to read and write only during his early years at Brecart, encouraged by my grandfather, yet his leisure pastime was doing crossword puzzles.

Pat Scullion was my first grown-up friend and there seemed to me nothing he could not do, except drive a car. Machinery terrified him.

However, weather, good or bad, meant nothing to him. In the heaviest rain or wildest winter storm he simply carried on, draped in sacks, drenched but as much a part of the outdoor scene as a tree. A heavy raincoat that my grandfather had given him was reserved for special occasions, such as churchgoing or when we had visitors.

Unwittingly, he gave me my first instruction in the facts of life. I could not have been more than about four years old when I wandered into the farmyard just in time to see Daisy, one of the cows, being assaulted, as I thought, by Norman, the Friesian bull, while Pat stood enigmatically by her head with a firm grip on both her ears. I watched the proceedings in consternation, amazed that Pat, normally so kind with animals, should aid and abet this unprovoked attack by the usually placid bull. He did not seem to mind in the least that I had witnessed the encounter, and when I asked him afterwards what had happened, he explained tersely and truthfully.

Armed with this new knowledge, I mulled the whole thing over in my inquisitive child's mind and determined to find out more about the phenomenon of reproduction and relations between the sexes, and not only in the bovine world. I had become aware of the reason for certain physical differences between males and females, but, at the time, judging by what I had seen of Norman's performance, there did not seem to be any great pleasure connected with this form of activity.

Another of Pat Scullion's multitudinous duties was to

groom and care for our two remaining horses, Molly and Billy, both greys.

About the time of the Norman and Daisy incident I had been yearning for a pony of my own, so, with my new-found knowledge of animal reproduction, I asked my grandfather if Molly and Billy could make one for me. Grandpa must have been rather startled by my suggestion and he evidently jibbed at explaining to me why Billy, a gelding, would not be able to oblige me or Molly, for I never understood why I didn't get the smart little grey pony I had in mind. I was given a donkey instead.

To the left of the house the River Bann swept right-handed in a bend up-river to Toome, the nearest village, about a mile away. Toome was in those days quite a thriving little place, and had long been a key spot in the troubled history of Northern Ireland. It was here that the road and rail bridge crossed the River Bann, carrying the main communicating links between Belfast and Derry, and it was an obvious place for ambush or road-block. Probably for strategic reasons, the police barracks of the RUC had been built beside the Toome end of the road bridge.

The economy of the village was based principally on fisheries, even though it was inland. The reason for this was Lough Neagh and its plentiful population of eels, together with other varieties of fresh-water fish.

The village itself straggled around the main Belfast to Derry road and its junction with the Ballymena road. Apart from the O'Neill Arms Hotel, there was only a handful of commercial premises, which included Doyle's Garage and McMillans Stores. The latter sold almost everything, including hardware, food, seed-corn, lamp oil, haberdashery and certain basic personal hygiene requirements. Anything not in stock could usually be ordered.

My favourite visiting place was, of course, the newsagents and sweetshop, known always to us as 'the Scotch Lassies', and run by two quite young sisters. Then there was a cobbler's shop and a little tailor's workroom. All of us at Brecart had our shoes beautifully hand-made and our tweed clothes cut and put together locally at a fraction of the cost of such things in any city.

Between the main road and the quay was the village square, lined on one side by a row of warehouses and stores and on the other by railway sidings. One of the stores was rented by Billy McQuade as an antiques emporium – in other words, a junk shop.

Billy was a great local character, always jovial and much in demand for his fine Irish tenor voice at wakes and ceilidhs. An accomplished and good-humoured poacher, he rattled around the countryside with his pony and cart collecting his stock and singing his heart out.

My two aunts were frequent visitors at his littered little mart, where all sorts of interesting finds were to be made, not least one that Aunt Amy had reason to remember. One day she noticed a charming china chamber pot perched high on a shelf and clambered up over other bric-à-brac to reach it. Triumphantly she retrieved it and jumped down again, only to find that it had been recently and copiously utilised. Whether Billy had acquired it lock, stock and barrel or whether he or one of his customers had been caught short was never established. Aunt Amy did not buy it.

The village square was the site for any visiting entertainment such as the circus or menagerie, and it was here, when I was about five years old, that I had my first experience of theatre. It was a gala occasion, advertised for weeks beforehand with colourful hand-painted posters plastered on every available wall space: a touring fit-up theatre company was coming to present its mammoth all-star productions of 'Maria and the Red Barn' and 'Sweeney Todd, the Demon Barber of Fleet Street'. Of course, my aunts booked seats in advance at McMillans for themselves and me.

When the great day came I was put to bed in the afternoon to rest, and in the evening we were driven up to Toome by Morrison, my grandfather's farm foreman. And there was the theatre: a rather bedraggled tent, smaller than the circus marquee, and with none of the noisy razzamatazz associated with the latter. But as I had no idea what play-acting was all about, I don't suppose my interest was dampened.

We filed in along with the rest of the carriage (and bicycle) trade and showed our tickets to a scarey-looking man whom I later recognised as the villain in 'Maria'. We sat on a wooden form in the front row, and oil lamps did little to brighten the gloom.

The aunts enjoined me to be patient and provided me with a bar of chocolate, so I settled down quite happily and lost some of my apprehension.

Finally, the great moment arrived. Our ticket-collector, now attired in some very strange costume, came forward to announce that we were about to behold a stupendous double-bill in which he would star, supported by his wife and splendid company, with musical accompaniment from the piano (which stood a few feet from us). Silence fell on the house.

Then came ear-splitting chords from the piano, the curtains were opened, and the show began.

Needless to say, I was terrified, sitting there in the front row. I had jumped, startled at the crashing piano, but this was nothing to what followed . . .

The raging tones of the villain, the tearful plight of the heroine, and the thunder and lightning effects were all too much for me. I dissolved into weeping that was in no way quelled by furious glances from the leading actor. My aunts did their best to comfort me, and eventually I must have got the hang of things, because we stayed until the end of the one-act 'Maria'. Perhaps my confidence had been restored by the rest of the audience, who reacted noisily to the spectacle, booing the villain, cheering the hero, crying with the heroine and applauding every exit. A good time was had by all, including the players who responded magnificently, and the pianist who thumped out frequent and deafening accompaniments.

Having survived 'Maria and the Red Barn' my aunts spared me further disturbance and we went home. I never did see 'Sweeney Todd', nor do I believe that the experience had whetted my appetite for a theatrical career.

Although Toome introduced me to the sophistications of urban life, it is downriver from Brecart that my heart and my mind will always turn, to Lough Beg, the Little Lough. As I grew old and strong enough to be able to handle a boat by myself I passed many rapturous and secret days here throughout my childhood and in my teenage years. I was the pirate or the explorer and Lough Beg was my ocean, its islands my new-found territories, its wildlife my discoveries. No boy ever had a more private and special sea.

Lough Beg glimmered less than a mile north of Brecart and the Bann flowed wide and tranquil past the house to fill its irregular basin, bisecting a featureless pastoral landscape dotted with small farms and scrubby patches of gorse and bogland.

To the east of the river the remains of my grandfather's land stopped short of the lough, although he still retained the shooting rights over a thousand or so acres on this side. Perhaps 'rights' is not the accurate word – we simply shot there because nobody else did.

The Bann swept past Salmon Rock and then opened out to form the lough, some two miles long and a mile or so wide, the centrepiece of what must be one of the loveliest, loneliest areas in Northern Ireland, wild and mysterious, immensely pretty and dangerously capricious. A sudden north wind and driving rain hurled in from the Atlantic can in moments transform the jewelled waters and sylvan shoreline into something very bleak and forbidding, very frightening. At the first menacing sign of a swift change in the weather, when the ripples swelled to sharp-edged wavelets and the woods took on a dark hue, I would row for all I was worth back to the river, or unfurl the sail in the dinghy and beat my way home when the wind actually got up.

There are a number of tiny islands in the lough, all rocky, some merely little hunched piles of boulders with scrubby thorn bushes maintaining a precarious root-hold between the stones, and some more extensive, boasting a few trees and patches of grass. The latter I was always advised to avoid, especially if there was any sign of woodsmoke and a boat tied up. Visitors were not particularly welcome at the site of an active poteen still!

From the point where the River Bann enters Lough Beg at the south to its exit in the north, a double line of stout wooden posts, each frequently crested by a perching cormorant or gull, marked the navigation channel for the bigger craft such as lighters laden with corn, Bann clay or coal.

Outside this channel the lough was full of traps for the cruising boatmen.

Fortunately, I don't remember ever having fallen into the water, which was just as well because I was never much of a swimmer. My aquatic baptism had been conducted by my grandfather when I was about five by the simple process of tying a rope around my middle and throwing me into the river from a bank. At least I learned how to make some sort of spluttering progress on the surface of the water and later refined my movements to an inelegant sidestroke. But I was never able to co-ordinate my breathing and my physical action, and even today, although I can manage quite a showy crawl, provided that I don't try to breathe, I still have to revert to the old sidestroke if I am to survive for any length of time in water.

After many hours spent alone on Lough Beg I eventually became quite a skilled navigator, and was even allowed to pilot the motorboat when we were driving duck over the butts long before I was given a shotgun for my own use. Some of the best hours I ever spent with my father as a child were those when I handled the boat, cruising about in the evening while he shot for the pot. Here was one point where our respect was mutual: he felt quite secure with me at the tiller, while I marvelled at his splendid marksmanship. I think we were quite proud of each other on those occasions.

Whilst my boating forays took me to every part of that lough, there was one place which became my special domain for years and years and where my imagination led me to all manner of adventures from the day I first grounded the boat on its scented shore: Church Island.

Church Island has a place in Irish history and a very special place in my memory, haunting and steeped in legend. The waterline is rocky and tussocky and abounding in clumps of wild mint that give it the delicate perfume that I always associate with wild and watery places. A narrow fringe of mossy grass encircles the tangled undergrowth and the dense, gnarled, lichened trees that allow only dappling shafts of sunlight to penetrate the mysterious gloom of almost the whole island. There may have been paths at one time, but for centuries Nature has taken control and closed in with its capping of dark verdure. To traverse the island one has to scramble through a scraggy, thorny jungle.

But the scratching, clothes-tearing effort is worth it for what one finds at the centre of the island. Here, at the highest point, in a brambled clearing, stand the beautiful ruins of an ancient Abbey, brooding and solitary and seemingly forgotten.

And it was all mine, every stone, every rock, every tree.

I was nearly always alone there, yet I don't remember ever feeling scared after my first tremulous expedition. I never saw anybody else there, and if I had I would probably have been terrified.

People did go to Church Island, if only for the Healing Tree. Somewhere in the undergrowth is a spindly old thorn tree, now very feeble and spare. Beside it is a boulder with a natural concave indentation on top containing always a saucerful of rainwater. Local folklore has it that many afflictions can be cured by dunking the affected part in the water and taking off any bandage or plaster and fixing it to the thorn tree. People came from miles around to the Healing Tree, and the thorn was always covered in a beard of discarded bandages, plaster and strips of cotton. I took the cure there in 1970 for tennis elbow – and it worked, I swear! Thank God I wasn't suffering from haemorrhoids!

I may have made Brecart, and its surrounding lands, appear to be rather grand. That it was not at all. The original estate had belonged for centuries to the O'Neill family, and was separate from their main seat at Shanes Castle. The Brecart estate was used mainly, I believe, for sport, and our house had served as a shooting box. Admittedly it was approached by about half a mile of carriage drive leading from the Ballymena road and entered through hefty iron gates flanked by heavy elliptical railings, but the lay-out of the house itself was quite farcical for our impecunious needs.

Its longest elevation was only one room deep, the rooms leading off a lengthy, shadowy corridor on both ground and first floors. Oil wall-lamps shed dim pools of light along it at night and getting from my bedroom to the nearest loo was something I dreaded as I scuttled from one end to the other, imagining demons at every patch of gloom. My room had been the gunroom and was evidently allotted to me because it was the warmest room in the house and well served with cupboards.

The front entrance was through a small square porch with two doors, the idea being that you opened whichever one was on the lee side in the prevailing wind. This gave on to a fair-sized hall, its chequered black-and-white tiled floor covered in the middle with a lion-skin rug, the head with its mouth wide open in what had once been a snarl but over the years had become a toothy yawn. On either side of the hall were the drawing-room and dining-room, with the kitchen quarters away at the far end of the building. Half-way between was a butler's pantry, presumably placed there in the past as a staging-post to give a breather to scurrying servants.

Next to the butler's pantry was the smoking-room, my favourite place in the whole house. This was my grandfather's special den, where only men were welcome and where there was always a lovely aroma of tobacco smoke mingled with wood smoke from the fire. Here Grandpa spent his evenings alone, reading or listening to his gramophone records, or tinkering with his crystal sets, which he made in cigar-boxes and presented to his friends.

Grandpa loved music and often in later years I would creep into the smoking-room when it reverberated to a symphony played at full blast on wireless or record and watch him as he 'conducted', eyes closed, arms flailing, totally transported.

This little room was full of trophies, pictures and photographs and other memorabilia special to my grandfather and those before him.

Another room remarkable for smells of quite another kind was the lamp room. Here were kept the drums of paraffin and all the spare lamps, and here the lamps in use were brought every day to be cleaned, refilled and trimmed. One old maid, Annie, seemed to be in charge of these operations, and wherever Annie went the stench of paraffin went too.

The upstairs at Brecart was chiefly remarkable for its total lack of bathrooms. There was only one in the whole house and this was downstairs next to the lamp room, and usually reserved for guests or for my grandfather, who was too big to fit into the slipper baths everybody else used in their own rooms.

3

SUPPORTING CAST

Perhaps it is a characteristic of my mentality that people are less clear-cut in my recollection than incidents and places. Certainly, although I spent so much of my childhood with my mother's family at Brecart my image of them as individuals is shadowy and only comparatively clear when connected with events that involved them.

Physically, Grandpa Hunter, however, could never be easily forgotten. He was a huge man, weighing over eighteen stone, and with a voice and presence that went with his girth. Except on occasions when he had to dress formally, his habitual daily attire consisted of Harris tweed plus-fours – his plus-eights, we called them – and always a bow-tie. His hirsute clothing accentuated his bulk and he was a formidable sight as he lumbered around. I would like to be able to say that he was nimble despite his size, but he wasn't. I was the only person who relished sharing a small boat with him on the river.

He was an immensely kind man, and always ready to laugh, which he did with great, gusty bellows. Yet, for all his jovial, good nature within the family, he hated being away from Brecart and had few friends.

I recall nothing of Grandpa's provenance and I have no idea how he acquired Brecart, whether it was left to him or whether he bought it. The latter seems unlikely because he was perpetually hard-up, and had managed to exist for years by selling off odd bits of land.

He had apparently been something of a tearaway in his early years, a heavy drinker and gambler, which perhaps accounted for his becoming very abstemious and rather withdrawn in later life. He never had a job in the years that I knew him, but seemed to potter quite aimlessly through his days, watching approvingly while other people busied themselves.

I was probably the only person aware of one of his major attainments, though I never confided this knowledge to anybody else. Grandpa must have been a candidate for the Guinness Book of Records for farting. He retired to bed earlier than the other adults in the house, usually only an hour or so after dinner was over. He would then lumber upstairs and look into my room, not realising that his creaking passage over the old floorboards often woke me. Satisfied that all was well with me, he would then retrace his steps along the corridor, heading for his room at the other end of the house. At the moment he turned from my door the concerto would start, in time to his steady tread rather like a distant pipe and drum band, and his wind-assisted progress was audible until he was round the corner.

For all his indolence and benign nature, Grandpa was something of a martinet and his word was law at Brecart. He also had certain stubborn eccentricities. Whilst quite a devout man, he never went to church, even for my christening, and hated churchmen of any denomination. He also scorned doctors and any sort of medical treatment for most ailments. He was reluctant to have a physician called to the house at any time, and never for himself. He averred that nature had her own way of curing – a belief that one day was to alter the pattern of my own life.

Another of Grandpa's little foibles was his attitude to cars. Sometime in the early 1920s he underwent some moment of uncharacteristic extravagance and went out and bought three expensive cars. These, he reckoned, would last him for the rest of his life, and he resolutely refused ever to purchase another one. And because these vehicles were so well-made and so rarely used, he was proved to be quite right.

The smallest of the three was a Chambers Coupé, apparently the only car that was coachbuilt in Ireland. It was a smart little thing, with buttoned leather seating and ivory knobs on the controls and window handles. There were tasselled blinds on the windows and a conical silver flower vase on the fascia panel.

The brute of the collection was the Cubitt, a massive open

tourer similar to the early Bentleys, and painted battle-ship grey. I don't remember this car ever being used and it stood grimy and neglected until its engine was removed and installed in the motorboat.

Pride of the fleet was a beautiful Sunbeam Tourer which served as the main family car to the end of my grandparents' life, being a six-seater with a canvas hood that was secured by leather straps when not stowed away at the back. The Hunter family became a familiar sight on the road to Belfast as they sailed along in their ancient vehicle.

And Grandpa *loved* bull's-eyes. He bought them in bulk in large glass containers and pressed them on all and sundry. After shooting days, when up to twenty guns had been out after duck, every guest was presented with a paper bag full of the sweets. I never saw a shooting man courageous enough to decline the offering.

With his love of music, Grandpa not only fancied himself as a conductor, but also as a singer. In those days we quite often had little musical soirées and the high spot of the evening had to be when he was invited to sing. He would lumber in, very genial and pink-faced, and launch into his version of 'I Must Go Down to the Seas Again', booming it out *con molto vibrato* in massive bass-baritone. That done, he would amble back to his smoking-room, well pleased with himself.

For all his eccentricities, my grandfather was a fairly practical man, not given to weird beliefs or theories. Perhaps that is why he scoffed at the legend of the curse on Brecart. In the light of future events it may have been as well that the legend did not worry him.

It is many years since the story was told to me piecemeal by my grandmother and my aunts, so I probably don't recall it accurately, though I'll never forget the gist of it.

Brecart had been built on the site of a priory or some such religious foundation that had been sequestrated after the Reformation. The story went that, before his charge was seized, the abbot or prior had drowned himself in the well in the courtyard and had pronounced a curse on the place to the effect that whatever family should inhabit Brecart would end in degradation and ruin.

Sadly, curse or no curse, that is exactly what did happen to the Hunter family, the ruin probably inevitable, the degradation quite horrible.

Granny Hunter was an altogether less noticeable personage. She was shortish, sturdy and always held herself very erect. Her features were quite plain, square-jawed and rather Germanic, and her habitual severity of expression was totally belied by small, very blue eyes that twinkled merrily and never missed a thing.

Her maiden name was Fane, and she had been brought up in England, before marrying my grandfather Agar-Daly and coming to live in Ireland. He had died soon after the births of my mother and my Uncle Richard, and Granny then married Grandpa Hunter, whom she had met in Dublin. They had four children, my uncles Bertie and Jimmy, and my two dear aunts.

That Amy and Dolly remained spinsters was more due to their isolated way of life than to any natural inclination, I'm sure. I also suspect that Grandpa saw off many would-be suitors because he found his daughters too useful around the house. They were attractive girls; Amy tall, shapely and rather languid ('Poor Amy. She has never been very strong, you know') and Dolly vivacious, red haired and extrovert, bouncing around on a very nice pair of legs.

They both doted on me, and gave up every moment to me when I was little, romping round the house or garden, going out in boats or for long rambles and taking me up to Toome on shopping expeditions.

They were inseparable throughout their lives, especially in later years when they lived in very straitened circumstances which they battled through together with a great deal of courage and still all the sense of humour of two splendid old ladies, slightly dotty but full of 'jizz', as they would say. They came back into my life near the end of theirs, and we all realised how much we had missed each other during the intervening long, long period,

Uncle Richard Agar-Daly and Uncle Bertie Hunter lived and died in Australia, and I never met them. Why they had decided to go 'down under' I don't know. On the outbreak of the First World War they had both joined the Australian

Light Horse, and their only spell in Europe was on their military posting to the United Kingdom.

The baby of the Hunter family was Uncle Jimmy. He hung around Brecart for years and was always there during my childhood. I suppose he regarded the place as his inheritance, although he never seemed to do much about it, apart from taking an occasional interest in the farming, and then only for brief periods. He was short, dapper, but very tough physically, and with his ginger hair went a hell of a temper. I was a little wary of him, but he was kind enough whilst not really having much time for me.

In fact, Uncle Jimmy didn't seem to have much time for anything. As with my aunts, perhaps any ambitions or purpose he may have had were quelled by my grandfather's overbearing presence. Grandpa kept a pretty tight hold on his family, for all his geniality. Maybe that is why my two other uncles had felt the need to go so far afield.

Jimmy did have one outlet for his energies. He had obtained some sort of reserve commission in the RAF, and was a part-time pilot, and, I used to hear, a very good one. His terms of service entailed only occasional training weeks on station and frequent weekend flying sessions. He was based on Aldergrove RAF Aerodrome, only a few miles from home, flying Vickers Virginia bombers, spindly biplanes with fixed undercarriages and lots of struts and spars, and the pilot and observer sitting up plainly visible above their elongated canvas box of a fuselage. These were the first aircraft that I ever saw at close quarters, and I thought them tremendous and very deadly.

The officers from Aldergrove were frequent weekend guests at the house. There was no telephone there in the early 1920s but we had our own exclusive signalling system. A day or two before the weekend a plane would circle round to attract attention. As soon as somebody dashed out from the house (usually myself) a message packet attached to coloured linen streamers would then be dropped onto the tennis court, telling us how many RAF guests to expect. All very exciting for a little boy on his visits to Brecart.

Some months after our return from India my father had
decided to go into general practice as a doctor. I suppose he
wanted to appear to be doing *something*, although for the
rest of his life he mainly subsisted on an allowance and
various generous hand-outs from his mother, who was by
then free from the financial restrictions and guidance imposed
by her more prudent late husband, the judge. Granny Todd
was one of the many birds that my father could charm from
any defensive perch in the trees. Fortunately for her (and
for my father) she had been left a comfortable income from
the Palethorpe family trust.

She lived in England, so I never saw her in those days, but
I somehow became aware of her influence over us as a sort
of benevolent fairy godmother. Years later I was to be very
grateful for the manipulations of her magic wand.

No doubt with Granny Todd's assistance, my father bought
a practice in Moneymore, a rather drab market town in
County Londonderry, some fifteen miles from Toome.

At first we lived in a rented farmhouse outside the town
and this suited me greatly. I can remember my first pair of
gumboots, which enabled me to slosh around happily in the
muck of the farmyard, and all this was grand for me, my first
real taste of freedom. My mother wisely let me run wild, but
she did draw the line at one or two Irish-isms that I picked
up from the farmhands and repeated unsuspectingly to her.

After a time we moved into a house on the outskirts of
Moneymore. All I can remember about it was that it had In
and Out gates coupled by a semi-circular drive which went
round an area of lawn in the centre of which was a large
monkey-puzzle tree. To the rear of the gardens there was a
fairly large stable-yard leading to a walled kitchen garden
and the one field that belonged to the house.

My first great excitement here was a visit to the monthly
horse fair that was held in Moneymore. My father gave his
gardener-groom five shillings and told him to take me to buy
a donkey. I should explain that in those days this was a fair
sum to pay in Ireland for a fine specimen of the ubiquitous
ass.

In the care of my watchful companion, whose name I have
forgotten, I was fascinated by the sights and sounds and

furious activity of a typical Irish horse fair. Scores of bucolic
countrymen in various stages of inebriation, and all seemingly
carrying knobbly sticks, shouted, haggled, argued and even
fought over their purchases and sales. The market square
was sheer bedlam, with animals of all shapes and sizes being
run up and down to show their paces while others milled
around amongst the onlookers. The fair was the great event
of the district and half the countryside turned up for it, if not
to buy or sell at least to see the fun, to enjoy a few jars of
ale or stout and maybe to have their fortunes told by the
ever-present tinkers.

I wanted to buy every donkey I saw, but my guardian
inspected a few very carefully before finally settling on a
nice-looking animal, larger than most and smooth-coated
from decent grooming and care. And so we set off home
with Neddy, who was to be my gallant charger for nearly two
years. He was a great walker, but had a habit of breaking into
a brisk stiff-legged trot which really rattled my teeth: I began
to feel that riding was a very overrated pastime.

Neddy was the first and most-prized of my acquisitions at
Moneymore. The second was a bicycle which Uncle Jimmy
gave me. The third I would have loved to do without: a
French Governess. From the start we cordially disliked each
other, and I have since never really taken to ladies with
moustaches.

Mademoiselle – I don't think I ever did know her full name
– was quite young, scrawny, dark-haired and sallow, her pale
skin highlighting that black smudge on her upper lip.

She had full and restricting charge of me for over a year,
except on the occasions when I was able to escape her
watchful and humourless attention. I think that even my
parents had sympathy for me, and tended to turn a blind eye
on her beady-eyed furies and a deaf ear to her voluble
complaints, but she was regarded as a necessary evil.

However, Mademoiselle had one virtue: she was a good
teacher. She gave me my first taste of academic discipline
and routine, and before her departure I was more or less
bilingual. After a while I was not allowed to speak any
English to her, even outside the schoolroom.

I would have dreaded those strict daily school periods with

her had there not been light relief provided by Sheila and Audrey McCausland, who lived in the Manor House in Moneymore and shared my schooling and the rigours of Mademoiselle. Perhaps a little older than me, Audrey was slender and curly-haired, and everybody said how pretty she was, but I rather fancied Sheila, who had long blonde hair and a bit more shape.

Apart from Mademoiselle, my worst affliction at that time was 'growing pains'. Night after night, and for several years, I would wake howling from that dreadful ache in my knees, and my mother would rub my legs with Jacob's Oil, which had a pleasant tingling effect on the skin, and gently put me back to sleep. Even my father was understanding about this.

Settling down to a humdrum existence in provincial Northern Ireland could not have been easy for my parents after their glamorous life in India. My mother must have felt the transition particularly, since her social and physical activities had become very limited, especially for a woman still only in her thirties. With a cook and two maids living in the house she was not exactly run off her feet, but she seemed to have had few outside interests in common with my father. She never rode to hounds, hated driving a car, gardened unenthusiastically and in general gave in to a pretty listless way of life – due in part to poor health stemming from a tendency to anaemia. Our proximity to Brecart, where we spent nearly every weekend and had frequent holidays, was the one bright spot in her existence.

My father, on the other hand, had thrown himself into his new life with gusto. He enjoyed being a general practitioner and soon became a good and kindly family doctor, popular and respected around the countryside. Many of his patients lived in isolated places in the hills nearby, approachable only along rough cart tracks, but these were the very people who knew they could call on him at any time. He would rush off at all hours of the day or night in his smart, tough little Humber two-seater, frequently having to walk the last few hundred yards. With the birthrate in Ireland as high as anywhere in the world, it was a good thing that he particularly enjoyed delivering babies, a skill well-learned from his days with Bethel Solomons in Dublin.

Probably because of Granny Todd's backing, money was not important to him. I often used to see him arriving home with the car full of payment in kind: sacks of potatoes, chickens and ducks, heads of cabbage or whatever his patients could afford. And for all his professional activity, my father's time in Moneymore was by no means totally taken up with work. He rode to hounds whenever he could get away, played golf regularly at Killymoon and had a gun in a pheasant and snipe shoot with two cronies.

The contrast between my father's hectic diary and my mother's enforced (or was it self-inflicted?) boredom inevitably led to chafing between them. I began to be aware of bickering and flarings of temper on both sides, and this was a worry that was to increase over the years. However, in the Moneymore days they mostly concealed their differences from me, and I wasn't too bothered by the little I understood of their problems.

One thing they did eventually agree on: the local pond was too small for fish such as they. My mother understandably yearned for a more sophisticated way of life and my father must have realised that he couldn't play at doctoring for ever. Sooner or later the fount of Granny's generosity might dry up. And besides, his professional interests were becoming more sophisticated. He wanted to broaden his skills.

And so it was decided to leave Ireland. My father was to go to Edinburgh for a spell to brush up on surgery, and we were then going to settle in England.

The Moneymore house was sold, my father went off to Scotland, and Mummy and I went to stay for a while at – guess where? Brecart, of course! I was nearly six years old.

4

SCENE CHANGE

In West Devon there is a cluster of villages and hamlets that share the same estimable suffix to their names: -worthy, meaning a small settlement. They include Alfardisworthy, Woolfardisworthy, Ashmansworthy, Chilsworthy and even Pyworthy. Central to the group is Holsworthy, a bustling market town, and it was to there that I was transplanted to put down roots in England.

As with so many English country towns and villages, the most enduring and impressive feature of Holsworthy is the church, erected in the Early English style about 1250, with later additions dating from 1366.

Our house stood across the road from this church and my room looked on to it and its churchyard. This view has always remained in my memory. Perhaps it was those early impressions that first kindled my interest in ecclesiastical architecture and the historical story-telling of graveyards.

It was not only the sight of the church which I was aware of but also the sound of it. The great tower contains a fine peal of bells that rattled our windows on Sundays and a carillon that boomed out at intervals every day. At one stage, when my mother was dangerously ill with pleuro-pneumonia, the bells were muffled and the carillon stopped for a few days, while she made a rapid recovery.

Our home was uninspiringly called The Elms. It was an ugly turn-of-the-century house with quite pleasant grounds, a lofted stable and garage building, a small field at the back, and a large brick barn which we never used.

My father practised from there, so the morning room became his surgery and eventually the breakfast room housed his X-ray equipment, an unusual toy for a country GP in those days and, I suppose, a gift from Granny Todd.

Holsworthy suited my father perfectly. His studies in Edinburgh had re-fired his enthusiasm for his profession, and here in Devon he was able to follow all his interests, both medical and leisure.

He had no partner, but came to a friendly arrangement with two old-established local doctors, both members of the Tetcott Hunt, and one of them was always ready to stand in for my father on his days out with hounds. He also enjoyed his shooting and even played rugger occasionally for Okehampton.

He tried hard to get fit for all these activities and each morning the landing outside the main bedroom shook with his heavy-footed skipping as he sweated away some of his prodigious liquid intake. As an ex-international player he must have been held in some reverence by his colleagues, but sadly, his years of physical fitness were coming to an end.

I still had a governess, but this time a very nice, jolly young lady, called Marjorie Sharpley. I went to her parents' house for my lessons, at first being delivered there by somebody from home, but very soon I was allowed to cycle to and fro. Now six years old, I was spindly but quite hardy.

I liked Miss Sharpley. She was firm with me, but in a kindly, good-humoured way. Apart from the usual periods of book-work, we used to go for long walks which were never boring because she kept my interest alive with information about the plants and trees and wildlife in the hedgerows and woods. I was lucky to be under her tutelage for about a year, by which time I was old enough to enter a local school.

I hardly remember anything about that school. It was quite small, and attended largely by farmers' sons, most of whom rode their ponies or horses to school. I wanted to ride my own little piebald pony, but was not allowed to, since the school was only a few minutes away, even on foot.

During my first few weeks in Holsworthy I discovered the benefits of financial credit. When I accompanied my mother on her shopping rounds I noticed that she got what she wanted by merely saying, 'Put it on my account, please.' I must have come to the conclusion that shops simply *gave* things to certain privileged people, because I amassed quite a store of sweets and comics just by using the magic words as I turned to leave. One of my first such purchases was a birthday present for my mother, a bottle of Parma Violets scent. My mother was marvellously convincing in her delighted receipt of the gift so the poor woman had to put up with an annual offering of the reeking mixture for years.

When the day of reckoning finally arrived for my shopping spree I was treated leniently. I suspect my father dined out on the story for weeks, but he did explain my mistake very clearly to me. However, I did get something out of it all: my first pocket money – a shilling a week.

Various members of the family came to stay with us, and my two doting aunts, Amy and Dolly, were frequent visitors. Having failed to fire my interest in live theatre in Toome, they now introduced me to a much more agreeable form of entertainment, the cinema. Film shows were held once or twice a week in a hall on the town square, and I found them enthralling, despite the constantly rainy pictures and the fact that I couldn't read the subtitles.

My other two main diversions in Holsworthy were Mr Prouse, and homing pigeons.

Mr Prouse was our gardener. He was very deaf and his garb consisted of heavy dark trousers, a long black jacket that I can only describe as a frock-coat, and a bowler hat which he never removed. Because of his deafness he rarely spoke and I found him unfriendly. However, I got my own back by creeping up behind him and putting live worms on the brim of his bowler. I was never caught out in this absorbing pastime.

My money-box was building up nicely until I discovered the joys of keeping pigeons. I was allowed to have one end of the loft screened off with wire netting and a little landing platform by the window. Common blue-bars and mealies could be bought for a shilling, but some of the trained mature birds cost half-a-crown, so my resources were strained as I tried to build up my collection. Finally, I did something that has been on my conscience ever since – I stole half-a-crown from my mother's handbag.

My money had run out and there was a particular bird that I coveted, but the dealer wanted a quick sale. Reckoning that I could save up and replace my mother's cash in a few weeks I crept into her room and found exactly what I wanted.

To this day I can remember feeling sick with worry over what I had done, even after I had in fact replaced the money.

One significant encounter took place early in our stay at Holsworthy. For the first time I can remember, I met my dear old Granny Todd.

She was as near to being an angel as I shall ever know. Her devotion to my father, her kindness to all, her tremulous desire to please everybody and her goodness to me never wavered. She had a little money, and for the last twenty years of her life she dispersed it willingly.

She was a lonely old lady, yet never intruded on others and only visited us on the rare occasions when she was invited. After my grandfather's death in 1921 she lived totally alone in hotels. Until the outbreak of war in 1939 she spent six months annually in London, four months in Bournemouth, a month or so in Newbury with her sister and brother-in-law, and the odd spell with us or with her daughter's family, the FitzPatricks, in Ireland.

As the years went by and as the calls on her income increased she continued to stay in the same hotels, gradually changing her apartments from elegant suites to the smallest rooms without bathrooms. But she never grumbled and remained sweet and cheerful.

She was totally blind to my father's excesses and deficiencies and seemed indeed to have spent most of her life under the dominance of the menfolk in her family, partly due to her self-effacing nature, and partly because she was reared in that late-Victorian tradition. First there had been her strict father, Job Palethorpe, a wealthy merchant and property owner, from whose hectoring implacability she escaped through marriage to an equally forceful man, kindly, but short-tempered and self-righteous. Then came my father, to whom she was utterly devoted, and whose every whim she tried to satisfy.

Granny Todd had always been very slender and pretty, and in age had lost none of her grace and charm. After her husband's death in 1921 she invariably dressed in sober semi-mourning, greys, blacks and lilac shades, but her manner was far from being sepulchral. She enjoyed a giggle as much as anyone, and was an inveterate theatre-goer. Her interest in the theatre perhaps found expression in my own eventual career, which I owe entirely to her, and from which I believe she derived some vicarious sense of fulfilment.

After a year or so at the little school in Holsworthy I was launched, at the tender age of seven, into prep school. The institution I was condemned to was Norwood School in Exeter, and as the day of my departure from Holsworthy approached I was terrified by the prospect of being sent off to live with strangers. It was no consolation to be assured that there would be lots of other boys in the same plight.

I was driven up to Exeter with my parents and after a brief chat with the headmaster – who surprised me by being very jolly and human – I was told to go off to my classroom (second on the left off the hall) and announce myself to the form-mistress, Miss Copleston. I was too dazed by the speed of it all even to blubber as my mother gave me a parting hug, but duly went off and knocked on the door second on the left, not having the vaguest idea what to do next. We must have arrived rather late at Norwood, because when I was bidden to enter I was confronted by a room full of boys already at their desks, all their faces turned expectantly towards me.

Quaking with uncertainty, I faced the mistress and blurted out, 'Please, Miss Cobblestones, I'm Todd.' It says much for the discipline she had already established with her little charges that there was not a snigger from the others, nor did she seem to have noticed my blunder. She simply said, 'Yes, I know. We were expecting you,' and led me to my desk.

That baptism of fire survived, the rest was easier as we were shown around the school and helped to unpack our belongings in the dormitory. It wasn't so bad after all, I decided.

I spent three or four happy, active years at Norwood. Few families are without their problems and vagaries, and once the initial brief period of homesickness is past a young boy at boarding school is cocooned, safe from such difficulties, whether emotional or practical. The organised routine of school life, the constant company of other boys, and the watchful caring of experienced staff fill all the hours of every day, and the average boy has little time to mope or worry about anything outside the confines of classroom and play-ground.

Even news from home is usually filtered to mention only the best and most encouraging facts of home life.

Certainly, that was the way it was with me, and I know that I was fortunate to be privileged to spend most of my formative years in this kind of refuge; blinkered, maybe, but at least shielded and reasonably carefree, and able to get on with the business of learning.

The news from my home during this period would have been very disturbing had I been told all that was happening there. Even before my departure for Norwood I had become increasingly aware of tensions mounting between my father and mother. They tried to minimise the effect of their personal problems on me, but I remember one devastating occasion when, after a stormy encounter between them, my mother, in tears, said to me, 'I'll divorce him. Would you like that?' I asked her what the word meant, and she explained that it would mean that we would leave my father and go and live somewhere else.

My reaction should have been predictable to her: I burst into tears and pleaded with her not to do such a thing. It was inconceivable that we could live without Daddy. My misery brought my father to the scene and both of them set about reassuring me. We all three ended up laughing and crying together – even my stiff-backed father – and my final consolation came when the two of them embraced each other.

Most of the fault, I suspect, lay with my father. His extravagance, his frequent trips to London where he and his cronies were very welcome at the Kit-Kat Club – no man could be an ideal paterfamilias with his weaknesses and selfishness. But my mother was not entirely blameless. Whilst she enjoyed the comforts of a well-found household and a reasonably enjoyable social existence, an underlying insecurity frayed her nerves and my father's convivial excesses obviously worried her. But, without the self-confidence to be firm, she simply carped and became a nagger.

There they were: two people who cared a great deal for each other, but who were totally incompatible. And there

was I: on the alert for signs of disharmony, and gradually
learning to keep my fears and feelings to myself.

After seeing how upset I had been my father almost turned
over a new leaf – at least, I think he tried to do so, even if
the next page was not without blemishes. Perhaps having
seen how much I cared for him he warmed towards me and
spent much more time with me. Even so, every now and
then some temptation proved too much for him. Once he
met my mother and me at Liverpool Docks on our return
from one of our trips to Brecart. As the ship berthed I was
looking over the rail from the boat deck with my mother.
She, of course, was trying to catch sight of my father on the
dockside, but I had eyes only for a glittering car that was
parked there, surrounded by an admiring crowd. My father
had told us that he had a surprise for us, but it never occurred
to me that it could be this pale blue Chrysler roadster, with
huge bonnet and yellow simulated-wood wheel spokes!

On this particular trip we stopped for lunch at Shrewsbury,
and I was taken to see my future school. I was greatly
impressed by the schools, with their beautiful grounds and
splendid buildings on Kingsland's plateau high above the
River Severn. Norwood seemed very modest in comparison.

I soon became quite a seasoned traveller, making frequent
journeys between England and Northern Ireland. My first
lone trip was made when I was only about seven-and-a-half
years old. I was taken to Belfast and put in charge of the
purser, along with several other boys also returning to school.
We were kept together as a group, given a huge supper, and
then bedded down in our various cabins. Next morning we
breakfasted and, as the ship berthed in Liverpool, we were
handed over to a representative of the shipping line who
took us by taxi to the Lime Street Station Hotel, where we
were given glasses of lemonade and biscuits. Then we were
introduced to the station master, an impressive personage in
top hat and morning coat. He in turn led us to the platform
and there the guard took charge of us. We were then
shepherded to the front of the train, where we met the engine
driver, before being settled into our compartment. This chain
of events was part of a time-honoured ceremony, and many

of us years later still retained the habit of having a word with the drivers of long-distance trains.

In most ways Holsworthy and Norwood gave me a kindly start to my life as an English resident, and saw me emerge as a fairly typical English schoolboy. Small-town country life broke me in gently to the demands of a semi-urban existence. I learned to manipulate my bike through traffic, to cope with shopping without the benefit of a charge account, and to contrive to keep myself mostly neat and tidy. And there were always the holidays when I could slip back into the wilder ways of Brecart.

5

ACTION BREAK

After a few weeks I settled in very happily at Norwood School and thereafter loved almost every aspect of school life – with certain traditional exceptions such as prep, exams and the worrying slog of those subjects which I found particularly difficult.

At Norwood I learnt the basics of organised sports and games. Always haunted by the spectre of my father's prodigious prowess as an athlete, I did my best in everything on the field or in the gym, and, fortunately, showed above-average ability. I enjoyed games, even cricket, although I had no natural skill with the bat, and much to my delight, I eventually managed to get my colours for both cricket and rugger. Swimming, however, remained my bugbear, and I only gained my proficiency certificate after several spluttering attempts to pass the tests.

During my first couple of years at Norwood my father's health had steadily deteriorated, his constitution being debilitated by increasingly violent attacks of malaria. It was eventually decided that he would have to undergo steady treatment and that he would benefit from a change of climate. This advice appealed to him enormously, and his chance came when he was invited to travel to South America as some sort of medical adviser to the then Prince of Wales and Prince George on the occasion of their visit to that hemisphere.

My fun-loving father thoroughly enjoyed the trip. After it he applied for a post as ship's surgeon on the Royal Mail shipping line, plying between England and Argentina, and was appointed to serve on the RMSP Arlanze. Whilst this gave him eventual freedom from his illness (and, no doubt, other freedoms as well) it had less favourable effects on my mother and myself.

The Holsworthy house was given up, we moved to a flat in Exeter, and I became a day boy at Norwood.

School was never quite the same for me after that. I still enjoyed my work there and made good progress in games and athletics, but I missed the evening routine of a boarder's life and I can remember often longing to walk up to school and join the others for all the fun we had at the end of the day. Cooped up in a flat, albeit a large one with a garden, was a far cry from what I had been used to.

My mother could not have been very happy, either.

But my mind has instinctively drawn a veil over much of that two-year period, and I remember little about it. Thank God there was still Brecart, where nothing much had changed.

I was eleven years old when yet another disruption unsettled my school life, but this time it was not unwelcome to me, and must certainly have been most welcome to my mother.

After some two years of tripping back and forth to South America my father's health was almost fully repaired, except for his by now chronic bronchial condition, which was not helped by his addiction to cigarettes. So it was decided that, after a few more voyages, the Guvnor (as he now liked me to call him) would settle back to his profession at home.

This time we moved to West Moors, in Dorset. Our house there was a very plain modern one with a good-sized garden. It was in a stuffy residential area, but my own favourite neighbours soon became the Owen family, Australians, very hospitable and easy-going, with a large brood of children. They gave me a glimpse of domestic freedom which I had never encountered before. Their house was an untidy shambles but nobody seemed to care, and in good weather the whole family lived more out of doors than inside. The children slept in tents in the surrounding woods, the garden was totally neglected, nearly all the meals were barbecued, and there never seemed to be any sort of timetable.

Our move to Dorset suited me beautifully. Not only did I escape the fetters of life in a flat, but I left Norwood and became a weekly boarder at nearby Queen Elizabeth's Grammar School at Wimborne. This gave me the best of both worlds: a real school life during the week and weekends at home. Not only was it a good thing academically for me to be at Wimborne, but it was considered by my father a sensible preparation for my entry to Shrewsbury.

So once again all was well with me in my scholastic world. I liked the boys, many of whom were scholarship boys from local schools, very bright and competitive, and I enjoyed living there in one of the three dormitories. I coped quite well in Form IIA, not quite the bottom form, and got into the under-13 rugger and cricket sides.

For three terms I was really happy at Wimborne, and was developing into a good average schoolboy, sturdy, fairly well-placed in my work (except the dreaded maths) and rather a star at games.

Then, in my twelfth year, I at last entered Shrewsbury School. It was a year that totally changed the course of my life.

To begin with, I had passed my Common Entrance examination with no trouble and was eager to show my father that I would be a worthy successor to him at sports and games. I had every reason to be reasonably confident that I would not let him down; I possessed a natural aptitude, was fast and agile for my age and enjoyed a rough and tumble. So all in all, my prospects were pretty good.

My father dropped me at school and then went on to Liverpool for some business reason.

I hardly remember anything of the first couple of days at Shrewsbury, where the time was mostly spent in settling in. From the moment of my arrival I had been feeling a bit queasy, but that was understandable after all the excitement.

Then, a day or so later, I really felt wretched, and was kept in bed and seen by a doctor.

Almost immediately I was moved into the school sanatorium. There had been an epidemic of scarlet fever and it seemed that I was one of the victims. All the symptoms were there.

My father, on his return from Liverpool, called in at the school, and was granted permission to drive me home. I was swaddled in blankets in the car and felt utterly miserable, not so much from the illness as from the disappointment.

My father could not have been happy about my condition, for he called in a second opinion as soon as I was bedded down at home. I remember my father and this other doctor examining me and taking various samples and tests. By now I didn't feel too bad at all, and wondered what all the fuss was about.

I was left alone for a short time and then my mother came into my room and sat on my bed, unaccountably upset and near to tears. Then my father came in and quietly told me that I was not very well and that a specialist was coming to see me. Meanwhile I was to stay very still in bed.

The specialist arrived from Bournemouth and again I was thumped and prodded.

Then my father and mother came back to break the news to me.

I had rheumatic fever and pericarditis, an extremely grave heart condition. In accordance with the teaching of the day I was to lie perfectly still, on my right side, with a bolster propping me in this position so that I wouldn't roll over. Even my head was not to be raised on a pillow. I was to use bed-pans and water bottles and would be spoon-fed. For a while I would have a trained nurse to look after me and then my mother would take over care of me. I could read and listen to the radio, and eat all I wanted, but must not raise my arms above my head or try to lift my head too high.

I would be like this for many weeks, my father said.

Looking back, I don't think I took in all that I was told. I'd had measles and mumps, and being in bed, spoiled and cosseted, had been really rather nice, with no work to do and lots of books and magazines to read. The prospect of an extended lie-in didn't bother me at all.

By now I was feeling perfectly normal, and was certainly more cheerful than my parents seemed to be.

It must have been dreadful for them. They believed that if I pulled through the crisis I would be an invalid for the rest of my life, but shielded me from this, telling me only gradually, as time went by. While all that concerned me was that I was being a bit of a bore for them.

And I hated using the bed-pan.

*

My period of sickness was divided into four phases. First, I spent three months or so lying on my right side, then about another three months lying flat on my back but with my head slightly raised on a single pillow. Following this I was allowed to sit more or less upright for a while, propped by a soft wall of pillows and with a cage over my legs to keep me free of the weight of the bedclothes. By now I seemed to have lost the power to move my legs much anyhow, and it was all I could do to twiddle my toes against the resistance of a sheet. Finally came the fourth period when I swung my legs out of bed and began a six-month phase of rehabilitation and recuperation.

One of the symptoms of pericarditis is a massive enlargement of the heart. In my case, the apex beat, normally easily felt by a finger-touch just in from the left nipple, had been pushed by the enlargement two or three inches towards the armpit, causing a loud tapping sound at each heartbeat, clearly audible throughout the room. This, I was told, came from suction between heart and lungs. There was no pain, but I could feel this tapping inside my chest and my pulse rate fluttered at up to 140 beats per minute, when the normal rate is about 76.

Lying on my right side was meant to reduce the pressure on my heart and to bring the apex beat more into its proper place as the enlargement decreased. Gradually the ploy seemed to succeed, and the tapping subsided. Because I was allowed no visitors for fear of over-excitement, I had never had the chance to show off my unique castanet concerto.

Throughout my confinement my mother was absolutely wonderful. As soon as she had mastered the knowledge required in caring for me – the keeping of pulse and temperature charts, the bed-bathing and rubbing with spirit to obviate bed-sores, the changing of covers and pyjamas, the handling of the dreaded bed-pan, the administration of various pills and medicines – she kept up her watchful and loving vigil daily, and often nightly.

My father cared too, and immediately started to plan his return to a settled home base. Meanwhile he wrote to me every week during his absences at sea.

So, once again, I felt the security of a united family, and
had nothing to worry about except my own situation.

Actually, truth to tell, I don't think I ever did really worry
about myself. I seemed to have accepted all the restrictions
that had been placed on me, and put out of my mind any
thoughts of what my life was likely to be later on. The future
seemed a long way off. I simply got on with the business of
making the most of things as they were.

It is impossible now to recall exactly what was in my mind.
All I know is that I never felt the need to shed a tear or to
seek any comfort. I almost enjoyed my unremitting daily
routine, and I don't think it occurred to me to feel sorry for
myself, even though I had been told that I would never lead
a normal life. No Shrewsbury, no games, no bicycles: either
I couldn't come to terms with this forecast, or I simply didn't
believe it.

The weeks rolled by inexorably and, strangely quickly. To
say that the days were uneventful would not be correct. In
such circumstances all sorts of little episodes became major
events: the progress of a fly on the wall can stir the imagination; finishing one meal and looking forward to the next one
can quicken a sense of anticipation; transforming audible
household sounds into mental pictures of what other people
are doing can be absolutely absorbing; being totally immersed in a book or a magazine can bridge the time gap
between the routine incidents of a day exactly like all the
others.

I am not aware of ever having been bored or fractious. I
became expert in timing my pulse without the need of a
watch, and took a lively interest in my condition. I slept a
lot. I developed a prodigious appetite, and I read and read
and read.

At first it was difficult to turn pages whilst jammed into
my right-hand-down position, but I soon learned to cope
with this, aided by a little cheating when nobody was there
to see. And I read everything I could lay my hands on,
devouring just about all the schoolboy magazines published
at that time: *Champion, Modern Boy,* the *Scout, Gem, Boys'
Own Paper, Rover* and, of course the *Magnet* with the antics
of Billy Bunter and company. I even read every line of *The*

Morning Post, including the ads. My father's *Wide World* magazine and my mother's weekly *Country Life* did not escape my attention, but I did draw the line at my mother's women's periodicals, except for an appreciative glance at the pictures of models displaying underwear.

Reading *Country Life* from cover to cover (as I still do) led me to a new interest, and I scanned every detail of the advertisements of houses for sale, cutting out photographs of those I particularly liked. A tin box which I kept by my bedside was soon crammed with details of the properties I would buy when I became rich. My lifelong interest in period architecture, furniture and fine arts stems from my early engrossment in the glossy pages of that beautifully produced magazine.

It was not long before my appetite for reading demanded more than such material. My mother gave me a complete set of the works of Charles Dickens and also took out a library subscription for me. Collected short stories, historical novels, biographies, all fed my hunger for reading matter.

Much of what I read obviously did not penetrate. I read fast and probably superficially. But the lasting effect must have been to make my mind more than ordinarily receptive to facts and opinions, and to raise my literary standards.

My last three months in bed were quite pleasant. I was sitting up by then and my bed was moved to the window, where I could look out over the front garden and see the road. The Owen children often went by on their bikes and waved.

Finally came the great day when, with my father and mother supporting me on each side, my feet were lowered over the side of the bed and I actually stood up. But that was all. I didn't even know how to make my legs move in the right direction, and I had absolutely no control over my buckling knees.

Never mind – the long lie-in was over.

I learned to walk again much more quickly than anyone had expected, with an enthusiasm that I must have been storing up for months.

For some days I needed to be supported during the short

periods when I was allowed out of bed, but gradually the muscles and joints of my legs responded sufficiently to allow me to shuffle across the room to a chair where I rested until I was ready for the return journey.

As soon as I was able to move unaided, the next stage was to potter about upstairs, carefully noting the variations in my pulse rate. For I still heeded the inbuilt cautiousness instilled by countless warnings about the dos and don'ts governing my particular malady. One of the problems of a heart condition is that there is nothing to show for it; no scars, no visible signs. At the first warning signal (usually about one hundred beats per minute) I lay still and let everything settle down to normal. I had always to allow for the fact that my heart would race a little with sheer excitement, even before I moved.

I had to be careful not to upset my parents or the doctor. I was still very much under supervision and had been told that I could drop dead if I put any great strain on my heart, but I reckoned that I knew better than anybody just how much my heart could stand. After all, I had studied it for months, and could literally *feel* its reactions. So I worked out my own recovery programme, which had to be totally secret, whilst I appeared to be sticking faithfully to the rules laid down for me.

I realised it would all take time, but I *knew* that I would succeed in the end.

Now that I could walk from room to room, my father carried me downstairs and his little study became my bedroom. The official verdict then was that this represented the full extent of my abilities: I should only walk very slowly and for short distances, I should never attempt to go up any steps, and I should resign myself to this prospect in the future. So now my full craftiness came into operation. If outwardly I appeared to accept this judgement quite cheerfully, inwardly I suppose now that there was the glimmer of a hope that I could always go that bit further. However, so far I was alone in my private opinions and lacked any fellow-conspirator in my planning.

Once I was downstairs it had soon been decided that I should spend most of the day out of doors, and a wheelchair was provided for me. I was pushed to a spot of my choice in the garden and supposed to sit there till somebody came to move me.

The rose garden became my favourite daily venue. About half the size of a tennis court, it was totally screened from view by a clipped conifer hedge, inside which it was surrounded, and criss-crossed, by narrow gravel paths, and I always asked to be trundled to it. Everybody evidently thought that it was rather sweet that I liked to sit and sun myself in this quiet, scented corner. Had they known my true purpose I would probably not have been the only person at home in danger of a heart attack!

I was allowed to turn my chair gently round to face different directions, but I had soon found that the wheelchair rolled along nicely on the gravel paths, so I worked out an exciting circuit which included fast straights and a few sharp bends. Over a period of weeks I steadily improved my times, always relating them to my pulse rates.

This latter was the overriding precaution in everything physical I did at that time and for months afterwards. To claim this now may seem preposterous, but that is how I remember those days. I had little else to think about, and I was all too well aware of the risks I was taking.

When I first swung my legs out of bed and stood up it was obvious that I had sprouted in my greenhouse environment. I was now tall for my age, certainly taller than my petite mother, but slender and rather flabby. My wheelchair exercises very quickly developed the upper part of my body, however, so that it thickened and became quite muscular. My physique has retained much the same shape ever since. And my height also never changed – for some reason or other I never grew a single inch from the age of thirteen. Perhaps I should go back to bed for a spell and see if I could add on the few inches that I have always secretly yearned for!

After about three months of downstairs living, during which I was walking about quite normally but only in short bursts (so far as anybody else knew), the great day came for my mother and myself to go to Brecart for a long holiday. She obviously needed the rest and the local vicar had agreed to tutor me so that I could make up for lost school time.

My father drove us to Liverpool for the overnight trip to Belfast, and we were met on arrival by Auntie Amy and Auntie Dolly. There was much cuddling and wiping of eyes, rather to my embarrassment, and eventually our train pulled into Toome.

Brecart had not changed much since my last visit over a year before. Pat still milked the cows and mowed the lawns; Annie still trimmed the lamps. Uncle Jimmy, however, had left home. My grandfather had scraped together enough cash to send his youngest son off on a world trip which was to take in a visit to his brother Bertie in Australia. None of us ever saw Uncle Jimmy again.

Grandpa did not join in the rapturous and tearful welcome which greeted our arrival. He treated me as if I had never been away, and never once discussed my illness with me.

It must have been a week or so after my arrival that Grandpa, who was adept at keeping me away from the female-filled house for most of the day, told me we were going down the river to see the new dredger working there. He told my mother and the others at lunchtime that he was going to row me around for a while so that I could troll a spoon for pike, a very gentle activity.

The moment we were out of sight of the house, Grandpa shipped the oars and said, 'Come on, boy, you row and I'll fish.'

I really was apprehensive. Careering round the rose garden in my wheelchair was all very well, but rowing a boat: this was something I had not yet contemplated. I can remember feeling my face go scarlet with a kind of shame as I started to protest, but the little boat was already nearly capsizing as Grandpa's huge bulk left the thwart and edged towards the stern. Falling into the river and swimming for my life, gumboots and all, was something else I hadn't envisaged. I hurriedly squeezed past my relentless grandparent and took my place at the oars.

No doubt my heart was pounding, more with fright than anything else, but for once I forgot to take note of it. I took the oars and pulled away downriver.

And nothing dreadful happened: no twinges of pain, no

palpitations, not the slightest breathlessness. Soon I was rowing steadily towards the dredger. Grandpa sat in the stern, placidly twitching his fishing line.

I knew then that I had found a fellow conspirator. It was a silent alliance – we never talked about my problem but it was wonderful for me to realise that I wasn't the only one who didn't believe all that he was told. There was a long way to go, for sure, but I *knew* that I was on the right lines.

That afternoon on the river with Grandpa confirmed all that I had been secretly thinking and gave impetus to my plans. Only Grandpa knew what I was up to, and so doom-laden were the warnings I had been given that for some two years my rule-breaking was unknown to my parents or to anyone else in authority.

Admittedly I was a great deal luckier than many people who suffer from rheumatic fever. But about 1955 I was told by a paediatrician who specialised in rheumatoid cases that my case had become textbook teaching and had done much to alter the treatment of pericarditis.

So perhaps, unwittingly, I did something towards improving the lot of others. And certainly, fifty years later, I am still tackling some pretty hefty jobs around the house and garden, and I have never heard any complaints about my other physical attributes.

At Brecart I was in the midst of all the places that I loved and the things I loved doing. I wandered round the country-side with the faithful and ageing Snooks and Major. I kept a rowing boat tied up and hidden at the boundary of our land and spent hours out on Lough Beg and Church Island. And I walked up to Toome along the river bank.

It was on my excursions to Toome that the two dogs seemed to have an agreed ritual. When we reached the edge of the Brecart townland, a wide, fenced ditch, Snooks always turned back and trotted home, whilst Major considered it his duty to keep me company. Nothing would induce them to alter this practice. Snooks could not be dragged any further, and Major would skulk along behind me if I tried to banish him home too.

Poaching and poteen-stilling were, as ever, the local leisure industries, and whenever I heard oars on the river in the evening I would go to the boat quay first thing in the morning to see if a salmon or a bottle had been left there as a traditional gesture of thanks. Sadly, the salmon had more or less vanished – but apparently the poteen had lost none of its fire.

My convalescence at Brecart lasted about six months and I made great progress both physically and mentally.

I was regularly checked over by Dr Keightley, a family friend who was the sole medical man that my grandfather respected, apart from my father. Jack Keightley was very pleased with my improved condition and allowed me several new freedoms, such as going upstairs and walking any distance providing I didn't rush anything. Naturally, he had no idea what I had been up to, and was therefore quite sure that the restricted lifestyle that had been prescribed for me was working effectively.

This was to be the pattern of my behaviour for the next couple of years: always to be a long way ahead of the rules that were laid down for me, yet always to be buoyed up by the certainty that I was doing no harm to myself whilst I expanded my covert activities. I got into the habit of leading a sort of double life. There were some awful frustrations involved in not being able to reveal my capabilities, but I had decided that this was better than being found out and put under stricter supervision.

But it wasn't always easy to sit and watch other youngsters doing things which I knew damn well I could do better myself. I had to bide my time, whilst the feeling of 'You wait – I'll show them!' burned into me.

Soon I was allowed to walk to my tutoring sessions at the rectory. I really enjoyed the hours spent working with the Reverend Tom. It was a gloomy, tree-shrouded house, but the gentle old rector was a wonderful mentor, and I think I learned more with him in a few weeks than I could have done had I never missed a term at school.

My mind had evidently been sharpened or made more receptive to learning by the wide range of subjects that I had been reading during the past year or so. Tom Egerton led me to a proper appreciation of literature, and to a liking for poetry, which had never previously interested me. English grammar, history, geography, Latin and French I took in quite readily; mathematics were still an insoluble mystery, but the old chap did his best to help me master the essential formulae.

Since my self-imposed strengthening regime was known only to me and Grandpa, my parents still regarded me as being delicate and planned for me accordingly. They had decided that Shrewsbury was out of the question, so a return to Wimborne had already been arranged. The West Moors house was sold and another one rented at Broadstone whilst a home was sought in the Wimborne area.

Eventually we found Clevedon Lodge, a pleasant, unremarkable house in an area of similar homes in nice wooded grounds on the outskirts of the town. My father took on the post of Medical Officer of Health in Wimborne and within a few months also bought a practice there.

By now I was well into my fourteenth year, and the muscular development that had been started in my wheelchair had been furthered by my rowing and other undercover activities, so that I was now quite sturdy. But still, when I returned to school in Wimborne, I was expected to live by a strict code of physical restrictions: no games, no running about, no bicycle.

Fortunately, most of the boys remembered me from before, so I was not treated as some delicate phenomenon. There was an instinctive kindness and sympathy towards me from everyone, masters and boys alike, and I was never made to feel an oddity. Only on the games field did I have to stand alone. Even then, the other boys did their best to include me in their informal scratch games: 'Toddy, will you umpire?' or 'Toddy, would you like to go in goal?'

And besides, the whole school very quickly became aware of my clandestine fitness campaign and aided and abetted it – although, astonishingly, no master ever discovered what was going on.

The temporary home we rented in Broadstone was a rather nasty Edwardian turn-of-the-century house, and it must have been a pretty miserable place for my mother. My father was all right, though. Now restored to relatively good health, he did not find his part-time duties as MOH at Wimborne too onerous. He had taken a gun in a shoot on a nearby estate, regularly played golf, and enjoyed billiards most evenings at the Conservative Club. My bedroom overlooked the side road, and nearly every night I would hear his brisk steps passing by, interspersed with the regular tap of the silver-knobbed Malacca cane that he always carried. I wish I had that cane today: the shaft was hollow and inserted into it was a glass corked tube some two feet long which was revealed when the silver top was unscrewed. Very handy when a little refresher was needed!

6

ACTION REPLAY

My first year back at school in Wimborne brought considerable improvements in my life.

I had caught up with my age group academically and
gradually worked up to being a leader in some subjects,
especially English. And although our move to Clevedon
Lodge meant that I was a day boy instead of being a weekly
boarder, at least I was given a bicycle which I was instructed
to ride sedately to and from school and out to the playing
fields at the opposite end of town.

Naturally, that bike, with the handlebars turned upside-
down to be more sporty, was pedalled furiously in competition with the others, especially at weekends when I got well
away from home and any supervisory eyes. It also became my
means of getting round the countryside. I explored Dorset's
places of interest, especially old churches and graveyards.
These had long fascinated me. One could often put together
the history of a village from the age and size of its church,
and from inscriptions on memorials and gravestones. Some
epitaphs might be sad, but others could be humorous.

Then there were the stark ruins of Corfe Castle on its
Purbeck hillock, and the great Roman earthworks at Badbury
Rings, where a group of us often went, for the forbidden
thrill of riding up and down such an exciting obstacle course.

By now I regarded myself as being physically perfectly
'normal', and safely able to do anything that other boys could
do. But still I was afraid to admit the extent of my activities.
There was probably still the nagging fear that I *could* just be
wrong, and that my freedoms would soon be curtailed if my
disobedience were to be discovered. When I first started to
trot along the road to Tom Egerton's rectory I had gone
through a period when my legs ached dreadfully, but I
realised that this was inevitable as the muscles came back

into use, so I was not worried. The pains came back when I first started my long bike rides, but gradually they receded again. All I cared about was that there were no more palpitations.

Home life at Wimborne was pleasant. We had a good cook who thoroughly spoiled me and she and the one living-in maid were privy to some of my subterfuges. Cook would prepare me generous haversack picnics when I was supposed to be spending the day with friends but was actually off on one of my cycling jaunts.

My mother was fairly content, though not in good health and becoming increasingly highly-strung. Her hobby was now hunting for antiques, and gradually the house was stuffed with things that she snapped up at country-house sales.

My father did just about as much medical work as suited him. He still drank steadily, but was fairly fit, and had found a new outdoor pastime: sailing. Nearly every weekend he went off to Poole to join the yacht that he shared with a couple of cronies, but when it was discovered that they were popping over to Dinard for a flutter on the casino tables, there was a very acrid row at home, and my crest-fallen parent went to sea less frequently. No doubt my mother had threatened to inform my grandmother.

The Guvnor had accumulated an assortment of friends around Dorset, including Augustus John, the artist, with whom he founded a Working Man's Club in some village nearby. The advantage of their awful tin hut was that Club licensing hours enabled them to drop in for a drink when other watering holes were closed.

One day at home I returned from school to see every boy's dream of the perfect motorbike standing by the front door: a Brough Superior. Whilst I enviously gloated upon it, its owner came out with my father, shook hands with me briefly, and roared off. Later I learned that my father's lunch guest that day had been Aircraftman Shaw, better known as Lawrence of Arabia. I would never have guessed it from the bony, ordinary-looking chap I had met outside.

I still spent most of my holidays at Brecart and, all in all, life was pretty good – with one exception: I was still not

allowed to play games. I knew darned well that I was perfectly
capable of taking part, but I just had to bide my time.

In my second summer at Wimborne I was at last allowed
to play cricket, and did quite well, becoming a member of
the under-sixteen side. As I never shone with the bat there
was little danger that I would over-exert myself running
between the wickets.

But other things were still forbidden: no rugger, no soccer
and no athletics. The latter was particularly galling, since I
knew that I was a faster sprinter than any other boy of my
age.

The Cadet Corps, too, was forbidden to me, so I rather
half-heartedly joined the school Scout troop. I was not
allowed to take part in some of the more energetic Scout
activities, but I did enjoy learning about local flora and fauna,
and built up quite a collection of grass-snakes, slow-worms
and lizards which were kept in a large glass-lidded show-case
at school.

Just before my sixteenth year I worked out a way of taking
part in the sports from which I was barred at school. I joined
Bournemouth Sports Club and began to play rugger again,
and also to take part in athletics.

My request to be allowed to go and watch games and
athletic meetings was sympathetically received, so I became
a sort of part-time sports correspondent for local newspapers
such as the *Bournemouth Echo* and the *Western Gazette*, and
some of the games I was reporting I had actually taken part
in – under my assumed name of Richard Andrews.

Perhaps a couple of years of pent-up energy and determi-
nation to prove myself motivated me on the field, and I
became marked as a promising player. The frustrating thing
was that, even though I was invited to play a couple of times
for Dorset Colts, I couldn't tell my parents.

My fitness and such skill and prowess as I had were due
more than anything else to my great friend and fellow conspirator Bobby Brewer. R. M. S. Brewer was probably the
most popular boy in the school. He was a year older than
me and something of a tearaway whose jaunty independence
did not always find favour with the school hierarchy. But he
excelled in every sport that he took up. He was a very good

scrum-half, a classy batsman, and as a lightweight was never beaten at boxing.

Brewer spent much of his free time training in a public sports park near his home, and I joined him. He knew about the restrictions that had been placed on me, but he also realised that I was as fit as anybody, and encouraged me to practise as much as possible. First of all we batted and bowled in the public nets, and during the winter we took out a rugger ball and practised running, passing, tackling and kicking, usually finishing our sessions with a cross-country jog and a dip in the River Stour, even when the river's edges were icy.

I also entered various local and South of England athletics events, including a Public Schools holiday meeting, at which I won the 100 yards and 120 yards hurdles.

But finally disaster struck: I ran at a Boy Scout county meeting at Poole, still as Richard Andrews, managing to win four events and the individual championship. At the end of the day I lined up with the other medal-winners to collect my trophies, when, to my horror, I realised that the presentations were to be made by Sir James Brooks, a friend of my parents. When I came before him it was questionable which of us showed the most consternation, and I muttered, 'Sir, can I speak to you later?' When I eventually had a chance to face him, I explained my predicament, which he already knew, anyway, and asked if he would keep my cups and medals for me and say nothing to my parents. He sportingly, if dubiously, agreed and I hoped my problem would be over for the time being.

But worse was to come.

Competing as Richard Andrews I had hitherto managed to evade detection, but this time a large photograph appeared in a newspaper which my father happened to see. And that did it – I was caught in the act.

I'll never forget the scenes at home: my worried mother in tears, my father furious, as he telephoned the heart specialist, and me quaking with fright. I couldn't wangle my way out of this.

The next day my father drove me to the hospital, where I had every conceivable examination, including blood tests,

an ECG and X-rays. Sheer nerves probably made my heart
behave most erratically, but they could find nothing wrong.
Finally, with my father present, the specialist gave me a
severe lecture, I might have dropped dead, etc, and then he
and my father broke into delighted grins and he told me that
I was all right, that I could now live a normal life. He went
so far as to say that I now had an exceptionally powerful
heart. I remember his words: 'Don't worry, son, that heart
of yours could pump sludge around.'

And so happily ended three years of doubt, deception and
frustration. I suppose the whole traumatic hiccup in my life
had done me no harm. Although I had missed many things,
Shrewsbury and lots of normal fun and games, I had also
gained. Queen Elizabeth's Grammar School, Wimborne,
had been good for me and only as a day boy could I ever
have carried out my schemes.

After that, a lot happened very quickly. I passed the School
Certificate Examination with five credits and two distinctions,
enough to gain me Matriculation Exemption, and I played
two parts in the school production of John Galsworthy's
Escape.

The play consisted of a series of scenes depicting a man
on the run from the police. Early in the play I took the role
of a lady surprised in her bedroom *en plein négligé*, a part
that I invested with mannerisms copied from a brief study of
my mother's boudoir habits, and that got me some laughs
from an indulgent audience. In the last scene I was the kindly
vicar who persuaded the fugitive to face up to justice, a
character whom I tried to base on Canon Keith, the cleric
who had instructed me in preparation for my confirmation.

Already I had developed a real interest in written drama
and attended regular play-reading sessions in which those of
us who wished to put in some extra study were encouraged
to read and discuss works by contemporary playwrights as
well as the obligatory classics.

Up to then I had found Shakespeare's plays pretty heavy
to wade through. However, in that year our set play for the
School Certificate had been *The Tempest*, and we were taken
to see a professional production in Bournemouth. At last
Shakespeare came to life for me, and from that time I became

an avid theatre-goer, either with school parties or with my grandmother's influence and help.

It was during that year that an idea for my future career became an obsession with me. The heady excitement of having articles accepted by local newspapers had begun to pall, and I wanted to be a dramatist.

I had enjoyed my brief experience of amateur dramatics, but it did not occur to me that I had in me the makings of an actor. It seemed to me that acting was fun but not something to be taken seriously as a job of work.

I actually started to attempt a play about the unfortunate Duke of Monmouth, but the sheer magnitude of the research required daunted me, and the more I read the more I realised that I could never encompass my subject in three acts. My play, had it ever been written, would have been nearly as long as the Duke's entire life.

It dawned on me that writing passable schoolboy essays and short stories – and sports reports for the *Bournemouth Echo* – was a far cry from writing a play, and I had no idea how to acquire the necessary skills and experience.

My parents were not well versed in such matters, and indeed my father now made it clear that he thought I should either go to university and study law or go into the army – both proper jobs for a chap, in his estimation – while my mother had romantic ideas about my entering the Diplomatic Corps, probably because I could speak French.

So I didn't rush to discuss my ideas with my mother and father.

Once again, Granny Todd became my confidante. I told her about my literary ambition and she, bless her, was delighted. The prospect of having a playwright in the family obviously thrilled her, and she lost no time in making it all possible.

One of Granny's acquaintances in Bournemouth was Italia Conti, who ran the famous Italia Conti Stage School in London. Miss Conti had a house in Bournemouth, and she and my grandmother frequently met to take tea together, so I was introduced to Miss Conti at my grandmother's hotel and put through quite an inquisition by that redoubtable and charming woman.

She told me I was not cut out to be an actor because I was too short but approved my desire to write for the theatre. However, she was adamant that I could never write plays until I had some experience of the theatre and some idea of the material needed by actors. 'Come to my school and learn what it's all about, dear boy. Noël Coward started with me, and look what he's done!'

I could never see myself with a fraction of Coward's talents, but Miss Conti's suggestion made sense to me. And Granny was agog at the idea. So we worked out a plan of campaign.

I should say nothing at home until the next time Granny came to stay with us. Then I was to broach the subject to my parents and Granny would back me up in the face of their inevitable opposition and would finally convince my father by offering to support me in London for at least two years. We both knew that he would not resist this ultimate temptation.

That afternoon in Bournemouth my future was settled, though not quite as I had intended, and by the end of that year, 1935, Granny and I had seen our strategy win through. I was to leave school the following April, when I was nearly seventeen, there being no point in my staying on if I was not going to university.

So, for another two terms, I just fiddled about at Wimborne. Being an ordinary schoolboy was boring. The thrills of London loomed, and I counted the days to the moment when, suffused with theatrical knowledge, I would sit down and dash off a brilliant first drama – probably a few months after I had arrived at Conti's.

I stood there appalled.

For some reason that I cannot remember I had arrived at the Italia Conti Stage School a day or so after the term had begun, and all the noisy activities of the place were in full swing. I had reported to the office and had been told to wait in the reception area until the secretary was free to give me my schedule of classes and list of requirements.

Conti's occupied two buildings facing each other across Lamb's Conduit Street in Bloomsbury. One was a rather ramshackle house where rooms – or 'studios' as they were called – were devoted mainly to the serious drama and elocution classes and where there was usually a fairly tranquil atmosphere, broken only by the occasional distraught wail of a budding Juliet on hearing of Tybalt's death, or by the adolescent roar of an angry, under-age Othello.

The other building was more modern and quite large, with studios opening off the reception area on the first floor. These studios were used solely for music and dance classes, except when male students were being instructed in fencing and sword-play. The only furnishings in these rooms were pianos and mirrors for the ballet classes.

To anyone waiting in the reception area the cacophony emanating from these studios was excruciating: at any one moment there might be *Swan Lake* being lustily thumped for a ballet class in one room, modern jingle for a clattering tap-dancing lesson in another, and musical comedy chorus tunes for a singing class from the third, all overtopped by the strident instructions or admonitions of the teachers.

This pandemonium assailed me as I waited there, self-conscious and ill-at-ease. Worse was to come. There I was, nervously wondering what I had let myself in for, when the classes all simultaneously ended and the three studios disgorged a chattering flood of animated, weirdly garbed students shoving and elbowing their way to the changing rooms.

The scene was reminiscent of the locker-rooms in the sports pavilion after a game – certainly the sweaty haze was the same – but there were two essential differences. I had never before been beset by a horde of girls in leotards and tights, and I had never before seen boys wearing tights, ballet straps, blouses and with rather long hair.

I myself had thoughtfully dressed that morning in what I considered would be correct for the occasion: my school tweed jacket, grey slacks and, of course, a neat collar and tie. Now I felt like an undertaker at Mardi Gras, and I studied the notice-board with deep concentration, though most of its messages meant little to me.

I was rescued by the secretary, who called me into her office to go through my schedule of classes and give me a list of things I would need, which varied from a pair of tap shoes to a complete edition of Shakespeare's plays. I thought I had enrolled only to study drama, but I was told very firmly that I was expected to do the entire school course like any other student. Later I realised the good sense of this. I would have to learn at least the rudiments of every facet of live theatre, for one of the merits of the Italia Conti Stage School in those days was that it was a thoroughly practical working stage academy, where any hidden talent might be detected and developed, and where a complete grounding was given in every aspect of theatrical work.

The school also acted as an agency, securing practical paid work for its students, many of whom paid for their studies out of professional fees. Those going through the school ranged in age from young children (Conti Kids) to adult actors and dancers coming back for refresher courses. During my own period there I appeared in crowd scenes in two Will Hay comedy films, had a small part in a government film concerning our national air defences (*The Gap*), spent several days filming a university athletics meeting with Robert Taylor in *A Yank at Oxford*, played leading roles in Conti's own production of *Where the Rainbow Ends* on two occasions, and experienced a season at the Open Air Theatre, Regent's Park, playing walk-on parts and understudying leads under the firm and critical direction of Robert Atkins.

There is nothing like practical experience, and the chance to work with and study experts, to form the groundwork for learning in any profession, especially if all this is backed up by good teaching and advice.

Small wonder that I became more and more absorbed in my new studies and activities. I had intended to gain some background for my literary ambitions, but I came away from there intent on being an actor – and never once even attempted to write for the theatre.

Just as well, probably. My profession has on the whole been kind to me.

And, although my poor mother had deeply-rooted misgivings about the dissolute life she was convinced I must be leading, my father didn't mind much one way or the other. On the day I left home to go to London he called me into his study and gave me the one piece of advice that he thought would be useful in my new world: 'There'll be times when you

will feel like a woman. Don't mess about with enthusiastic
amateurs – they never know what's wrong with them. Go to
the old prostitute – she always keeps herself clean.'

Italia Conti herself took certain drama classes. I seem to
remember that she concentrated on the more romantic subjects such as *Romeo and Juliet* or *Twelfth Night* where she
delighted in using all her silvery tones and still-discernible
prettiness to demonstrate female artifice to her students. She
was indeed a most charming and beguiling woman and very
kindly. Her house in Bournemouth, right on the cliffs, with
its private path down to the beach, was always available for
ailing youngsters or for the less privileged ones who simply
needed a holiday.

Her sister, Bianca Murray, was a daunting person who
undertook the bulk of the senior drama coaching, and she it
was who gave form to whatever latent talent I had. Mrs
Murray's leathery face appeared to have taken on some of
the hue and texture of the tobacco in the Russian cigarettes
she chain-smoked, and her deep, gravelly voice was probably
the by-product of incessant nicotine as well as years of vocal
athletics. For all her fierce expression, especially as she
massively inhaled a prodigious drag on her cigarette as
though she hated it and wanted to consume it totally, she
had a great sense of fun and humour, which she released in
thunderous back-alley guffaws.

She was a stern and exacting mentor and I learned from
her basic lessons which gave me my first real understanding
of what plays and playing were all about.

Marjorie Anderson's class in elocution and voice production was one that I enjoyed. I thought she was a charming
person, and could always recognise her beautifully modu-
lated tones as presenter of *Woman's Hour* on BBC Radio
until her retirement a few years ago.

I fared less well in the other classes.

My singing has always been hideous, even by bathroom
standards, but I was forced through my discordant paces in
the musical comedy lessons. At least my efforts provided
amusement for the others, if not for the unfortunate girl with
whom I was paired, usually Doreen Symons, a very pretty

girl whom I greatly fancied. Sadly, our duet sessions put paid to any hopes I had of her. Red-faced with embarrassment, I lumbered through the awful minutes, gasping with relief when the moment came to end the song and go into the final embrace, which I would have enjoyed had I not by then persuaded myself that my exertions and nerves had induced halitosis, body odour and sweaty hands. Even now, the mere sound of 'Tea for Two' can terrify me all over again.

Ruby Hilary, too, went through considerable anguish in endeavouring to improve my ballroom dancing. My shuffling and tripping progress around the room usually left me bereft of willing partners, so Miss Hilary had to volunteer to pilot me herself. She was a strong woman, and a born leader.

I was dropped from the ballet and tap classes within a few weeks. The spirit was most unwilling and the flesh just could not master the necessary agility.

But I was an enthusiastic, if clumsy, participant in the Greek dancing classes, which were held in a large hired hall, where we contorted ourselves in all manner of strange exercises, or pranced around the room throwing, carrying or catching balloon-like objects with supposedly controlled abandon. Alas, my object in attending these classes was not to improve my deportment, but to feast my eyes on Dinah Sheridan, quite the most lovely girl I had ever seen. Tall, slender, willowy, golden hair streaming, Dinah only needed a green and bosky background to be the original classic nymph. As she wafted elegantly through our Greek dancing sessions she was my dream of absolute perfection.

Dinah looked on me not unkindly, and we occasionally dodged lessons in order to hold hands in the local cinema, where they had double seats costing sixpence each for the afternoon performances.

She is still lovely and utterly charming today – and still, romantically, calls me Sausage.

In general, I adjusted quickly and happily to Conti's. I was there for about eighteen months during 1936 and 1937. Not long, one might think, to learn all the basic skills of a professional actor – certainly not by the standards of modern drama schools – but here the benefits of practical experience in the theatrical world, so much a part of Conti's curriculum, accelerated the training process.

Our leisure moments were mostly spent in the Express Dairy café next door. Here we sat around in chattering groups drinking milk-and-a-dash (the dash, I hasten to add, being simply a few grains of coffee) or eating our snack lunches of egg and beans on toast. And then of course there were the breaks that came when I got a job in a film or on stage.

The Will Hay movies were great fun to work on, and Conti's produced the leading young actor, Jimmy Hanley, who was the envy of us all and had reached almost star status.

But my two seasons in *Where the Rainbow Ends* were the highlights of my early professional appearances. This lovely old show was Italia Conti's own production, and was staged for some weeks each Christmas and New Year at the Holborn Empire. It had a rattling good jingoistic story about England and St George, and all the elements of a marvellous spectacle for children – and their parents – with dragons, a witch, a genie of the lamp and a brother and sister in peril until the timely intervention of St George, revealed in his shining armour.

Roger Quilter's music was enchanting and formed part of his Children's Overture. Sir Roger himself always conducted the orchestra on the first night, Boxing Day, the last night, and whenever Royalty was present. At other times Leslie Woodgate took the baton. His niece, Florence, was one of the leading dancers.

Many famous names have appeared on the *Rainbow* cast lists, including Noël Coward, Gertrude Lawrence and Jack Hawkins.

I was entrusted with two leading parts, the Slacker and the Witch. The Slacker's downfall was considered to be the acting highlight of the show, and certainly stretched my inexperienced capabilities. But the Witch provided me with a skill not known to many actors: I was 'flown' on a Kirby wire from the wings onto the stage and later from the stage back into the wings.

The art of 'flying' demands certain disciplines. For example, one can never turn through a complete circle on stage while the wire is slack. This would risk putting a kink into the wire which would probably tighten and snap on take-off. Also, one must be careful not to anticipate take-off and jump, as this would put a sudden strain on the harness and the fine steel wire, with a similar result. The theatrical aeronaut remains still and relaxed, allowing the strain on harness and wire to be taken gradually.

My entrance was made from offstage, perched on a platform at the top of a pair of steps some twelve feet high – a wobbly process at the best of times, especially for someone who has difficulty standing on a chair to replace an electric light bulb. On the given cue, the wire would tighten, I would be hoisted up a foot or so and then swung onstage, landing as decorously as possible when the wire was lowered by the controlling technician.

'Flying' offstage was the reverse process. On cue I braced myself, hoped that the wire had not fouled anything, and wafted off to the steps again, grabbing a safety rope until my feet were firmly planted on the platform.

As the Witch, I was festooned in a shroud of grey muslin rags, topped with a straggly grey wig, and plastered with a hideous greeny-grey make-up. As the final touch of artistry I blacked out my teeth, except for one fang in front, and, of course, I carried a broomstick. My entrance and exit were accompanied by a loud, maniacal cackle and I spoke my lines in a high-pitched, rasping shriek. No three witches on a Scottish heath ever smote their roles with greater enthusiasm.

That same eagerness proved my undoing on one occasion. Carried away by my own performance, I failed to find the mark for my exit, and flew off in an arc, missed the safety rope and the steps, and flew backwards on stage again, by which time my cackling laugh had risen several octaves. After a couple of pendulum movements I was eventually lowered – onstage. Stung by the howls of laughter from the audience, I tucked my broomstick between my legs and shuffled off, grimacing evilly at the house. It was the high spot of that day's performance.

With several dozen high-spirited youngsters going through their paces in the show, there were inevitably moments of indiscipline, and Conti's chauffeur, Ted, was a major contributor to these. Taking part in the show as an extra stage-hand was Ted's annual perk, and this amiable Cockney derived a great deal of amusement from his various duties, one of which was to stand inside a hollow plaster tree which was an important prop centre stage in some of the scenes. The tree had canvas arms meant to look like branches, and Ted manipulated these to grab the young heroine lost in the forest during one of the frightening moments. He also had to emit warbling hyena cries on certain cues.

All this Ted did with gusto and with frequent profane remarks *sotto voce*, designed to 'corpse' those on stage, usually only too successfully. Frequently the cast were hard-pressed to stifle their giggles.

On one occasion, Albert Davies, who played the young hero, told Ted that his parents were in the audience, and promised to bring him one of his father's cigars next day if Ted didn't try to corpse him. Ted agreed and behaved impeccably, but unfortunately Albert forgot the cigar next day. At the point in the show where Ted should have produced the hyena call, Albert gave the necessary cue, but it was followed by silence. Albert tried again, and again there was silence. Albert gave the cue a third time, and there came a rich Cockney voice from behind the tree, 'No cigars, no effing hyenas.'

Albert corpsed.

However Ted, a great royalist, was as good as gold when the then Queen Elizabeth occupied the Royal Box with the two little princesses, Elizabeth and Margaret.

During my period at Conti's my leisure time away from the school went through some mixed patterns, ranging from the fairly U to the very non-U.

Always I was provided by Granny Todd with an adequate though not substantial weekly allowance which was occasionally augmented by my own earnings and even by a few hand-outs from my father. I invariably had enough for my needs, but from time to time had to save up furiously – and often dietetically – to finance any little extravagances. Still, nearly every week I could count on at least one good blow-out when Granny took me to dinner, either at her hotel or at some restaurant.

At first I had a bed-sit in Gower Street, opposite the Royal Academy of Dramatic Art. Granny had arranged these digs for me, probably because she thought they were in an area appropriate to my new studies, but after a couple of weeks I went as a paying-guest to a house in Onslow Square, South Kensington, owned by a friend of Granny's. Here I was very comfortable and well-found, and stayed for two or three months, thoroughly spoiled by my kind hostess.

However, I was now beginning to find my way about London, and felt that I needed more freedom of movement. So my next choice of accommodation may seem extraordinary: I took a room at the London Central YMCA Club. I had been seeking some sort of club which I could afford and which had good sports and leisure facilities, and in the YMCA there were an excellent and very reasonable restaurant, numerous reading rooms with a good stock of books, music rooms where recitals were frequently given, and six first-class tables for billiards and snooker. The sports complex provided a competition-sized swimming pool and a large and very well-equipped gymnasium, and there were also a rugger club and wrestling classes.

So I took a very comfortable room there and reverted to an almost school boarding life, looked after by a kindly staff of matrons, porters and maids, and lived well within my income, with a bit to spare for other interests.

Those were the days of débutantes and coming-out balls and parties, and Granny saw to it that I was on the lists of acceptable young men who contrived to live quite busy social lives at very little cost to themselves. All that was needed was the requisite entrée, two sets of evening dress, and the ability to buy a bottle of champagne at the 400 Club or some such late-night venue. All this I managed without too frequent recourse to the overdraft facility which Granny had set up for me at her bank in Davies Street.

Fortune seemed to smile on me. One night, having delivered a young deb to her home in Kensington, I walked out miserably into the pouring rain without even the price of a bus fare, prepared to trudge wetly the miles back to Bloomsbury with resultant awful effects on my dinner-jacket. I had gone only a few steps when I saw a pound note glistening on the pavement. At the same time a taxi hove into sight, so with my lucky discovery I was able to ride home in comfort.

More than once, in later years, something equally fortunate has turned up in the nick of time. Somebody up there must have kept an eye on my welfare . . .

For almost a year I contrived to keep a happy balance between my Bloomsbury and Mayfair activities, and with Miss Conti's advice and encouragement, I auditioned and was accepted for the whole 1937 season in the Regent's Park Open Air Theatre Company, playing small parts and walk-ons, but with the chance to understudy some leading roles.

We were directed by the great Robert Atkins, revered as a fine director and a memorable character. Burly and booming, Mr Atkins controlled his players with a voice that could put pigeons to flight and actors to shame, and was heeded by stars and supers alike.

I was fortunate in those weeks at Regent's Park to be able to study some great actors at work, amongst them Ion Swinley, Phyllis Nielson-Terry and, above all for my taste, Balliol Holloway, an impressive, craggy old man who was superb as Malvolio, Jaques and Caliban. I wish I had his sonorous voice, and wonderful stage presence.

The jewel in our band of players was the delectable Vivien Leigh, then in the brightest days of her beauty – and, like myself, a great and unsuppressible giggler. She played Anne Boleyn in our production of *Henry VIII*.

In that play I understudied Giles Isham as the Duke of Buckingham (thank God the star never missed a performance, because I trembled at the awful realisation of how inadequate I would be in the part) and walked on as the Bishop of London in the coronation procession, suitably robed, mitred and grey-wigged. My only duty was to flank Queen Anne in the slow, dignified parade across the stage and up some steps towards a symbolic throne, bearing her crown before me on a velvet cushion. Nothing too onerous, one might think. But I had not reckoned with the difficulty of supporting the precious headpiece without a tremor whilst negotiating the steps in my long robe.

Inevitably, at one performance my solemn progress was marred by the tiniest of trips, enough to send the crown teetering to the edge of the cushion. I grabbed it with one hand just in time to prevent it from actually crashing to the ground, but in this tense moment the blameless Bishop of London mouthed a very audible 'Bugger!'

This was too much for Miss Leigh. She corpsed, and was joined by most of the courtiers and churchmen around her, including myself.

She never reproached me for reducing her great moment in the play to a helpless shambles, and fortunately I don't think Robert Atkins heard about the incident.

It was during that summer that Laurence Olivier, darkly handsome and already famous, must have been paying court to the lovely Miss Leigh. His visits to her tented dressing-room were frequent, and always induced conjecture amongst us lowly members of the company.

I enjoyed that season immensely, and, I believe, learned a lot from it. I even had the chance to play Orlando in *As You Like It* for one performance when the leading man was ill, and was especially elated to be asked by Robert Atkins to join the company the following year.

1937 also marked one of the most tragic episodes in my life . . .

One evening I was called to the phone. A man who described himself as being from Associated Press asked me if I could give him any details of my mother's death by drowning in Ireland.

Stunned and totally confused I replied that I didn't even know about it. Could he tell me anything? He couldn't.

I then tried to phone my father, and for call after call I couldn't get through. Our Wimborne number was constantly engaged. Not knowing what to do, I abandoned my efforts.

Later that night I was called to the phone again. It was my father. It had been his efforts to get through to me that had kept our phone busy.

He had had the same query from Associated Press, and wondered if I knew anything. We then decided that he would drive up to London to fetch me, after trying to contact Brecart to find out what had happened.

Miserable hours passed while I packed and waited for the Guvnor.

Late that evening he arrived, and we started our drive to Dorset. On the way he told me that he had been unable to contact Brecart, but that he had spoken to a solicitor in Ireland and asked for details, and also for wreaths, etc., to be arranged if necessary. He had also made plans to charter a plane for us the next day.

It was an awful journey home.

I should explain the background to all this.

Weeks previously, my mother and father had had a serious row. I don't know the details, and can't ascribe any blame. I did know that my father was by no means an ideal spouse, but I also knew that my mother had become increasingly neurotic during the past year. She was also bitter about my going to London and about my chosen career, feeling that I had succumbed to my grandmother's influence.

This may have been true, but I couldn't see any harm in it, and really didn't know how to cope with my mother's displeasure.

She had finally decided to separate from my father, at least for the time being, and to go back to Brecart to think things over. She had written to me on her arrival there – the first I knew about the whole affair – in terms that were pretty caustic about both me and my father. I had not replied, simply because I did not know what to say. I thought she would cool down in a short time, anyway. At my age I had no experience of writing wise, placatory letters.

I had been dreadfully worried, nevertheless, and on this occasion couldn't turn to my grandmother for advice.

And then came this shattering news.

On the morning of our arrival home, a telegram arrived for my father stating that any wreaths from him or myself would be returned, and that we would on no account be received in Brecart by the Hunters.

The solicitor also phoned to say that as far as he could ascertain my mother had been found drowned by the riverside and that a verdict of suicide was expected.

The charter plane was cancelled. My father and I spoke little to each other: what was there to say, except to question

why? We were both desperately upset, and I saw my father
sitting hunched at his desk, sobbing. I pretended I hadn't
noticed, and went off to blubber in my own room.

It had been a cruel blow to both of us, and the Hunters'
attitude, inexplicably bitter, had compounded the hurt.

After a couple of uneasy days at home I returned to
London by train. I only remember one thing my father said,
just as I was leaving: 'I wish we could have her back, you
know.'

I wished the same.

Apart from the loss of my mother – and I had always
been closer to her than anyone – I never heard from my
grandfather and grandmother Hunter again, nor, for many
years, from my aunts. Nor did I know what had befallen
Uncle Jimmy. I suppose the Hunter family blamed my father
and me for what had happened to their favourite, but their
bitterness was extreme beyond belief.

So – no more Hunters for me, no more Brecart, no more
Ireland. And no more family life, either, for a very long
time.

7

THE WELSH PLAYERS

Towards the end of 1937 my way of life became slightly more expansive, helped by the proceeds from the Open Air Theatre and a film which I appeared in financed by Cadbury's, the chocolate-makers. It was a half-hour version of today's TV commercials, made for exhibition in cinemas and produced with considerable quality.

During the weeks I spent filming in the Birmingham area I stayed in the old Grand Hotel, and thoroughly enjoyed my taste of the good life. I especially savoured cosy dinners in the Grill Room tête-à-tête with Joan, a very attractive local girl, who seemed to appreciate my taste in wine. I re-formed my friendship with Joan when I was in the Army a couple of years later. She then dubbed me Ricky-with-the-Tuft, an allusion to the moustache I had grown as part of my wartime camouflage.

On my return to London I sublet a flat in Dolphin Square for a few weeks, and then moved to a furnished apartment in Clarges Street, just off Piccadilly. I was still officially a student at Conti's but I only attended occasional classes under Bianca Murray's tutelage.

I managed to play an occasional game of rugger that winter and on New Year's Eve, 1937, I was probably the last person to climb the statue of Eros in Piccadilly Circus. From then on the monument was boarded up on festive occasions.

During my months in Clarges Street I had ample opportunity to follow my father's advice regarding the sort of ladies I should consort with, but frankly the idea didn't appeal to me.

Piccadilly, Bond Street, Curzon Street and Clarges Street bounded the area where high-class tarts plied their ancient trade, and many of them appeared to occupy flats in the area, or in Shepherd Market. Drawn up at regular intervals along the pavements, they prowled their allotted beats as watchfully as any sentries, each in her uniform of black suit and silver fox fur cape, and frequently accompanied by the obligatory miniature white poodle.

Whenever I walked back to my flat in the evenings I ran the gamut of their greetings, such as, 'Hello, darling. You look lonely. How'd you like a nice young virgin?' At first I was quite flustered by all this attention, and hurried along with a muttered 'No, thank you,' but after a few weeks they got to know me by sight and evidently accepted that I was not a potential client.

One particularly good-looking girl with page-boy blonde hair was posted on the corner of Clarges Street and Piccadilly, and we recognised one another with a sociable time-of-day for some weeks.

One bleak winter evening, quite early, I was scuttling head-down through the drizzle, and, rounding the corner into Clarges Street, I passed my acquaintance. I had only gone a few yards along Clarges Street when I heard a hurrying clack of high heels behind me.

Before I could get out the customary 'No, thank you,' the girl said, 'Don't worry. I know you don't want me, but would you like to have tea with me?'

She went on to explain that she lived in the flat across the road from mine and had noticed that I seemed to spend a lot of time alone, and that she had often wondered whether I would like to join her for a cup of tea, but that she hadn't liked to ask.

Now, however, she didn't intend to hang around any longer in the rain, so would I like to pop over to her place in a few minutes – just to talk, she stressed.

It would have been gauche and churlish to refuse, so I agreed to join her.

I expected to find myself in some exotic boudoir, draped in silks and heavy with incense, the way it was in the movies. The sitting-room I entered, however, was almost a replica of my own furnished apartment across the road, and my hostess began briskly to set out the tea things.

'Milk and sugar?' would never have been Mae West's opening gambit.

In no time I forgot my nerves and chatted away, munching scones and telling her about my theatrical ambitions. She seemed to be genuinely interested.

Eventually we got around to her own story. Apparently she had first gone 'on the game' when she was twenty and her parents had died, leaving her to fend for herself. Her earnings were enough to keep her in that pleasant flat. Her clientele came mostly from being on the books of the American and German Embassies and certain big companies.

What really staggered me was her assertion that she almost never went to bed with her clients. 'Most of them just want somebody to take out to dinner,' she told me. 'They usually get so drunk that they don't mind if I tell them to go home and be good boys.' But it seemed that many of those who did get as far as the bedroom had very weird needs. She apparently kept a cupboard full of equipment for the purpose – whips, slippers and such.

I would like to be able to report that I had a continuing relationship with this girl similar to that enjoyed by David Niven with his Nessie, but I never saw her again. No doubt her telephone bookings kept her busy.

After one more season in *Where the Rainbow Ends*, several of us at Conti's were interviewed by a man who was forming a new repertory company in Wales.

Robert Thornley was a plump, pudgy-faced gay who seemed to delight in exaggerating everything traditionally camp: shrill giggles, arch sidelong looks, and little fluttering hand movements, constantly sweeping back the lock of hair that fell over his eyes. His heavy Lancashire accent was further complicated by an explosive stutter so that he spoke in staccato bursts, his sentences tumbling upon each other in rapid fire. One felt that he would have been happier in drag, yet he always wore dark suits that never quite fitted him and sober ties that were knotted never quite centrally.

He was withal a thoroughly endearing man, kind and generous to a fault and with a sense of humour that suited his characteristic chuckles and giggles. He laughed at himself as much as anything.

Above all, Robert had a deep love for the theatre in all its aspects. He was one of that irrepressible band of small-time impresarios who have somehow kept world theatre alive, struggling constantly against the lack of funds, often cheerfully enduring considerable personal hardship and always hoping for a huge success that would give them access to the well-heeled backers. They are fighters, not always scrupulous in small ways but never ill-meaning, rarely profiting themselves and forever optimistic. Some never know the glamour of a West End theatre, some fall out, disillusioned and penniless despite their enthusiasm, and a few move up the thespian ladder to fame.

Fortunately, I believe that Mr Thornley eventually found a wealthy Mr Buckley, from Bolton, and had a degree of success after the Second World War.

The auditions for the Thornley company were held in a room at Conti's. I was present because Miss Conti had apparently recommended me. Whether it was because she thought I had any outstanding talent or because she thought that I should have a taste of the real hard work and atmosphere experienced in repertory companies, I never discovered. Perhaps a bit of both.

We listened while the amiable Mr Thornley explained his plans. The group was to be called the Welsh Players, and would play a limited season in the principality under the aegis of the Miners' Welfare Trust, an organisation that provided for welfare and entertainment in the colliery areas. The season would open at Ebbw Vale, and then go to Merthyr Tydfil, and the intention was to find a permanent home in the area, and to form a repertory company. The opening extravaganza was to be Edgar Wallace's *On the Spot*.

Immensely persuasive, he convinced us all that this was to be the chance of our lifetime: to join a distinguished company and play to packed houses in plush theatres in one of the most glamorous areas of Great Britain. The salaries would not be high but would be adequate for all our needs, and would, of course, be increased once the company had become established.

After my first reservations about Mr Thornley's mannerisms, I soon warmed to the whole concept. I, along with

Michael Darbyshire and some other youngsters that I had
not met before, agreed to join the Welsh Players. So at last
I was to be a full-time actor!

The Workman's Hall, Ebbw Vale, South Wales – there's an
address to conjure with, then!

This was the unlovely setting for the first production of the
Welsh Players in 1938. Our ridiculously youthful company
duly presented *On the Spot*, a play depicting the characters
and times of the Chicago gangsters of the 1920s and '30s. It
had originally been seen in London with Charles Laughton
playing Tony Perelli, and with Charlotte Francis playing Min
Lee, his Chinese paramour.

Our chief claim to distinction was that Miss Francis was
our resident director, and, of course, she played our Min
Lee as well. I appeared as Angelo Verona, one of the thugs,
a role that called for the skills and characteristics of a young
George Raft. I waded into the part with a swarthy make-up,
a stuck-on thin black moustache, my first built-up shoes (later
to be a permanent feature of my professional wardrobe) and
an enthusiastic bash at a heavy Italo-American accent. I must
have been awful, but I got kind reviews from the local papers.
That part of South Wales had for long been theatre-starved.

The Workman's Hall had been built, probably around the
turn of the century, partly as a theatre-cum-music-hall, and
partly as a meeting house. It had a proscenium stage, very
bare dressing-rooms, and the auditorium itself remains in my
memory as a curious mixture of court-room, church and
theatre, with lots of wooden benches on several levels.

We were quite a success, and stayed on at the Workman's
Hall with an extended repertoire for a month or more.
We were all young hopefuls, having our first experience of
belonging to a permanent repertory company in the pro-
vinces. Names, sadly, I cannot remember, and all my keepsakes of that period were lost during the war. One I do,
however, remember was Betty Rogers, an extremely pretty
and charming girl with whom I formed a close and lasting
friendship until I joined the army and she, as Sally Rogers,
became a popular radio personality.

Robert Thornley kept our enthusiasm and spirits high with

his stuttering chatter while he rushed around plotting and planning our future existence, and Charlotte Francis drilled us with her own special thespian philosophy: which was that all acting ability and emotion comes from the genitals. 'Darling, bring it from the genitals!' was her oft-repeated cry from the stalls, as she peeled another orange from the ever-present bag beside her. This frequent exhortation was applied to the volume of our voice production as much as to our depth of feeling.

Apart from our work in the modest atmosphere of the Workman's Hall we all lived a pretty frugal existence in Ebbw Vale. Michael Darbyshire and I shared a room in a little terraced house and such spare time as we had was spent outside the grimy ganglions of the town, with its tightly packed centre of grey-faced streets, the surrounding green hills scarred by coal pits, factories and bare slag heaps. We walked those hills whenever we had the chance and looked down from the brightening colours of spring onto the pall of smoke that hazed our working world below.

Betty Rogers had digs in nearby Tredegar, and most evenings I walked back with her over the hill between the towns rather than leave her to take the bus alone after the show. We followed a sheep path for a couple of miles or so, and soon got to know where the gates were in the wire fencing. Chattering along with Betty was fine, but returning alone in the dark and in silence gave me the occasional stomach-churning moment when I sensed another living presence. Fortunately, it always turned out to be a sheep.

The next leg of our tour for the Miners' Welfare Trust was Merthyr Tydfil, then a depressed and depressing town right in the heart of the Welsh coalfields.

We were to be there for two weeks, presenting two different plays, each from our Ebbw Vale repertoire. We were all quartered in a bleak temperance hotel in the centre of the town and played in a ramshackle, faded theatre that must have seen better days – it could hardly have seen worse ones.

Those were hard times for the mining fraternity. Unemployment shed a hopeless gloom everywhere, from the shabby interior of the hotel to the streets themselves, always peopled by groups of idle men hunched in cloth caps and mufflers, the dismal round-shouldered huddle of men with nothing to do and nowhere to go.

Perhaps I exaggerate, but that is what I remember most about Merthyr Tydfil in 1938 – that is, except for one radiantly heart-warming incident.

We did badly there. The big old theatre needed greater crowds than we could draw in those frugal times. We had an audience, but not a large enough one, so that before the end of our first week it was clear that we could not afford to stay for a second. Even poor Robert Thornley looked close to tears when he called us together and told us that there was only sufficient cash to cover our hotel expenses but none for our salaries. We would have to pack up and leave, and he hoped our fares back to London would be covered. Then, with a characteristic flutter of the hands and a rather broken giggle, he turned out his pockets and shared out every penny he had among those in the company who were skint.

That was on the Thursday, and we were a very woebegone little bunch as we wandered back through a chill evening to our hotel.

The news of our plight must have got around.

On the Friday night we were all leaving by the stage door together when we were confronted by a group of men. An elderly spokesman stepped forward and, in the lilting tones of the valleys, delivered what might have been a prepared address.

They had heard of our problems and were sorry. They had been to our show and had enjoyed it; they hoped we would stay one more week; they had talked to others in the town and had organised a little whip-around, and would we please accept it and stay on. They hoped their help would be enough to cover our needs.

Thereupon he handed us a bag of money in notes and silver.

Here was true kindness – from men who for the most part were in even more dire straits than ourselves.

Needless to say, we *did* stay for another week.

That moving moment was a turning point for the Welsh Players. First of all, our hotel cut its rates to a seemingly impossible low, then, in our second week, business perked up, and the peak of our good fortune was reached when the irrepressible Mr Thornley greeted us with the news that he had found a permanent home for us in Abergavenny.

The placid market town of Abergavenny is set amidst some of the most spectacularly beautiful countryside in Britain. Nestled in the Usk River valley, the surrounding pastoral scenery soon climbs to the heights of the Black Mountains to the north and the bluff hill of Blaenavon to the south. Enchanting stream-cut valleys, some with romantic ruins such as Llantony Abbey, push their woody fingers down from the high places. Crickhowell, where the Usk is fast-running and shallow and ideal for fishermen, is nearby, as are the lush plains of Hereford and the historical sites of Monmouth and the Welsh Marches.

For me there could have been no more ideal setting in which to live and mingle my profession with my country pastimes. Abergavenny was bliss after nearly two years in London, especially as my father had now given up the Wimborne house, stored most of his belongings and furniture, and left me with no home to go to.

Our theatre, in the town hall, was adequate and comfortable. The company lived in digs scattered about the town but, helped by Granny Todd's continuing allowance, I opted for a little temperance hotel – not because I was abstemious, but rather because the place was clean, comfortable and cheap.

Soon we were settled in Abergavenny and becoming an efficient little company of actors and technicians, complete with our own designer, Leo Starr, and stage-management crew. We drew good audiences from the town and surrounding country and won the support of the local tradespeople who were most helpful in lending us furniture, pictures and anything else we needed to dress our sets.

How we had the time for outside interests I find it now difficult to comprehend. We were a weekly rep which meant that we presented a new play every week, with all the concentrated lines-learning and rehearsal that this entailed, plus, of course, the current production being performed each

evening. We were not a big enough company to allow leading
actors to alternate nor were standards of production allowed
to become slipshod or haphazard. But the redoubtable
Charlotte Francis drilled us very precisely, and we worked
really hard to learn our craft.

I believe that those of us who had a period of grounding
in repertory theatre companies were fortunate. Today that
opportunity for young actors is sadly almost non-existent.
So often over recent years I have seen the deficiencies of
abundantly talented performers who have made names for
themselves in television series but are totally lost for stage-
craft when they attempt to take on a live theatre appearance.
And there are screen actors who, when faced with more than
half a page of dialogue, can't get it right until the twenty-third
take.

Somehow we all managed to enjoy our brief leisure time
in Abergavenny, especially on Sundays, which were free for
all but the stage staff. I rode most weekends with pretty
Peggy Roberts who knew some marvellous hacking paths
around the hills and valleys; Evan, a young local schoolmas-
ter, and I enjoyed our pints at various inns, and he frequently
lent me his nippy Riley sports car for jaunts through the
countryside while Peter Trier, a trainee land agent who
worked on a nearby estate, fixed me up with some rabbit
and pigeon shooting and became almost a lifelong friend.

The summer of 1938 was a memorable one for me. I was
making a life of my own and the loss of my mother and my
home – and Brecart – had ceased to matter so deeply. And
I had really found my *métier*, in a profession by which I have
contrived to live happily and reasonably fruitfully for many
years.

A couple of months after our arrival in Abergavenny,
Mr Thornley was offered the rental of a large mansion at
Llanfoist, a mile or two away, for thirty shillings a week.
We would all pay equal shares towards housekeeping and
maintenance, and Mr Thornley undertook to provide the
necessary furnishings by hire-purchase out of company funds.
So about twelve of us became the tenants of Llanfoist Hall,
a square-fronted Georgian house facing across the lovely
river valley, surrounded by parkland and fields.

If we thought we were lucky before, now we dwelt in Elysium! There was plenty of room for all of us, we hired a devoted live-in housekeeper who became fiercely proud of her post with the famed Welsh Players, while our young theatre electrician volunteered to double up as houseboy and keep the communal rooms tidy and the garden decent.

Our only near neighbours were Colonel Baker and his family. John Baker, the elder son, became a great friend and we used to shoot together. The sun shone brightly on us all that summer. But heavy clouds were piling up.

For several weeks before the Munich crisis our theatre audiences had dwindled. In those anxious days people stayed at home to listen to the radio news, and there was an air of apprehension everywhere.

Then Mr Chamberlain returned from Munich waving his scrap of paper and promising peace in our time. But the damage had already been done to the Welsh Players at the Abergavenny Town Hall: a few more weeks of reduced attendances and our little company was in deep trouble. We had no capital reserves and our running costs were not being met out of income. Once again, we all took salary cuts and pared our living expenses.

Our devoted housekeeper stayed with us, was quite prepared to chase creditors from the door, and with the aid of Peter Trier and John Baker I was often able to supply the ingredients for rabbit and pigeon pie. But we knew in our hearts that we could not survive for long like this, even though we tried to put on brave faces in the town for fear of turning away even more of our followers.

Finally, in December, some of our furnishings were repossessed whilst we were all at the theatre for a matinée performance. Quite clearly, the Welsh Players were not going to be playing much longer. Robert Thornley asked us to hang on until the New Year, as our Christmas holiday shows might help to pay off the worst of the bills. We faced a bleak festive period ourselves. However, for a few more weeks hang on we did.

Christmas Eve was a miserable day. We had a show that night and scarcely had enough to cover our bus fares, let alone do anything about Christmas fare. Rabbit and vegetable soup had been prepared, and the nearest we could get to a turkey were a few scrawny winter wood-pigeons.

After the show we all caught the bus home. It stopped for us at the bottom of the drive up to the Hall, and we scrambled out to begin the trudge up to the house. We were a bit concerned to see so many lights on in the house, because we tried to keep our electricity bills down, but it was only as we entered the hall that the truth became clear.

A decorated Christmas tree stood there, and everywhere was garlanded with holly, paper chains and streamers. Coal and log fires blazed, and as we crowded into the drawing-room we were greeted by a fusillade of champagne corks.

Beaming hugely, there stood the entire Baker family, and all our friends. Goodness knows how they and the housekeeper had kept their lovely secret from us. The laden buffet table was soon denuded and the celebrations went on till the small hours.

Nor was that all. We were told that we were to lie in next morning and not to worry about our Christmas dinner – it was all arranged.

Sure enough, a vast turkey was cooked in the Baker household and borne in triumph to our dining-room, to be served to us by Colonel Baker and his helpers. Dickens himself could not have described a more cheerful and heart-warming scene.

First, the miners of Merthyr Tydfil, and now this . . .

I learned more than mere thespian tricks during my time with the Welsh Players.

8

THE DUNDEE
REPERTORY
THEATRE

Early 1939 saw the final demise of the Welsh Players. Our little company split up and returned piecemeal to London, though most of us hoped that we would work again together.

I did bits and pieces of theatre work in London, and had nowhere else to go (though fortunately Granny Todd was in town, and still helped me along). Brecart was no longer on my visiting list, the Wimborne house had been disposed of, and my father was wandering around aimlessly, though for a time he rented a charming little cottage at East Horsley in Surrey, and I spent a few weekends there.

One of the parts I played was in a perfectly awful production at the Arts Theatre. The play was a horrendous piece by a rather potty Irish ex-monk. The story was something about the problems of a widower and his daughter, and I was the daughter's boyfriend. Every so often the leading man would pick up a photograph of his defunct spouse and burst into a doleful dirge, the lyric of which began:

> 'One kiss, one sigh,
> As you pass by,
> The sorrow of it all.'

I must say, I echoed that last sentiment every time I went through a performance of the dreadful play, but it was work. The girl who played the daughter was distinguished by the euphonious name of Triphena Gay, I remember.

The best thing that came out of that play for me was a note from Robert Lennard, a good film and theatre agent, saying he had seen and liked my performance and, if I did not already have an agent, perhaps I would like to make an appointment to see him at his office. And so I met one of the nicest men I have ever known, one who eventually was to transform my career and my whole life.

At last I felt a complete professional actor: I had an agent, I was in work, and the future looked rosy.

Robert Thornley had kept in touch with me and one day phoned and asked me to meet him for tea at his hotel, a shabby little place in Villiers Street. When I found him there he said he had managed to put together enough finance to launch another repertory company and asked if I would join him again. I was only too delighted to accept.

The only problem was the location of the new venture. In the theatrical magazine *The Stage* there was a small column of theatres advertising for a permanent company, and we jotted down a short list of possibles. The final choice was made by the simple expedient of Thornley closing his eyes and jabbing the list with a pin. The point went home at an ad for Her Majesty's Theatre, Dundee.

And so, in these unlikely surroundings, the Dundee Repertory Theatre was born, a company that was to become one of the most respected reps in Britain.

Mr Thornley agreed a deal with Her Majesty's Theatre and soon put together his company of actors. The opening play was to be *On the Spot* again, and this time the lead was to be played by Francis L. Sullivan, a famous screen and stage actor of heroic girth who was ideal for the former Charles Laughton role.

Perhaps fortunately for all concerned I was unable to repeat my rendering of Angelo because of my current job in London, but I was to join the company in Dundee after the first week and start rehearsing for the next production.

Like so many of Robert Thornley's schemes, all did not go according to plan.

The theatre was enormous and very run down and stood in a faded area of Dundee surrounded mostly by jute factories. It was soon apparent that the project could never be viable, but the indefatigable Mr Thornley was not prepared to accept defeat. In the space of some three days he put together a consortium of businessmen prepared to finance the reconstruction of another hall and to form a board of management for a permanent company.

The Forester's Hall, a large building in the centre of the city, was chosen as the shell of the new theatre, but construction work would not be completed until the end of the year. It would be up to Robert Thornley to keep his company together through the second half of 1939.

Once again Mr Thornley's inspiration and the enthusiasm of a hopeful young company prepared to do almost anything to survive kept us going.

First, we took up professional residence at the 'Little Theatre', a tiny place which belonged to the Dundee Amateur Dramatic Society. With their help we coped very well. And when our lease there expired we spent a few weeks in the Byre Theatre in St Andrews. Then in August we opened a season at the Good Templar Hall in Broughty Ferry, a fishing village suburb of Dundee. Not ideal venues, but we had to keep our company together somehow until our new theatre was ready.

By now I was playing golf regularly at Carnoustie and St Andrews. My keenness for the game became so obsessive that I frequently played nine holes in the morning at a local course, then snatched a hurried breakfast and started rehearsal at 10.30. Theatre work then went on all morning and most afternoons, followed by the show at the end of the day. In between times, lines had to be learned!

But war clouds were hanging heavy over all in those days. My father had already been recalled to the army as a member of the Regular Army Reserve of Officers, and was commanding a Field Ambulance unit. Everywhere the preparations for conflict could be seen, and again – shades of the previous October in Abergavenny! – the radio news bulletins overshadowed the day's routine. The Good Templar Hall was not exactly overcrowded each evening, but still we had carried on. After all the months of waiting it was hard to believe that we might never occupy our nearly completed theatre.

A state of war with Germany was declared on Sunday, 3 September, 1939. And for me there was almost a sense of

exhilaration that at last we were going to clout the belligerent
Nazis where it hurt. We had beaten their forefathers only a
few years ago (with a little help from our friends) and we
would quickly do so again, of that I was sure. Great Britain
and the Empire, together with France and her impregnable
Maginot Line, would soon stop any German advance westwards and would drive into Germany as soon as our full
forces were mobilised. The press and radio media had helped
to build up our confidence and resolve with encouraging
articles and talks about the great potential of the Allied
Forces. We could hardly understand why Hitler had been so
stupid as to invade Poland and bring down on himself our
mighty wrath.

One thing was clear to me: I would have to move fast if I
was to take some active part in the great adventure.

Twenty-four hours later, on the Monday morning, I was
at St Andrews University Reception Unit in St Andrews,
volunteering for army service.

There was nothing exceptional or heroic about this. Tens
of thousands of others had already joined the Territorial
Army in anticipation of the need for a trained stand-by force.
My itinerant profession had made it impossible for me to
join the TA, so I was months behind many others.

Strangely enough, my father in his letters had never
urged me to join up before my official age-group call-up,
but I was sure he would approve of my hurried trip to St
Andrews.

I went to the University Reception Unit because if you
were a university student and held certificates from a recognised Officers Training Corps unit at school or university,
you could be enrolled as a potential officer, and could select
your preferred arm of the service.

That I had never even been in the OTC at school owing
to my physical disability, and was certainly not a university
student, did not deter me. I presented myself at the Reception Unit where a friendly and helpful young officer of the
Royal Scots, who was attached to the OTC and had already
been briefed by my bona fide student friends, filled in the
enrolment forms for me as a second-year student reading
English, who had qualified for OTC certificates at Wimborne

in 1936, and I signed my name on the dotted line, noticing the penalties for false declarations.

All went well, and I was enrolled as a member of His Majesty's Forces, subject to a final medical examination.

For this I was required to strip off in front of three stolid elderly Scottish doctors who went through the ritual of thumping, prodding, listening and urine-testing which appeared to bore them into virtual stupor.

It was the first time I had faced a medical check for years, and I was very nervous. I had been through all this too often. But my racing pulse did not seem to bother the panel at all, and I was told to get dressed and fill in another form. I obeyed, almost to my complete undoing.

Under the heading 'previous ailments' I naively wrote 'pericarditis'. As I had already passed my medical test it did not occur to me that my past history had any present bearing.

When I handed the form back to the senior doctor the old physician nearly bounced out of his chair . . .

'Pericarditis! You've had pericarditis?'

Within moments the three of them were galvanised into life, their actions like those of speeded-up comic strip characters. I was told to strip off again and the examination process was repeated. I was made to jog, jump up and down and do press-ups. Each time the thumping and listening became increasingly intense as the old chaps took it in turns. I had obviously made their day.

They questioned me about my illness and the years since. By now I was bitterly regretting my stupidity in correctly filling in the form.

I was told to go into another room and wait. During that miserable few minutes I had already made up my mind that there was nothing to stop me having another go with a different panel.

Quite quickly I was called back to face my inquisitors, who had shed their lethargy and appeared quite lively and benign. I was told that I had passed my medical and that I was now entitled to be enrolled in the army. They even shook hands with me as if I had graduated with honours.

Within minutes my enlistment in the army was completed,

and I caught a train back to Dundee in time for the afternoon rehearsal.

I had been told to expect my call-up in January 1940, so I had about three months to get ready for the great day. The delay surprised me as I had expected to be drafted almost immediately, but I was well pleased with myself as we rattled back over the great Tay Bridge. Dundee had never looked so good to me, skirted by the broad, shimmering river and framed by a background of rolling green hills. I decided that I was going to make the most of the next four months.

I told Mr Thornley that evening that I had joined up and would be leaving in January. Our new theatre was to open in December so Mr Thornley suggested that I should do the opening production and the Christmas show, and then have a short break before reporting for training.

Meanwhile, I remembered the false testimony on my enlistment forms, and decided to get some smattering of military knowledge so that I would not be totally unmasked when I reported for duty.

In a bookshop I managed to find some pamphlets on army parade-ground drill and weapons drill, and studied them assiduously, going through the motions of marching, saluting and handling various weapons, and practising fieldcraft. But what I failed to appreciate was that my pamphlets were pre-First World War and dealt with drills and weapons from the Boer War or the Indian Mutiny. At my future training centre I would find little call for skills in operating a Gatling gun or assembling a horse-drawn field kitchen.

Fortunately, a recruiting officer took a room for a while at my digs, and, once he had recovered from the hilarity of reading my pamphlets, taught me all I needed to know to pass muster.

Soon the great occasion arrived as we opened our new permanent theatre. On Wednesday, 20 December, 1939, the Dundee Repertory Theatre was launched with a gala performance of *Hassan*, by James Elroy Flecker. God knows why Robert Thornley chose this unwieldy vehicle. It was beyond our scope, both materially and in sheer manpower, and contrived to run some two hours over schedule.

Messages of goodwill had been solicited for the occasion and George Bernard Shaw's reply was very much to the point: returning Mr Thornley's letter, Shaw had simply scribbled in the margin, 'Don't waste your time on messages. Make the plays attractive and you won't need flapdoodle.' Sound, if terse, advice.

So from the unlikely seed of a pinprick in a Charing Cross hotel grew a company which flourished to considerable theatrical prominence and which still exists today, after many vicissitudes. I am proud to have been one of its founder-members.

Before the opening production in our new theatre, I had received a note from the War Office telling me that my call-up had been deferred to April, so I decided to stay on in Dundee.

As the early weeks of 1940 sped by, I became increasingly worried that I would never see any active service. Nothing much seemed to be happening in the war so far as we in Britain were concerned, and the letters I received from my father, now in France, were becoming more and more confident of an early stalemate and negotiated peace. He seemed to be thoroughly enjoying his recall to the colours and sounded very fit and happy.

Many of my student friends were taking their finals and some had already completed their courses and, to my annoyance, gone into uniform.

It was agreed that I should leave Dundee a couple of weeks before my call-up, due on 15 April. I was impatient to get away and was concerned that I had received no further word from the War Office. I wrote to the appropriate department to remind them of my existence and also to give them my address during April in London.

Meanwhile my final Saturday performance arrived, and at the curtain call I was presented with a very handsome leather writing compendium, which still survives. And so I departed for London and my long-awaited military service – but the official letter waiting for me on my arrival told me my call-up had again been deferred and I would not be required until August. There was some sort of bottleneck in the Officer Cadet Training Units for the infantry.

I had plunged into a fairly hectic social programme in London, and my funds were quickly running out. There was only one solution: by mid-April I was on my way back to Dundee, feeling pretty subdued. Mine was certainly not to be the return of a hero . . .

In June 1940, France fell to the German invader, and I had a telegram from the War Office: 'Regret Major A. W. P. Todd missing, presumed prisoner of war.'

'Poor old bugger,' I thought, 'I hope he's all right.'

And in July my waiting ended. My second and final farewell Dundee appearance was in *Tony Draws a Horse* on 3 August. I had been told to report to ITC, KOYLI, at Strensall, Yorkshire, by 18.00 hours on 15 August.

9

A TEMPORARY GENT

It is not my purpose here to pose as a war historian, but only to chronicle events which directly affected me. Certainly, Hitler must have got wind of the British Army's intention to deploy its significant new reinforcement, Private Todd, RAP.

On 16 July, the day I received my call-up papers, the worried Führer issued his 'War Directive No.16', announcing final preparations for Operation Sealion, the invasion of England.

I was fortunate in my introduction to army life. Strensall Camp, in 1940 the site of the Infantry Training Centre, the King's Own Yorkshire Light Infantry, was a pleasantly situated permanent army depot a few miles from York, with excellent buildings and facilities, a handsome officers' mess, tree-lined avenues and the inevitable huge barrack square surrounded by solidly built soldiers' quarters and administration buildings. Between the guardroom, the officers' mess and houses lay a fine cricket and athletics field and football pitches were laid out beyond the troops' quarters.

Feeling decidedly shaggy in my travel-rumpled clothes, I was directed by a very smart duty NCO, wearing a red sash and the white-backed green chevrons peculiar to the KOYLI, to the lines of 'Volunteer' B Company at the far end of the drill square.

Sergeant Davis and his brother, Corporal Davis, were the epitome of regular light infantry soldiers, immaculate in dress and military bearing, with neatly clipped moustaches, and the husky gravel voices of typical drill instructors, and also a rich vocabulary and sense of humour that were to make our future sweaty exertions almost fun. Sergeant Davis was our instructor in nearly all our training for the next three months, gruff but kindly, and the Corporal was his fall-guy, the demonstrator who showed us, with considerable acting talent, how and how not to set about our tasks. Together the brothers provided a splendid double act.

I was lucky, too, in the company to which I was posted. Volunteer B Company was so called because its intake was all from ex-regular reservists recalled to the colours, or volunteers who had enlisted from choice, all of whom had done OTC training – all except me. Despite my efforts in Dundee to read up the various manuals, therefore, I had a lot of learning to do to keep up with the others. All the same, unlike many who were conscripted in those days, I actually enjoyed most of my primary training. At least there were no whingers in my platoon, and the old sweats did a lot to help those of us who lacked some of the skills.

For the first few weeks, all our spare time seemed to be spent sweeping, cleaning and polishing, in addition to the morning routine of tidying everything for inspection before first parade, measuring the exact distance between beds, and laying out our gleaming equipment and webbing precisely according to an official diagram. I had always been pretty tidy by nature, but since those days I have been fussy almost to the point of being impossible to live with.

Our platoon was thirty-six strong. I can't remember the names of many of my companions but probably the most illustrious was the Hon. Richard Wood, younger son of the Earl of Halifax, who was the British Ambassador in Washington. Dick and his great friend, Geoffrey Jamieson, had both played cricket for Eton and were each about six feet six inches tall.

As Light Infantrymen, our drill differed from that of other infantry regiments, especially in marching, where our pace was 120 to the minute compared with the 90 of the Guards and others. This suited me perfectly, with my somewhat truncated legs, but was very hard on such as Dick and Geoffrey.

I think all of us enjoyed those weeks at Strensall. We were soon very fit and there was something of a school atmosphere in our barrack-room existence, helped by the Yorkshire humour of our old sweats and the Davis brothers.

We genuinely took pride in our own turn-out and even in the glittering orderliness of our quarters. The spit-and-polish, white paint on the outside steps and stones, and parade-ground drill strangely enough made sense to us, and there could have been few smarter platoons in the army at that time. Besides, we were keen to get good chits and not delay our move to Officer Cadet Training Units.

Apart from our routine in drill, field training and weapons training – and learning how to stick a bayonet into a hanging sack with the teeth bared whilst emitting a snarling roar calculated to strike fear into the enemy – there was little time for more light-hearted pursuits. In October I got a few games of rugger, and needless to say, with Wood and Jamieson standing in our line-outs, Volunteer B Company were top of the ITC table.

Most evenings were spent in the camp canteen, which was cheap and cheerful and staffed by volunteers from the district, worthy ladies who included the wife and daughter of Archbishop Temple, then Archbishop of York. He himself frequently dropped in to join us, rubicund, jovial and totally at ease amongst a crowd of down-to-earth Yorkshire lads.

Even at that early stage in our training, we had an emergency role in the event of invasion or enemy landing. We were to be rushed in buses to a nearby RAF field to take up ground defence positions. I suppose, with our old P14 rifles and a few Bren guns, we could just about have fought shoulder to shoulder with the Local Defence Volunteers with their shotguns and pitchforks, but fortunately, the RAF and the Royal Navy saved us from the test.

During August I had a telegram handed to me by my Company Commander. To my delight it simply said, 'Meet me Peanut Bar Ritz Thursday 1830 hours Father.' Knowing the Guvnor's liking for this particular watering-hole, I had no doubt that the message was genuine and that he had got home to England somehow. I explained the circumstances to my OC and was immediately granted 48 hours' compassionate leave.

Once at the Ritz there was no mistaking the broad back propped against the bar. The old man gave me a huge grin. 'What'll you have?' was his greeting.

Then, with frequent interruptions for refreshment, his story unfolded.

He had been serving as the registrar of a base hospital somewhere in the Cherbourg area up to the evacuation from France. When his hospital was overrun he and some others stayed behind to care for the wounded, and were of course taken prisoner. He himself had been slightly wounded but was still able to carry out his medical duties. In fact he still looked dreadful. He was very stiff and still had bandaging on his chest and back and his face was grey and sunken.

After some weeks, the remnants of the base hospital staff and prisoners were herded into a train bound for a POW camp somewhere in Germany.

On the first night of that journey he had managed to jump off the train undetected, and to make his way back to the coast, helped and fed by sympathetic French country folk, and still not too much troubled by his wound. Arriving finally at a small fishing port, he lay up for a few days, watching the movements of small craft in the area. Then one night he untied a rowing boat and set off into the night, heading in the general direction of England.

He was lucky. Next morning he was picked up by a British patrol boat and brought home, by now pretty exhausted and sore.

He had been taken to the military hospital at Banstead in Surrey for treatment and observation, and on this particular day had been allowed to come to London to meet his son.

Scarcely the fittest of men in recent years, the last few weeks had obviously drained him, and he was never to recover completely, although of course I did not know that at the time.

After dinner in the Ritz Grill I saw him off by taxi for his train to Surrey, and then wandered round to the Bag of Nails, one of my own favourite health resorts, for a few nightcaps. Next day, my pockets somewhat lighter, I returned to Strensall.

Some weeks later five of us in the platoon were notified of our posting to Sandhurst for our final pre-commission training. This was a stroke of luck. The Royal Military Academy, Sandhurst, had recently been converted from its peacetime status as the pre-eminent army officers' training centre to its wartime equivalent, an Officer Cadet Training

Unit, with a curtailed course of four months instead of the previous eighteen. But it still had all its peacetime facilities and staff, and was impressive by any standards.

The offices, cadets' living quarters and halls of study and dining halls were contained in two main buildings: the Old Building, a magnificent porticoed and colonnaded Georgian structure, and the New Building, long and comparatively modern, in red brick with stone quoins, a set of four interconnected blocks and a large central dining hall.

The grounds were quite magnificent, with a tree-lined lake near the New Building, splendid playing fields, parkland and a rougher training area. The Commandant and his officer staff had extremely good-looking houses on the Camberley perimeter, and there were extensive buildings ranging from the Chapel, the hospital, gymnasium and transport lines to the NCOs' quarters.

Broadmoor Criminal Lunatic Asylum was conveniently nearby for those who succumbed to the strain of the curriculum.

I was posted to No.16 Platoon of C Company, in the New Building, where I found myself sharing a room with B. A. P. Todd, a taciturn, lean young Scot unrelated to me. Nearly all cadets had single rooms, but there were a few doubles usually occupied by brothers or closely-related cadets. Obviously, the orderly room had thought that R. A. P. Todd and B. A. P. Todd were kin. Fortunately, Brian Todd and I were very compatible, similarly tidy and, above all, sound sleepers.

One of the benefits of Sandhurst at that time compared to other OCTUs was that the civilian staff was still maintained, so that every five cadets shared an ex-soldier civilian servant, who kept our uniforms, boots and equipment in perfect order, did the room chores and even polished our bayonets, brasses and boot-studs. They were also able to tell us about the various instructors and their particular foibles, and exactly what to expect of each training session. Brian and I and three other cadets shared Bill, who was senior servant and a very wise and helpful old bird.

Our room was on the second floor of the end block of the building, at the end of a long, stone-floored corridor along

which our platoon's rooms were ranged, with the bathrooms
and servants' cleaning rooms in the middle.

My first encounter with Company Sergeant-Major Lord
was not propitious. We had a muster call on our first evening
at Sandhurst, when certain routines were to be explained to
us and particulars to be noted. We were told to report, just
as we were, to an area at the side of the New Building.

We fell in in three ranks, not sized off, and a rabble we
must have seemed to the great CSM. A man of splendid
physique and bearing, fiercely-moustached and stentorian of
voice, he was a presence of tremendous dignity and steely
discipline before whom lesser military mortals would excus-
ably quail. But with all that, in fact, went real kindliness,
true caring for his charges, and a great sense of humour.

One of Lord's immortal drill-square ear-splitting com-
mands was, 'Mr King of Jordan, sir, stand *still*, sir!'

After his spell at Sandhurst, CSM Lord became Regimental Sergeant-Major of the 3rd Battalion, the Parachute Regiment. He was taken prisoner at Arnhem and the record says
that when his POW camp was re-taken by the British he
greeted the relieving unit with a cup of well-brewed tea in
his Orderly Room where all was scrupulously tidy, with
records of the camp inmates correctly filed and every prisoner
in good heart and order.

Nevertheless, something about me must have particularly
offended him, because as he moved along the front rank,
ramrod erect, with pace-stick jutting aggressively under his
armpit, he came to a quivering halt before me, only inches
away. I could not read his expression because I couldn't see
it. I was looking straight before me, neck well back into my
collar, and my vision reached no higher than his upper tunic
buttons.

After what seemed an eternity, he shattered the atmosphere and my nerves with: 'Mr Todd, sir, you're a dozy, idle
man, *sir*!'

Even though I tended to agree, I was not sure what answer
I should give, if any. I risked raising my eyes sufficiently to
look up beyond that fierce moustache and thought I detected
two beady brown eyes lurking in the shadows behind the
peak of his cap.

'Sir!' I quavered.

Then I swear I saw the twitch of a smile.

'You should have told us that Mr Todd was not your brother, sir, and you could have had a room to yourself.'

And he moved on.

As time went by we showed signs of being a poor marching company by Lord's standards, so he rectified that by arranging for the pipes and drums of the Scots Guards to give us some rhythm and swing. For four solid hours one day we were marched backwards and forwards to the skirl of the pipes and the beat of the drums, whilst our instructors roared and barked at us. Thereafter, not surprisingly, we became the best drilling company at Sandhurst.

One subject universally unpopular was fieldworks, which included the siting and digging of weapon pits and trenches, and the preparation and breaching of minefields and wire defences. Our instructor in wire defences was a lean and humourless civilian ex-soldier known as Take-a-Bight Knight. He assured us that the way to handle barbed wire was not to be afraid of it but to grasp it firmly at all times, take a bight in it. Since his clothes were mostly ripped to shreds and his hands hideously scratched, we were naturally loath to follow his example.

It was in our living quarters and off-duty life style that we were particularly lucky at Sandhurst. We still enjoyed the benefit of the peace-time kitchen staff and had our own servants to serve us at dinner. There was The Fancy Goods Store also, near the dining hall, where we could buy all manner of things to augment our rations, such as wines, port and sherry, or even extra sausages, as well as cleaning materials and toilet articles.

We had Band Night once a week when the officers dined with us, and the FGS did a roaring trade in wines and extra goodies. We also had Dining Out night once a week, when those who so wished, if not on Passive Air Defence duty, could go out to dinner in Camberley or London, subject to a pass.

Another part of the lighter side of life was the end-of-term concert, which was excellent and in which I would have dearly liked to take part, had I not sworn never to admit to

anybody that I had been an actor. I didn't want to finish
up as a divisional entertainments officer organising ENSA
parties, much as I admired the work they did.

A large part of our concert in C Company was written by
William Douglas Home, the now-famous comedy playwright. His co-author-cum-leading artiste was Simon Phipps,
now Bishop of Lincoln.

I seemed to be coping pretty well with the requirements
and had no fears about being commissioned in due course.

Then it happened . . .

It was a Dining Out night, and there were only a few of
us cadets left in our two C Company blocks doing PAD Duty
(fire-fighting and rescue).

I had just had a bath and was walking along the second-
floor corridor to my room, clad in pyjamas and with my towel
slung over my shoulder. As I left the bathroom, although no
alarm had been sounded, I became aware of the woom-
woom-woom drone of an enemy intruder twin-engined
plane, a sound with which we were quite familiar. During
that period of sporadic bombing raids on London many
German aircraft overflew Sandhurst.

I had walked on only a few paces when the quiet of the
evening was shattered by a heavy explosion nearby.

'Christ!' I thought. 'That was close.' I broke into a trot,
realising that I had better get dressed.

Then I swear I saw it. Clearly printed in my mind is the
sight of the second bomb as it came through the ceiling only
yards in front of me and went through the floor of the corridor
before exploding somewhere below. The photo-electric cell
of my mind stopped that frame of the moving picture and
left it like a snapshot in my memory.

It could only have been a fraction of a second before the
building all around me was going upwards and outwards,
and I was sailing through the air with the rubble. A second
or two later I thumped down on a lawn some thirty or forty
yards from the building, bits of debris raining down all round
me and the air thick with dust and smoke. I had literally
been blown through walls that weren't there any more and
had travelled quite a distance.

My first instinct was to be bloody angry. 'There's been a

mistake,' I thought. 'Nobody is supposed to have a go at me in this war! I might have been hurt, damn it!'

Then I scrambled to my feet and made sure that I was in fact intact. All my limbs seemed to be working perfectly, and I felt no pain anywhere. All I could feel was that for some reason I was very wet, as though I had just got out of the bath. I supposed that I had been near a burst pipe, or something.

I don't remember how I got back into the building, but I knew that I must try to get help for those caught in the collapsed end of the wing. All the electric lighting had failed so I had to scramble as best I could to the corridor connecting all four blocks. As I reached it, I saw figures running towards me from the far end, torchlight stabbing the gloom and dust.

The first cadet to reach me shone his light on me, said 'Oh, my God!' and was promptly sick. With the arrival of the others and more light, I nearly had the same reaction. What I had thought to be warm water was in fact blood, trickling from puncture wounds and abrasions all over my face and body. No Hammer horror film ever showed a more gory monster.

Perhaps because I had actually seen the state I was in, I now felt pretty sore and queasy. I was glad of the help of a couple of cadets as I walked to the hospital, which was close by. When I arrived I was made to lie on a stretcher, given a cigarette and a cup of tea and an injection. Meanwhile, others were being carried in, and it was clear that quite a few cadets had been hurt.

When I had been cleaned up and examined, I was told that there was nothing seriously wrong, but that I would have to go to the operating theatre in the morning to have removed various bits of brick, wood, glass and metal that had lodged in me, a procedure that I didn't exactly relish. After that I was given a sedative and slept.

Fortunately it emerged that my legs seemed to have taken the worst of the blast, and from upper-thigh to midriff I was unharmed. Altogether, I had been very lucky. Five young men were killed that night, and a dozen or so had been hurt.

Brian Todd had a miraculous escape. Our room was over

a Hall of Study, which occupied the height of the ground and first floors. One of the pillars in the Hall of Study reached to the floor of our room. When the building collapsed, the pillar remained intact, sticking up through the rubble, and Brian was found very quickly, rigid in shock but otherwise unhurt, perched on its top.

After my morning session in the operating theatre I was removed by ambulance to Lake House, a pleasant place near the chapel that had been the adjutant's home and which was now to be used as a lying-in hospital centre until the proper hospital had its windows restored and other damage repaired.

For the first couple of weeks I was too sore to take much heed of anything but my own aches and pains. I was fairly severely bruised, and a mass of small cuts and punctures. These were dressed each morning and the process included the draining and re-plugging of the deeper holes in my legs. What seemed like yards of stuck-in gauze had to be pulled out, and then replaced by similar lengths of gauze saturated in an oily mixture of acriflavine which were prodded into place . . .

Fortunately, however, I healed very quickly and as the years went by there was hardly a mark left to show for my battering. One annoying effect, however, was that I could not be passed-out with my C Company intake, and had to wait another few weeks while I caught up with the training I had missed.

But eventually, in the early spring of 1941, I graduated from Sandhurst at the traditional passing-out ceremony where the outgoing company marches up the steps of the Old Building, through the portico and on into the interior, led by the Adjutant on horseback, his charger presumably well-used to this distinctly un-equine custom.

That evening, splendid in our new uniforms and glittering Sam Brownes, a large group of us decided to celebrate in London with our various girlfriends. As it happened, we wanted to go to the Café de Paris, but we could not all get table reservations. A handful of us decided instead to dinner-dance at Hatchetts to the music of Stefan Grappelli and the Hatchetts Swingtet.

That was the night that the Café de Paris was destroyed in a German air raid. Some fifteen of my friends were killed.

Hatchetts was not touched.

Later that spring, perfectly fit again, I reported back to Strensall as 180649 2nd Lieut. R. A. P. Todd, a newly-joined officer of the KOYLI and a temporary gent for the duration of the emergency – which now seemed set for a lengthy future.

I and the other junior officers lived in the main officers' mess building, where we each had our own bedroom, not at all spartan, and each was provided with the luxury of his own batman, a privilege which we enjoyed for the rest of our service.

Life for me during that time at Strensall had an unreal quality about it. Here we were, in the middle of what was soon to become a world war, yet in a way untouched by it. True, we were training hard, but we lived extremely comfortably, dined well despite the increasing wartime shortages, and were frequent guests at nearby country homes for tennis, cocktail or supper parties. Wines collected over years flowed freely at the weekly Band Night dinners, when the depot band, bugles and orchestra played on the lawn or in the hall, the various courses rounded off with coffee and fine vintage port.

Whilst we enjoyed the good things of life in our off-duty hours, I and my brother officers would put in a full day's training. The senior officers and the more experienced juniors were in charge of the instruction and administration of the large through-put of conscripts who arrived constantly in batches, and the newly-joined like myself were put through various courses of instruction to fit us for eventual posting to active service units of the regiment.

Most young officers remained for about six weeks at the depot before being posted away, but I was lucky enough to spend four months at Strensall. In addition to spells of basic infantry training with the advanced conscripts, I did a course as a trainee carrier officer, learning to drive the tracked armoured Bren carriers and their tactical use; then became the trainee MT officer, driving various types of truck up to

3-tonners and getting some idea of their maintenance. I particularly enjoyed brief training as a dispatch rider, which entailed some fairly hilarious cross-country rides on BSA motor cycles over the surrounding heathlands, when our rough-riding resulted in frequent bike-buckling falls. Fortunately, my landings were always cushioned by springy heather.

The one activity which I really loathed was the weekly cross-country run. Everybody in the camp had to take part in this form of masochistic drudgery, except for senior officers and those on guard duties. The course was plotted each week by a junior officer from the duty roster, and he had to give up an evening to marking out approximately four miles of surrounding countryside. I was not built for long-distance running and found it thoroughly boring. I usually contented myself by jogging sweatily for long enough to finish the course and end up amongst the stragglers. This eventually came to the notice of Colonel Wieler, and I was quite sharply told that he expected a better effort.

This reprimand came just as it was my turn to plot and mark out the course, which I duly did with enthusiasm and premeditated malice. There were no written rules as to the layout of the course, except that it should be some four miles in length, so I felt quite justified in picking a route that would suit me.

A mile or so from the camp was a disused canal. The towpath was completely overgrown with enormous nettles, but there was a narrow single track along it occasionally used by ramblers. I decided that this track would comprise the middle two miles or so of my course.

When our run started, I hared off as fast as I could for the first mile, arriving well up amongst the leaders at the canal bank. When I reached the nettle-bordered track I slowed right down to my usual comfortable jog, with about three hundred men lined up behind me, and with ample opportunity to recover my breath over the next couple of miles. Despite the curses of my followers and the occasional agonised yell as someone strayed into the bed of nettles, I was determined that if anybody was to pass me they would have to swim for it.

As we eventually swung off the canalside, I again ran as hard as I could for the last mile, ending up a creditable fortieth or so.

One of the more incongruous subalterns at Strensall during that time was Lieut. Morris. In his late forties, portly, bald and short-sighted, and of weighty academic mien, he was in fact a well-known lawyer who had served in the First World War and had volunteered for service a second time. We admired his spirit, but felt rather sorry for him, convinced as we were that he would spend his service in some undistinguished military backwater.

In fact the benign Mr Morris outstripped us all and was soon promoted to brigadier. Furthermore, a dedicated socialist, he became a Member of Parliament in 1945 and was later created a peer of the realm. Seeing him bravely essaying a PT parade, one would never have foretold his distinguished future.

Morris and I collaborated to produce and write the annual camp concert, a mixture of fairly lascivious sketches written by me and music provided by the Band and Bugles and our very good string orchestra, under the leadership and baton of Band Master Raisin and Bugle-Major Jaeger, a brilliant bugler and Posthorn blower (if there is such an expression). After the war he became Band Master of the Irish Guards and conducted that splendid ensemble at many Royal Premières and other occasions that I was fortunate to attend. He went on to be Director of Music at Kneller Hall, the Army School of Music. I admired him immensely and remember him with great respect. I would like to think that he might blow a ghostly Last Post when my time is served.

Morris was in overall charge of our production, but I particularly enjoyed my self-appointed task of auditioning, selecting and rehearsing the female element of the show, selected from our decorative squad of ATS girls.

Eventually, in the late summer of 1942, all the good things of Strensall came to an end for me, and my posting to 2/4 Bn., KOYLI, came through.

I took leave of all my friends, and set off with my regulation paraphernalia of equipment, sleeping-bag, camp-bed, canvas bucket and wash-stand, clothing, boots, button-stick, housewife (pronounced huzif, and nothing to do with any uxorious mate), and God knows what else to my first experience of a real active service unit.

Didlington Camp, near Thetford in Norfolk, was a dismal collection of Nissen huts huddled wetly in the midst of mile upon square mile of dank, coniferous forest.

I reported to the adjutant and to the CO, the latter a rather grey officer, older than I had expected. I then met my company commander, and was next taken to my quarters. I would be sharing one of those Nissen huts with a dozen or so other junior officers, my patch being a bare rectangle of concrete on one side near the centre of the hut, the most dreary part, since the only windows were at the ends of the corrugated iron building. Lighting was provided by a couple of hanging Tilley pressure lamps.

Over the next few days I did my best to transform my patch of concrete into a recognisable area of human habitation with the help of my batman and a carpenter from the Pioneer Platoon. My camp-bed was central to the decor, with a converted orange box at the head to serve as a bedside table and shelving, and, on the other side, a stoutly made lidded box which stood on end as a wardrobe. My folding camp-chair and canvas wash-bowl on its tripod, both in a delicate shade of pastel green, completed the furnishing of this little pied-à-terre.

An army blanket in a restful tone of slate grey insulated my bare feet from the cold floor when I was at my ablutions.

The domed walls and top of a Nissen hut made it difficult to affix pin-ups, so my only art exhibit, hanging by a wire hook from a stanchion, was a tranquil little large-scale 1:25,000 map of the area, its muted greens and browns tastefully mounted on three-ply and shielded by a transparent covering of talc.

On the evening of my arrival I met Platoon Sergeant Wilson, and he took me round the camp layout. Wilson was a sturdy long-serving Territorial NCO, very experienced and quite unflappable, with all the droll humour of a typical Yorkshireman. He must have been in his late thirties, and his capable demeanour made me acutely aware of my own inexperience, despite the moustache that I had grown in an attempt to camouflage my callow features. I was twenty-two then, and this was my first actual command, a platoon of thirty soldiers, many of them older and a good deal more rugged than I.

It was through the sensible, dependable Sergeant Wilson that I came to understand the working relationship that can flourish between a young officer and his supporting NCOs. With his help, and that of my three corporal section leaders, I began to learn my job and to know my platoon. They were mostly ex-miners, very tough and loyal. The majority were survivors of the fall of France débâcle, but the remainder were young, green conscripts, and it was to be my responsibility over the coming months, with the help of my NCOs, to train them into an efficient fighting unit.

At Didlington I soon found, also, that a platoon commander, whatever his age or worldly experience, is regarded by his little bunch of troops as something of a father figure. To me they brought their problems, whether personal ones – many of the men were separated from their young wives and families – or questions of pay and allowances, or simply day-to-day difficulties with some aspect of their training. I would then do my best to advise or give some assurance, and, if the case was beyond me, take it up to my senior officer, the company commander.

Didlington Camp was no Utopia. The gloom of its surrounding forest made it dreary, and the nearest town with any pubs was Swaffham, about nine miles away – quite a hike for even the most dedicated beer drinker. There was no public transport and army vehicles were not to be used for recreation purposes.

It fell to me, therefore, to hatch a plan to relieve this lack of welfare for the thirsty soul.

We had, as a battalion, an emergency role for airfield defence in the case of ground attack. For this purpose we had been allotted a squadron of requisitioned civilian buses, manned by RASC drivers who were quartered with us. Apart from a very infrequent test alert, these buses were never used and the drivers were left hanging around aimlessly day after day.

I suggested to the CO that these vehicles should be given regular use to keep them in good running order, and that their drivers should have frequent practice at night-driving under blackout conditions. To complete their preparation for emergency calls, a full human load would add the necessary sense of responsibility. All this systematic practice was to be strictly only for the benefit of the drivers and their buses, of course!

The CO thought it was a good idea, and the brigade commander later agreed.

So Todd's Tours came into being, and Didlington became more bearable for all.

Five bus-loads of men went off on three evenings a week; on Tuesdays to Newmarket, on Thursdays to King's Lynn and on Saturdays to Norwich. This variation of route was, naturally, all part of the plan to enhance the drivers' skills! Furthermore, as the organiser of this special training, I obviously had to accompany the little convoy on most occasions, to ensure the orderly conduct of the whole operation – especially on Saturdays to Norwich, where I had a regular arrangement to hire a bathroom at the Castle Hotel. For half a crown I enjoyed half an hour of towelled and steaming luxury. This was followed by a meal in the hotel dining-room, accompanied by one or two other brother officers, and occasionally a little diversion with a Norfolk damsel of my temporary acquaintance.

There were periodic mishaps, of course, one of which concerned our storeman, a weedy little lance-corporal who lived under the disciplinary yoke and watchful eye of the Quarter-Master-Sergeant, a large and plain-spoken humorist.

The storeman, whose sole purpose in life was to safeguard the custody of his supplies, and who slept in the cluttered Aladdin's Cave portion of the hut where they were kept, came to the Staff Sergeant with a real tale of woe.

'Staff, I've lost t'key to t'storeroom.'

'How, son?'

'In t'latrine, Staff. It dropped out of my pocket into t'pit when I were sitting on t'pole.'

'Well, tha'll grope for it, lad. Tha'll grope for it!'

With my mother in
Ireland around my third
birthday

Brecart in 1925. The home farm courtyard lies beyond the iron gates to the left

My father: in the Irish Rugby side against France in 1913

In the army in India around 1921 (*seated, extreme right*)

Back in uniform, 1940

The last photograph of him, taken while on leave in Ireland in 1941

Granny Todd

Uncle Jimmy at Brecart during the twenties – before the Brecart Curse descended on him

Myself when thirteen, having just learned to walk again

With Bobby Brewer during one of our training sessions, in 1936

Playing Banquo (*extreme right*) with the Dundee Rep. in 1947

With Pauline Jameson, playing Orlando to her Rosalind, in *As You Like It* for the same company

And he did.

Then, in the autumn of 1941, 46 Infantry Division was moved to the South East to become part of XII Corps, commanded by Major-General Bernard Law Montgomery.

10

SCENE SHIFTING

Our battalion was in luck so far as quarters were concerned in our new XII Corps Area, perhaps as compensation for our miserable camp at Didlington.

We were stationed at the former Small Arms School at Hythe, on the Kent coast. Our barracks consisted of a modern hutted camp, well laid out and with a proportion of brick-built permanent structures.

At last the battalion was being forged into an efficient force, nearly up to strength and with rapidly improving arms and equipment.

The 2/4 Bn. had had, in common with many others, a totally debilitating experience in France the previous year. On 27 April 1940 the battalion had landed at Cherbourg as a second-line unit, pathetically ill-equipped and woefully ill-prepared for battle. It had been embodied as the 2/4 KOYLI in August 1939, but as the platoons were being formed they were scattered all over South Yorkshire, Nottinghamshire and Lincolnshire, and when the battalion moved across the Channel it was the first time it had ever been collected together in the same place at the same time.

Within days, on 8 May, the war exploded, and the Germans broke through Holland, Belgium and Northern France, a great armour-headed bludgeon smashing towards the Channel ports. Ten days later the KOYLI entrained, knowing neither its destination nor its role.

There followed four weeks of utter confusion. Frequently bombed and strafed from the air, sometimes marching, sometimes entrained, the unit was engulfed in a shambles of dispersed formations, hordes of civilian refugees and the muddle of defeat.

On 8 June the regiment was allotted the task of holding some four miles of the Seine which included two bridges.

There were no supporting weapons whatsoever; no artillery, tanks, mortars; just rifles, bayonets, and a few light machine guns. Contact was made with forward elements of the enemy, and then, early in the morning of 9 June, the bridges were blown and the forward companies ordered to retire across the river as best they could. This they managed to do by swimming and in whatever boats they could find, B Company Commander, Captain Viscount Gormanston, being shot and killed as he swam across in search of a boat.

The withdrawal accomplished, they joined the British forces retiring to Cherbourg, constantly on the move from one pointless defensive position to another, none of which could have been held against a concerted attack, until they embarked for England on 17 June, the day the French capitulated.

Thus the 2/4 KOYLI in which I served had known the frustrations of inadequate preparation and equipment for its first taste of battle in 1940 and had felt the bitterness of defeat. The experience was common to most units of the British Army. Wherever the fault lay – with nearly a generation of politicians, planners, statisticians and commanders – the British Army went into battle woefully unready. Mistakes were made at all levels, and since wars are won by those who make the fewest mistakes, the principal value to be gained from defeat is in the lessons to be learned from it.

One man who had seen all this and had learned from it was General Montgomery. In my opinion the leader most responsible for a whole new attitude of aggression and confidence in our officers and men was Monty. His famous victories, his flamboyant though ascetic personality, his brilliant leadership, his politico-military opinions have been recorded in vast detail, yet it is not generally recognised that his eventual effect on the morale and training of the British Army probably started in his XII Corps, in south-east England in 1941.

I know, because I and my colleagues were among its first amazed victims.

Up to the time of our move to Kent our training had been similar to that of the rest of the British Army: as supplies of new equipment became available there was inevitably a lot of time spent on learning their efficient and skilled use. Route marches and drill parades, too, were a weekly part of the curriculum, together with physical training. But, as I remember those days of mid-1941, there was no great sense of offensive urgency at any level. Senior officers of field rank and above, I suppose, were fully occupied behind their desks on problems of organisation and administration. Certainly I don't remember ever seeing one in PT kit.

When we did take part in exercises above battalion level, the hypothetical enemy was usually represented by elderly colonels waving flags. We endured these occasional affairs with no great enthusiasm, especially if the weather was unpleasant. We knew that our test would come eventually but we were in no hurry to meet it. And meanwhile, for us juniors, it was still nice to change into service dress for dinner in the mess.

Then came General Montgomery.

The first noticeable effect of Monty's attitude when we joined XII Corps was an order enforcing *all* officers and men to attend early morning PT parades, and that meant even staff officers and garrison commanders. There were a great many very red faces to be seen daily sweating under the unsympathetic eyes of impressively muscled army PT instructors.

All sorts of tales were rife about General Montgomery at that time. One heard of his ruthless weeding out of his commanders and staff, and of the awe he instilled among those supporting him, an awe not unmixed with dread and dislike. One also got the impression that he was a very prickly thorn in the sides of his seniors. Certainly he had a way of getting what he wanted.

Whilst our training was hotting up, we still had various defence responsibilities. We were, after all, stationed on a part of the coast very near to France, and my platoon was selected for one of the most bizarre defence duties imaginable: we were to defend and hold the Dymchurch Redoubt.

The Redoubt is a large, circular sunken fortress barely visible above ground, a relic of the Napoleonic era. Its main armament in 1941 consisted of two six-inch naval guns manned by the Royal Artillery. The task of my platoon was to secure this fortress so that the guns could operate in the event of either ground or sea-borne attack.

It is surrounded by a wide, deep, stone-walled dry moat, which only takes in sea water in the event of storm or high tide. The quarters for my thirty men and over one hundred gunners were below ground level, in a vaulted catacomb of rooms and passageways. All the walls were immensely thick, the outer ones pierced by gun and rifle positions.

I had three sections each of ten men: one section always at readiness, one on stand-by and one stood down and following normal training routine. I myself, though I slept in my cell at the Redoubt, carried on with daily training as usual.

In the event of attack, two of the sections would remain in the Redoubt, manning their two bren-guns and their rifles, the third would be placed in slit trenches in a wire-encircled perimeter, and the Redoubt was to be held to the last man, while the bulk of XII Corps withdrew to higher ground. One old Lewis gun was sited as additional fire power and the coastal road which passed through the perimeter was mined at each end with a Fougasse, an ancient device consisting of buried explosives topped by barrels of oil. The idea was that, when detonated by remote control, these Fougasses would crater the road and set the area alight, thus providing an anti-tank obstacle.

No doubt it was information about the formidable defences of the Dymchurch Redoubt that deterred the German Army from invasion!

The whole of the coastal strip was heavily prepared with anti-invasion works. The beaches were mined, coils of Dannert wire were strung about everywhere and steel anti-tank traps lined the sands, while concrete pill-boxes were dotted around at crossroads and likely enfilade positions. The outward face of Britain had changed enormously in the past year and these defensive signs had come to be regarded as being as natural as the trees and hedgerows.

This part of Kent was traditionally a holiday resort area, and one of the area's chief claims to fame was the Hythe to Dymchurch miniature railway, which in happier times had transported thousands of children and adults along its three miles or so of narrow track. The Dymchurch terminus was just across the road opposite the Redoubt; as I was looking at it one day an idea began to form in my mind.

My platoon's 15-cwt truck was used only for transporting stores and men on training, so my stood-down section had to hike to Hythe when on pass in the evening. Remembering Todd's Tours at Didlington, I asked the CO if he would consider suggesting to Brigade that the rolling stock and equipment might be requisitioned for use by the nearest RE Railway unit.

It was not long before permission came through, so on several evenings each week a delighted squad of soldiers mounted the model carriages and were trundled off to quench their thirst. More than once, smart and a bit self-conscious in my service dress, I was a passenger on the Dymchurch Flyer.

While the Dymchurch Redoubt nobly kept the Germans at bay, I myself was detailed to a special training group preparing to form beach patrols, small parties of men who would carry out reconnaissance on the shores of occupied France. The object would be not to fight, not even to make contact, but by stealth to gather information.

It was just what I needed. Here at last was a chance to do something active, and I reckoned that my days spent handling small boats in Ireland would be an advantage. Here, too, was the awakening of a new, more aggressive spirit in XII Corps.

We trained for a few weeks in the grounds of Sandling Park, near Hythe. One or two useful new weapons had been issued to us, including a new plastic grenade which had no safety fuse but exploded on impact when thrown. But before I even sat in a boat as part of my beach patrol training, I was detailed instead to attend the XII Corps Battle School, a two-week blast of blood-letting and another of Monty's little innovatory divertissements.

The Battle School was based on a battered mansion near Folkestone, and the surrounding estate was littered with the most hideous obstacles and man-traps that a bloodthirsty imagination could devise. Rats' Castle, or The Slaughter

House, as the mansion was locally dubbed, was rather less than basic in what it provided for our shelter. There was no furniture, most of the windows had been blown out by blast from the activities of the previous course and the food was of a dreadful soup-kitchen variety. But these were the least of our tribulations, and we soon learned to forage for wood for hot water and to dry our sodden clothing. Some of the staircase banisters were already missing before we got there.

The whole object of a battle school is to simulate as nearly as possible real battle conditions. Tactics were not part of the teaching, except for team-work, but we learned a few new tricks such as how to surmount ten-foot walls in three-man teams and how to cross Dannert and conventional barbed wire obstacles without pausing.

Fierce competition was the keynote of the exercises. Close to Rats' Castle was a steep-sided conical hill thinly covered with slippery grass. Each day before breakfast we had to run across the park in full battle order with packs and rifles, up, over and down the hill and back to the garden area, where each man then had to fire ten rounds onto a target as he gasped for breath and tried to keep his helmet from tipping over his eyes. Each individual time and target score was totted up – and it didn't pay to come anywhere near bottom.

Apparently, on a previous course to ours, General Mont-gomery had arrived to witness this early-morning pipe-opener. He asked if anybody had been sick from the exertion, and when the commandant said, 'No, sir. Very fit lot, sir,' Monty gave him to understand that he had not been doing his job properly. 'Even when a man has puked from fatigue, he still has forty percent of his energy left,' the General told him briskly.

My memory of those two weeks at the battle school is mostly of interminable cross-country obstacle courses where from time to time we came under fire from live bursts of Bren and rifle shots. Another little amusement was to have us all crawling in line down the conical hill while concealed crack shots fired single rounds between us and just above our feet. The object of this was to learn to keep our heads down and to get used to the sound of rifle fire aimed at us so that we might detect the source of the shots.

The effects on us of this jolly two-week holiday in the peaceful Kentish countryside were salutary. I surprised even myself. Normally quite a fastidious, mild little soul, within a few days I was charging about like a bull terrier, plunging into the muckiest obstacles, ripping my denims to bits on wire and cheerfully slurping down as much of the awful food as I could get hold of.

As the survivors of these courses returned to their units and began to spread the teaching, so thoughts were being turned from defence to attack, and the basic groundwork was being done for the eventual re-invasion of France. And much of the responsibility for this new aggressive attitude was General Montgomery's. He had good reason to know about the horrors of battle: he had fought in the trenches in France from 1914 to 1918. Historians may deride him, fellow-commanders may have criticised and disliked him, but to the troops and to us junior officers he was a great soldier.

I must have returned to the battalion from the battle school with a fairly good report, because I was told that I would probably be going back there as an instructor. My feelings about that were mixed; I had survived the two weeks, but going through it all again for an indefinite period would probably transform me into a homicidal maniac.

I was saved from this fate by a posting order to an officers' transit camp in London, in fact the Great Western Hotel in Marylebone. There I was told that I would remain for forty-eight hours and then receive a railway pass and further instructions. Meanwhile, I was to draw some special equipment from the stores.

In the stores, a chirpy corporal looked me up on his list. 'Oh, yes! Mr Todd, KOYLI. You need arctic kit, sir.' His glee was obvious but not infectious.

I was issued with a large pile of clothing apparently designed for the Himalayas. String vests, white socks and leg-warmers, a white smock and white denim trousers; snow goggles, white silk gloves and white gauntlets, fur balaclava helmet and a huge kapok-lined coat so stiff that I could barely struggle into it.

'Well, that's it,' I thought. 'It's Russia. Bloody hell, what a prospect!'

My worst fears were confirmed later when I was issued with a railway pass to Glasgow and told to report to the port officer at Gourock.

I phoned my father in Banstead Military Hospital and he agreed to meet me at Euston Station the next evening.

Right on time he appeared, walking very erect down the platform. I saluted him in my best Sandhurst style, then we shook hands. He looked dreadful, his face drawn and his uniform hanging off him.

We spoke only briefly. It was a strained little meeting. There wasn't much either of us could say. I hadn't felt like this since the first day I went away to boarding school. Now I was supposed to be a grown-up warrior, and to behave accordingly.

Finally, we shook hands again.

'Well, goodbye, old chap. Good luck.'

'Thank you, sir. Goodbye.'

He stepped back, saluted me, turned about, and stalked off briskly down the platform.

I never saw him again.

The port officer at Gourock handed me a sealed envelope which I was to give to the senior officer on board the ship on which I was to embark immediately.

Once on board, I reported to the senior officer, and presented my papers. 'We sail for Iceland this evening, Todd. You will go to the Transit Camp in Reykjavik and from there to join 1/4 KOYLI at Reydarfiordur.'

Iceland. So the mystery was solved, and I must admit to great relief. At least I was not to perish on the steppes of Russia.

I knew, of course, that our sister-battalion, the 1/4 KOYLI, had been in Iceland for a year or so, but there my knowledge ended. I had no idea what Iceland was like, except that it was an area over which there seemed to be a constant deep depression, according to BBC weather bulletins.

We sailed from the Clyde in the early evening, and picked up our naval escort some miles out. This consisted of a cruiser and two destroyers. Quite a strong force to guard a single ship, it seemed to me.

Almost as soon as the coast of Scotland disappeared from view we ran into a gale, a real North Atlantic stinker, and the officers' dining-room was almost empty when I went in for dinner. Fortunately I am a good sailor, so I enjoyed my meal and felt especially smug when I noticed a few green-faced officers tottering hurriedly out. I had a comfortable cabin on the main deck amidships, so I went to bed about as well placed as I could be, in the circumstances. The ship was a fair-sized converted P&O liner, more suited, I suspect, for gentle cruising in the Indian Ocean than for battling through freezing Atlantic storms, and she rolled and pitched convulsively.

There were only a handful of army officers at breakfast next morning, and nobody seemed to be in a particularly chatty mood. During the entire three-day voyage very few passengers ever appeared from their cabins.

I went up on the boat deck during the morning, gingerly moving from one good handhold to the next. The scene was at once exhilarating and quite terrifying; to my landlubber's eyes it seemed impossible that even our big liner could survive those mountainous waters. The boat deck must have been fifty or sixty feet above the normal waterline, yet when we were in a trough the waves reared yards above our funnels. The ship would climb up a steep wall of water, perch seemingly stationary at the top, then lurch forward and begin the sickening plunge down the slope, shuddering as the propellers lifted out of the water.

The next stage in this fearsome progress was the most frightening to me; as we reached the bottom of the slide the bows dug deep into the next wave and the whole fore-end of the vessel simply disappeared from view under what looked to me like an impossible load of water. Many times I wondered if the rest of the ship would simply follow the bow to the bottom of the deep. I have the greatest respect for those who face this sort of thing as part of their lives. That trip to Iceland in 1941 was an experience I shall never forget; and hope never to repeat.

From my perch on the boat deck I noticed that the two destroyers were nowhere to be seen, and the cruiser, less than half the size of our ship, came only intermittently into

view as it crested the waves half a mile or so ahead of us. By
lunchtime she too had turned away and left us. A ship's
officer told me that the destroyers had turned back early in
the night, unable to take those seas, and the cruiser also was
in difficulty. He assured me, however, that no U-boat or
German plane could operate in these conditions, which was
something to be thankful for, at least . . .

When Iceland hove into view on the third day the storm
had abated to a lively blow. Our sighting was of what looked
like a smudge of ragged white cloud on the horizon, but as
we steamed on we realised that we had been looking at
snow-capped mountains. Then a very pretty picture-postcard
scene began to unfold, with a base of dark, almost black
shoreline surmounted by a strip of vivid green land and
topped by the sparkle of ice-caps that glittered in the sunshine. In the middle distance was the colourful cluster of
Reykjavik, mostly white but dotted with brightly painted
houses in blues and reds.

As we sailed into the bay to our berth there were signs of
the aftermath of the storm everywhere: small boats smashed
together, others driven on-shore, and larger craft sunk in the
shallows or floating keel-up by their moorings. Icelanders
said it was probably the worst gale in living memory.

The next part of my journey to join the battalion at
Reydarfiordur was delayed a few days, as the storm had also
held up the coastal ship that regularly made trips around the
island, so I had an opportunity to explore Reykjavik and see
what the Icelandic capital had to offer.

Not a great deal in those days. It was a township of about
30,000 people scattered rather haphazardly round a bay. The
roads were pretty rough and only a few main streets were
metalled, and there was no European uniformity about the
houses and buildings, many of which were of wooden construction, having corrugated iron roofs and being gaily
painted in reds, blues, yellows and greens. And there were
no trees. In fact, there was not a tree on the whole island,
except for a small area in the north covered with stunted birch
not much bigger than gooseberry bushes but ironically
known locally as the Forest.

After the fall of France in 1940 Britain was left to face the
power of Germany alone, to hold out in defence of her islands
and to preserve a springboard for future counter-attack into
Europe. A mammoth and daunting task faced Churchill and
the British people. The threat to Britain's shipping was the
gravest menace of all. Germany controlled the entire west
coast of Europe, and the enemy submarine fleet ranged
the seas for thousands of miles, harassing and hitting our
convoys, most of which therefore had to reach Britain by the
Atlantic route rounding the north of Ireland. Clearly, without
the supplies made available by the United States of America,
without Lend Lease, without food and materials from our
colonies, the British would starve, and whoever held Iceland
would control this route. If the Germans were to occupy
Iceland therefore, and use it as a base for naval and air
operations against our sea lanes, Britain would be crushed.

So in June 1940, a British force was dispatched to Iceland.
It consisted of 49th Infantry Division, supporting units of
Royal Artillery, Royal Engineers, and elements of the Royal
Navy and the Royal Air Force. The islanders, a stoic, rugged
people, obviously did not relish their neutral country being
occupied by a foreign power, but it seemed they felt that, if
there had to be invaders, better the British than the Nazis.

The British had been in Iceland over a year when I arrived,
and everywhere there were signs of the military occupation:
army camps, vehicles, notice boards and armed troops. Relations with the Icelanders were on the whole excellent. I
myself never met anything but friendliness or, at worst, a
dignified aloofness from those fine people.

Later I was to see more of this fantastic volcanic island,
but during my first few days in Reykjavik I was able only to
wander round the capital. I found two hospitable spiritual
homes in the town: one was the Oddfellows Hall, which was
open to the public and which supplied excellent and very
cheap smorgasbord lunches; and the other was the Borg
Hotel, a sizeable and comfortable place which served pretty
good food, mostly based on fish and lamb or mutton, and
which held a dinner-dance every evening.

At one of these functions I caught the eye of one particularly attractive little blonde who did not appear to be attached

to anyone in particular, so I decided to chance my arm and ask her onto the floor. She declined very politely but firmly, and I detected a pretty stony look in the eyes of her companions. Chastened, I went back to my table, and hoped I hadn't given offence. Nevertheless, I noticed Hulda continued to look my way a lot until she left – alone, so far as I could tell.

'Damn,' I thought, 'what a waste.'

The next evening I was at my same table and again Hulda was there, chatting to her friends but not dancing, and once more looking across towards me quite often. Eventually, to my astonishment, she came over to me and asked me if I would dance. I rose and clumsily steered her round the crowded floor. She hurriedly explained that she thought I was very nice, but that she could never dance with me again, much as she would like to, because her friends would not approve. That's the way it was, she said. I said I understood and was sorry.

All too soon she was gone.

I again dined at the Borg on my final evening in Reykjavik, and, once more, she was there, but this time came nowhere near me, nor even gave me a glance. 'Oh, well,' I thought, 'I can't blame her.'

Then a waiter brought a note to my table. It was from Hulda saying that she would shortly be leaving, and would I meet her outside at the end of the street. Naturally, I rushed to pay my bill and retrieve my coat and cap. I turned left out of the Borg and waited on the corner.

She came out of the hotel and walked towards me. She was enchanting, her slender body buttoned into a long coat, high-collared and wide-skirted, trimmed with a fur-bordered hem, and her blonde tresses capped by a round fur hat. But my spirits flagged a little when she took my arm and said that she wanted me to walk her home and to meet her family.

Once at the house the awkwardness that I had foreseen kept me nervously on the edge of my chair. Her parents were as hospitable as could be, considering that neither of them spoke English. A nice, middle-aged couple, they nodded and smiled approvingly at everything I said, though they understood not a word. Hulda translated, and seemed perfectly at ease, rather to my surprise. Father produced glasses of schnapps which I found pretty fiery.

Then, at about midnight, the parents left, shaking my hand warmly. Hulda and I sat and talked for a while, and then, mindful of my long walk back to camp, I said it was pretty late and time for bed.

Hulda agreed, and I rose and moved into the hall, turning to get my cap from the hallstand. As I picked it up, I heard her say, 'What do you want that for?' I looked round, and there she was, half-way up the stairs.

Suddenly my situation dawned on me. And yet, much as I would have delighted in such an opportunity under more discreet circumstances, I doubted if I could do myself or Hulda justice with the kindly parents looming over me.

I don't think I made a very good job of explaining this to Hulda, but she seemed to understand and had none of the reactions of a woman scorned. We exchanged addresses, dallied a little longer in the hall, and then I trudged back to the camp, not sure whether to feel regret or relief at my ignominious departure.

It seemed that in Iceland women, who were very much in the minority, made their choices and these were accepted by all and sundry.

Somebody should have warned me.

The little coaster ploughed her sturdy way from Reykjavik along the south coast eastwards to Reydarfiordur, my final destination. I was her only passenger, and what I could see of the Icelandic coast was not particularly inviting. The island is a rugged volcanic mass about the size of Ireland, but with a population then of less than 150,000 people, whose livelihood came almost entirely from the sea. In the villages huddled in the shelter of the larger fjords every house had curing lines outside where fish were hung to dry and even the stony fields and tiny vegetable patches were fertilised with a top dressing of rotting fish. The reek was something you got used to quite quickly, especially as the air was otherwise so crisp and pure.

It is a land of wild and fantastic scenery, barren and fearsome in most parts. Great jagged mountains, perpetually snow-capped, tower over gorges and fissures, ending in mighty cliffs at the sea's edge or in boulder-strewn scree slopes where nothing grows.

The interior of the island is not unlike the popular conception of the surface of the moon. It is a desert of black lava dust and cinders, and the plain is dotted everywhere with tiny extinct volcanoes. When I was there there were no permanent roads crossing this wasteland, just tracks usable for only a few months of the year and marked by lines of rocks. Pony trains were as common as vehicles.

To complete the weirdness of the terrain there are geysers spouting boiling water and steam, sulphur pools bubbling and frothing, vast glaciers gleaming and the most incredible sunsets in vivid rainbow colours.

All I saw of this from the ship were occasional glimpses of the grim coast, the mountain snows and the vast bulk of the great glacier, Vatnajokull, until, on the third day, we swung in to the Reydarfjord.

The fjord is about fifteen miles long, a mile or so wide at the entrance and tapers down to the mouth of a little stream inland. First, we passed a tiny hamlet, just a collection of one or two small houses and huts clustered round a jetty. Then, as we nosed up the fjord, its edges widened to strips of grass, never more than a few hundred yards wide, but enough to provide grazing for sheep, ponies and a few milk cows. Beyond this narrow green fringe the mountains rose up steeply to some three thousand feet, their slopes broken by innumerable streams and fissures still full of snow.

And so we arrived at Budareyri, my home base for the next few months. It was a fairly large village, brightly painted like all the others, and now enlarged with Nissen huts and various army stores. A long wooden jetty was its main feature, and the largest building the inevitable fish factory.

I was met on the jetty and taken to Battalion HQ. The CO, Lieutenant-Colonel J. F. Walker, was one of the most likeable and efficient senior soldiers I had ever met, and remained a valued friend of mine until his death in 1979.

He greeted me warmly, and told me that I would have a few months to settle down, and that then he had a job for

me to do. I was to train a group of NCO instructors and then
to organise a mini-battle school on the lines of the one in
Kent. He wanted the battalion to be brought up to date on
the latest forms of training in the UK, while continuing to
practise for its new role as part of an arctic and mountain
division.

I realised then why I had been posted to Iceland, and
looked forward to my future responsibility. But I would not
be able to undertake this until the following spring, as it was
already August and we were now approaching the dark days
of the arctic night.

B Company Officers' Mess was very comfortably housed
in a large modern villa sited right on the edge of the fjord
beside the narrow rough road about half a mile from Budareyri. Here I joined the rest of the company officers, each
of us in a pleasant bedroom and enjoying a cosy off-duty
existence in well-furnished quarters. In addition to each
officer's batman we had a cook, so we were not short of
house-help. Our food would have been rather monotonous
– fish, including whale-meat, lamb and mutton, and horse-
meat plus basic army rations – had our cook been less
adventurous. Surprisingly, our company commander, a
powerfully-built rather taciturn man, was also something of
an epicure, and specialised in producing succulent savouries
based on such unlikely ingredients as porridge oats mixed
with fish-roe.

Our house was typical of many in Iceland, in that the front
door was reached up a flight of steps, and the living-rooms
were all on that first-floor level. The ground floor rooms,
habitually buried in snow in winter time, were used in that
season as storerooms, and in summer as a single-storey
apartment which could be let or lent to visitors from the
dusty main towns.

The views from the house were spectacular. The front
looked across about half a mile of fjord to a massive range
of mountains that lowered their snow-capped bulk steeply
down to the water's edge. The rear vista had a narrow
foreground of rough, boulder-strewn pasture leading up to
a scree slope beyond which another range of mountains
sharply crenellated the skyline. On clear days the sun glinted

on the icy tips, and as it reddened towards evening it painted the hills and gorges as a fantastic kaleidoscope of vermilion and purple, orange and green.

The battalion had been in Iceland for more than a year now, and had overcome very tough conditions during its first winter there. Over seven hundred Yorkshiremen, many of them miners more used to tunnelling under the earth's surface than scaling forbidding heights, the remainder town-dwellers who had never even seen a rugged mountain or faced physical privation, suddenly found themselves doing duty in a sunless arctic waste.

And they adapted to these conditions magnificently.

Invasion was expected at any moment, so securing and guarding some two hundred square miles was the first priority and this was done as rapidly as possible. Defensive positions were either dug or erected and camouflaged, and made as weather-proof as possible. Nissen hut living quarters were built and dumps of stores and ammunition strategically placed.

Ingenuity was the keynote of all these early defensive preparations. Little of the material was supplied by the army, but flotsam and jetsam were collected from the water's edge. Sledges were improvised to carry three-inch mortars and ammunition, and toboggans made of sheets of corrugated iron were used to transport rations and stores to the outposts. Cliffs overhanging possible landing places were mined so that thousands of tons of rock could be exploded onto the shore line.

Icelandic days begin to shorten in August, and the first light snows fall in September. The sun is seen for the last time about mid-November and thereafter daylight lasts literally only minutes. In clear weather it is never totally dark, however, because the snow reflects some light from the stars and the *aurora borealis*.

I was probably fortunate in having missed that first year in Iceland and in not having experienced the fighting and the hardships of a disastrous campaign in Norway, but I felt somewhat green compared with my brother officers and men who had been through it all. Fourteen months in the army and I had not seen a shot fired in anger.

I tried my best to catch up with the others, at least as far as training was concerned.

I took over an excellent platoon that had for some time been commanded by the splendid Sergeant Grinsell, a really fine soldier and a man of great humour and good sense. He wasted no time in teaching me the tricks of the arctic and mountain trade.

On my arrival we still had a few weeks of daylight left and every moment was used to bring me up to the standard of the others in tactics and arctic survival techniques. Thus when I was not following the routine training programme with my platoon I was off on my own trying to master the basics of skiing, helped by a Norwegian instructor, or floundering around on Swiss Army snowshoes. Smaller than their Canadian counterpart, they had little ski runners underneath, so that on hard snow one could slide as well as mush. Perhaps because my legs are short I found the wide-legged waddle hard to accomplish, and had a habit of treading one shoe onto the other, with the result that the only part of me that maintained forward impulsion was my face.

Because the weather was already beginning to deteriorate, at this stage I had no actual mountain training, but was put through the rudiments of rock climbing on cliffs nearby. For this we had no special equipment other than ropes, and our boots' steel toe-caps.

It was the climbing that really gave me trouble.

I have absolutely no head for heights. Even as a child, tree-climbing was something I never attempted, and to this day, I cannot look out of the window of a tall building without feeling the sickening urge to be drawn outwards and downwards.

In climbing, therefore, all I could do was to hang on and try never to look down. Naturally, I never mentioned this to anyone at the time, and I think I got away with it – except once:

A group of us were roping down a short, steep cliff. I was quite near the bottom when I foolishly looked down – and froze. Perspiration broke out on my face and my hands. I didn't dare to move a finger, but just clung there.

Above me was one of my corporals and within seconds I

heard his quiet voice, 'Hang on, sir. I'll get you down.' He must have noticed my predicament, and quickly took the strain on the rope, long enough for me to pull myself together and complete the descent. He never mentioned the incident afterwards, and neither did I.

I would like to thank him now.

The days soon shortened and the cold became more intense. By November we were restricted to the winter schedule: long hours of inactivity, with only such training as the weather would allow. Even the half-mile between B Company officers' mess and the company lines in Budareyri became quite a hazard. Keeping the men's spirits up, especially round Christmas-time, was a major preoccupation. A lot of time was spent on keeping paths and tracks passable and gramophone records, books, newspapers, radio programmes from the UK and games such as chess, draughts and dominoes also helped. By far the most popular radio programme was the special weekly Forces request programme featuring Vera Lynn.

The end of February brought a return to reasonable conditions – and another fright for me . . .

A decision had been taken in 1942 that all personnel in fighting units of arctic and mountain forces should belong to a special medical category. A1 Plus. And, of course, whilst superficially I was as fit as anybody, I still had that previous cardiac disability on my medical records. So the MO decided that he had no recourse but to send me to Reykjavik for special tests.

Reykjavik was a changed place. Since Pearl Harbor on 7 December 1941, the Americans had moved fast, and a strong contingent of our allies was already there, superbly equipped and dashing around in jeeps.

My two days in Reykjavik were spent at the American transit camp, palatial compared with the drab places I had stayed in previously, and the Americans I met there were a friendly, cheerful lot.

I had to undergo three separate medical check-ups: a superficial examination at the British general hospital; a complete pilot's test, blowing up tubes of mercury or something, being spun around in a swivel chair to check my balance after jumping up and down from a chair, having my pulse and blood pressure tested; and a session at the American hospital, where they had more sophisticated cardiac-testing equipment. Once more I was pronounced to be one hundred per cent fit.

My relief can be imagined. At last the old ghost had been laid, and I was officially sound in wind and limb. My return to Reydarfiordur was jubilant, and then the real fun of training for arctic and mountain warfare began.

One sad bit of news arrived for me and was not totally unexpected: I had a telegram from the War Office in London to say that my father had died. So that was that – I was now on my own, save for Granny Todd, who was still going strong in her frail way in Ireland with the FitzPatricks; no parents left and Brecart gone, since my Hunter grandparents were both dead and I had heard that the house and land, left to the aunts, had been sold.

11

A BLOODY GOOD PERFORMANCE

The spring and summer months of 1942, busy and hard though they were, seemed like a holiday after the rigorous and benighted days of winter.

We were now pretty well equipped for our job, and properly clothed for Icelandic conditions. We had been issued with heavy woollen socks, vests and long underpants. These and warm sweaters were covered with white arctic trousers and smocks, and completed by silk gloves worn under snow gauntlets. Snow goggles and fur helmets were used when we were in the hills, and reasonable skis with Kandahar bindings were available. Everything possible was painted white: rifles, bayonet sheaths, automatic weapons, boots and sledges were all made to blend with the background.

Instead of the usual army packs, we carried large canvas rucksacks. Each man was issued with a white quilted sleeping-bag, and every second man also carried a two-man arctic tent. The entire load weighed about eighty pounds with weapons and ammunition – no mean burden in deep, soft snow, floundering along on snow-shoes up a steep mountain slope, or trekking on skis.

In our mountain training we lived mostly in the two-man arctic tents. These were light, quite flimsy affairs, easily erected and just – but only just – big enough to house two men and their equipment and spare clothing. Each had a built-in canvas floor, in the middle of which was a flap some twelve inches square. This flap was a very essential part of our daily existence. Once the sun had gone down, men were more or less confined to their tents because of the bitter temperatures, and this is where the mid-floor flap came in.

Once it was opened, the square patch of snow thus revealed was spooned out for drinking, cooking and washing,
melted and heated over cubes of solid paraffin burned in
tins.

The resultant hole in the snow could then be put to other
uses: as a receptacle and, more importantly, as a loo. But
most of us were creatures of habit, so the need rarely
arose.

It had been found during the British Army's first winter in
Iceland that regularity of bodily functions was essential. In
the low temperatures and the rarified atmosphere of the hills
there had been frequent cases of giddiness and fainting, and
the MO had established that this was nearly always due to
men becoming constipated by putting off as long as possible
the shivery process of exposing their nether regions to the
icy blast.

So a procedure was laid down that required every man to
visit the latrine after breakfast, and to report the result to
his senior NCO. Shades of childhood!

One of the few advantages of arctic training is that snow
is easy to handle. Trenches can be prepared in no time, the
soil dug out being banked up as a shelter against blizzards
or high winds, as a bullet-proof shield, and as cover from
view. A man can dig a fox-hole with a firing parapet in
seconds. And of course a defensive position is difficult to
spot at any distance even in good light.

Once burrowed into the sleeping-bag one soon learned to
stay motionless until the body heat had warmed up the
interior. Every move merely sucked in cold air – a fact
that I still observe when tucked into some chilly English
country-house bed.

We were instructed by Canadians in arctic survival
methods and by Norwegians in mountain warfare tactics.
Most of us became proficient touring skiers, and could cover
fair distances with our heavy loads. And skiing was, of
course, our main spare-time recreation. There was nothing
more exhilarating than a good ski-run down from the hills
to the mess, where a tin bath would be filled and steaming and
a good meal ready.

Fishing, too, was popular and the Icelandic rivers provided

great sport. In spring and summer football was organised on the few stony flat fields available.

In April 1942, Colonel Walker told me to start my battle school. I trained a small group of instructors, and we set about choosing our terrain and constructing all sorts of fiendish obstacles. I laid out a schedule every bit as tough as the one I remembered from Kent, and the officers and NCOs who went through it were spared no more than I had been at Rats' Castle.

In July, however, the KOYLI were relieved by the Lincolnshire Regiment, and moved to take over their quarters in Akureyri, a charming town in northern Iceland, and towards the end of August, 49th Division was withdrawn from Iceland altogether, and replaced by American forces.

We arrived in Ross-on-Wye on 26 August 1942. The weather was glorious, and we could not have been allocated a more attractive spot in which to enjoy the brilliant sunshine. Ross-on-Wye is a pretty town perched on the banks of the river and surrounded by beautiful scenery, heavily wooded and very different from the barren hills and plains of Iceland.

However, the hot weather knocked us out: after a long period of cool temperatures and a fat-based diet we wilted in the heat and a local pioneer corps unit was brought in to carry out the routine chores of barrack life while our men just lay around or cooled off in the river.

In a week or so we collected our travel passes and set off for a three-week leave, myself in civilian clothes because I was going to spend my leave in Ireland, staying with my Aunt and Uncle FitzPatrick at their home just outside Dublin and, as Ireland was a neutral country, no uniforms were allowed to be worn there by British servicemen.

At Dun Laoghaire I was met by Uncle Fintan in his car – the worthy judge pink-faced, white-moustached and dapper as always. I was surprised at this because petrol was extremely scarce in Ireland at that time, and even more surprised when he offered me use of his second car. I thanked him, but worried about using up his petrol ration. His reply, given with a twinkle, was typical: 'Oh, that's all right. You see, I try a lot of black market cases, and I get some very good addresses that way.'

I hope he wasn't serious, but you can never tell with an Irishman.

My stay with them was my first taste of home life for years, and I loved every second of it. Aunt Eileen's humorous good nature matched that of her husband, and they were both wonderfully warm and kindly to me.

My three young cousins were all still at home, and of course there was Granny Todd, very frail now, but as sweet as ever. She had left London when war broke out and had stayed at Roebuck Mount ever since.

Life in Ireland at that time was a curious mixture of studious neutrality and loyal fervour for the Allied war effort, especially in Dublin. The highest proportion of volunteers for the British forces came from Ireland, and bus conductors rarely charged a fare for anybody on leave: 'Are you from the forces? Ah, that's all right, then.'

Despite the veto on British uniforms, I saw dozens of servicemen who didn't possess any civilian clothes merely wearing raincoats over obvious khaki or blue.

Most curious of all to me was that favourite health spa for officers, the Wicklow Bar. Here I spent many a gregarious session with others of my kind, while at the far end of the room were seated a handful of Germans in full uniform, internees from crashed aircraft or sunken ships. It was very much a case of live and let live in that cheerful atmosphere.

Neutral Ireland was in many ways like a holiday resort compared to beleaguered Britain. There were shortages of fuels and manufactured goods, and though clothing was rationed, food was plentiful. I got through prodigious amounts of beef and butter, and it was an almost-forgotten freedom not to have to observe a strict black-out after dusk.

Back in Ross-on-Wye, the battalion reverted to training for a normal infantry role. Our preparation as an arctic and mountain force seemed to have been abandoned.

Within two or three weeks I was detailed by Colonel Walker to go to Catterick Infantry School of Signals on a two-month course to train as a battalion signals officer. Due to our lack of wireless sets and normal army communications in Iceland, we had no signals officer at that time. The fact that all entrants for the course were required to have had two years' experience in signals procedures and equipment had to be ignored. I had never learned the Morse Code, let alone operated a wireless set.

Comfortably housed in large modern buildings, I joined what was regarded as being one of the most difficult specialist courses that the army had to offer. Apart from mastering the intricacies of operating, 'netting' and fault-finding procedures on a range of the latest equipment, there was a crash course in Morse Code, flag signalling and signal lamps, in addition to the extremely complicated jargon of radio signals procedure. Even those who had trained in these skills for two years or more found the prospectus pretty unnerving. I could make no sense at all out of the sheaf of pamphlets and papers that was issued to me on arrival. However, I was there to learn and hoped for some sort of divine inspiration.

None came. At the end of the first day I was ordered to report to the commandant's office. The commandant was in a blazing rage. I was to be RTU'd (returned to unit) forthwith. Not only was I wasting their time, but my CO had no business sending me on the course without the required two-year standard of proficiency. Furthermore, he, the commandant, was going to write to the War Office complaining about the whole affair.

I looked for an opening. Finally, as he paused for breath, 'Permission to speak, sir, please?'

'Well?' said he, glowering.

I then launched into a heart-rending account of our privations in Iceland: how we had no wireless sets as they would not work out there because of magnetic interference; how we had no field telephones because they could not be operated in sub-zero temperatures; and how we were trying desperately to catch up with our more fortunate comrades in the UK.

It was a bloody good performance, though I say so myself.

I won't claim that the commandant burst into tears, but he certainly mellowed. 'All right. I'll give you a week to catch up. Then you'll be tested again. Go and see the chief instructor and see what he suggests.'

The chief instructor, a very pleasant man, reckoned that if I was prepared to work night and day for the next six days, it could just about be done.

And, thanks to him and my own retentive actor's memory, it worked. In one week I crammed in two years of technical knowledge and procedures. Superficial it may have been, but at least I passed that second test, and once I had caught up with my fellow-students, life at the Infantry School of Signals was not at all bad. I enjoyed some bibulous evening forays into Darlington and also got some good games of rugger for the School of Signals and for Catterick Garrison. Army rugger in those days was of a very high standard since so many leading players were in the forces, and Catterick Garrison was a fine team which even included a few international players.

The day before we all left Catterick, our results were published. I had got a Catterick D, for distinguished, so the old blarney must have worked well.

Back at Ross-on-Wye I looked forward enthusiastically to training a signals platoon in 1/4 KOYLI, which, as part of the 49th Division, was earmarked for a leading role in the forthcoming Second Front offensive into Europe. But within days all my hopes were rudely dashed: I received a War Office posting as signals instructor to the Regimental Depot and Training Centre, now removed for some reason from Strensall to Berwick-on-Tweed. I almost regretted my Catterick D. I reckoned I might as well have joined the Pay Corps as finish up instructing at a training centre.

So Christmas 1942 was spent at Berwick in a miserable hutted camp perched above the windy cliffs outside that historic town on the River Tweed. Fortunately for me, however, there was a shortage of accommodation at the camp, so I and two other officers were quartered in a small hotel in the town, where we lived very comfortably.

Also, a friendly lady who ran a small restaurant opposite the hotel kept her establishment open once or twice a week after normal hours so that I could dine in solitary state on tripe and onions, one of my favourite dishes.

Which was all very well, except that it was not getting me any nearer an active part in future military events. I applied for acceptance into the Commandos or the Parachute Regiment, but nothing came of it. I had a feeling that my application never got beyond the Orderly Room. Detesting my idle job, I tried hard to think of some other way out of it.

My means of escape arrived in the new year in the shape of a regular KOYLI officer who visited us one day. He was on the staff of 42nd Armoured Division and listened sympathetically to my grumbles. Then he came up with an idea: he would speak to General Aizlewood, his divisional commander, and see if the general would request my posting to 42nd Armoured Division as a liaison officer at Div. HQ.

The plan worked. Early in 1943 I was posted to General Aizlewood's formation, and reported to HQ 42nd Armoured Division in its temporary location in a big house in Yorkshire, where the division was on a large-scale exercise.

Within minutes of my arrival, I was dispatched on my first mission as an LO. I was to take a message from the Div. Commander, General Aizlewood, to the Corps Commander, General Dempsey. The trip was made in an armoured scout car, one of those marvellous little mini-tanks which were as ubiquitous in an armoured division as jeeps had become in infantry divisions. It was a tough, tiny iron box on wheels, with a top speed of about sixty, an engine that emitted an exhilarating scream of power, and an ability to be driven in reverse nearly as fast.

I was thrilled with my vehicle and my new importance. Fortunately, also, my map-reading was pretty good, so I directed my driver to the pin-point reference I had been given with no trouble, even though it was already dark. I found the corps commander sitting on the steps of his huge mobile HQ. As I waited to be led to him there was quite a bit of hurried coming and going of staff officers and I marvelled at the speed and brevity of the general's questions and remarks. Here was obviously an incisive intellect, and I just hoped that when my turn came I would not be reduced to stuttering confusion.

I shall never forget my brief minutes in General Dempsey's

presence. It was no surprise to me when a year or so later he was to command the 2nd British Army – our entire British land force – on D-Day. To my great relief he received my message without comment and dismissed me with a curt nod. I scuttled back to the safe refuge of my scout car.

During the remaining days of that exercise I picked up the rudiments of my job. A liaison officer is a sort of junior dogsbody, at worst a kind of errand boy. But he is also his general's contact man, and sometimes his eyes and ears when communications are difficult, and I knew I was going to like the job.

The exercise completed, we moved in convoy to the new divisional area based on Warminster and adjacent to the huge training area of Salisbury Plain. Divisional Headquarters was in an idyllic spot: Redlynch House near Bruton, in Somerset.

Redlynch House belonged to the Earl of Suffolk and Berkshire, and was kept up in almost peacetime condition by Lady Suffolk, the former actress, Mimi Crawford. The household was still overseen by the Suffolks' butler, and much of the furniture and pictures were still *in situ*.

The setting was really beautiful, rich parkland and wood-land, with a lake which we were allowed to fish. So, once again, I was one of the lucky occupants of very comfortable quarters, even though I had been allocated one of the ser-vants' smallest bedrooms.

However, despite our home comforts, we were busy pre-paring for the imminent Second Front. I and other junior officers went on a local tank-driving and gunnery course. My previous experience as carrier officer at Strensall stood me in good stead, and I was soon driving Crusader and Covenanter tanks with reasonable safety. My training as a signals officer also came in handy, as much of an LO's work on active service is concerned with keeping radio contact and knowing the procedures.

The spring and early summer of 1943 was a busy and pleasant one for me, and had included another leave in Ireland with the FitzPatricks.

Then my routine was abruptly exploded: news came that 42nd Armoured Division was to be broken up. Apparently there had to be a cut in the armoured establishment, and as the junior formation we were the ones to go. It was a real blow.

'Hell!' I thought. 'I'm damned if I'm going back to the regimental depot to wait for a posting.' I decided to make one more application for the Commandos or the Parachute Regiment.

It so happened that the same week that we had been told of the division's fate, I had to go to the headquarters of the newly formed 6th Airborne Division near Amesbury. I made up my mind to carry out my mission – I forget now what it was – and then try to find out a quick way into airborne forces while I had this golden chance.

I need not have bothered: it was, in a sense, airborne forces that found me.

Whilst I was there, word apparently had reached the Assistant Adjutant and Quartermaster General (AQ) that a young KOYLI officer was visiting. Lt. Col. Shamus Hickie, himself a regular officer in the KOYLI, sent for me.

Colonel Hickie, a lean, dark Irishman, wasted no time. 'Todd,' he said, 'we have formed a Light Infantry Parachute Battalion. It's still under strength and needs officers. How would you like to join it? I can arrange a posting for you as soon as there is a vacancy at the Parachute Training School.'

Fate had led me straight to the one man who was responsible for all officer-postings to 6th Airborne Division. Within minutes I was on my way back to Redlynch, a Para-elect. And within a very few weeks instructions came for me to report to the Parachute Regiment Depot and pre-selection school at Hardwick Hall, in Derbyshire.

So far, in the summer of 1943, my three years of army service had had little impact on the course of the war. I had worn the dark green fore-and-aft cap of a Light Infantryman, the balaclava headgear of an Arctic trooper and the black beret of an Armoured officer – but I had never seen a shot fired in battle, except for a few anti-aircraft shells. I had been wounded in my pyjamas and stuck on a scree-slope. I had lost my father and my grandparents.

I was beginning to feel a fraud.

Awful things had happened in North Africa, in the Far East, in the Pacific and in England – but I myself had suffered less fear and danger than the average civilian in London. I had, on the whole, enjoyed a package tour of interesting places and unusual activities at no cost whatever to myself.

Maybe now I could give my share of effort . . .

Not without fear.

12

'FOR I SHALL KEEP MY TROUSERS CLEAN'

The Parachute Regiment centre was a cheerless hutted camp set in parkland overshadowed by the great Elizabethan mansion of Hardwick, built to the command of Bess of Hardwick, ancestress of the Dukes of Devonshire.

I reported there with a hundred or so fellow volunteers for parachute training. We were to spend two weeks at Hardwick undergoing pre-selection tests, and those of us who survived the procedures would then go on to Ringway, the airfield near Manchester, where the Parachute Training School would give us our actual jumping instruction.

The object of the Hardwick course was to weed out any who were physically or temperamentally unsuitable for parachute units, and the whole curriculum was aimed at subjecting us to tests of physical fitness, nerve and spirit.

The selection standards of the Parachute Regiment were extremely high – and they needed to be. Every man was a volunteer, and, apart from being physically sound, had to be of exemplary character and discipline.

What impelled these men to volunteer?

To answer that I cannot do better than quote from *With The 6th Airborne Division in Normandy*, written and published in 1948 by General R. N. Gale, who had been appointed in May 1943 to form and command the Division:

'Above all it was confidence bred of a belief in their cause, in themselves and in their country. It is difficult to capture the atmosphere which this confidence spread wherever these men were. It could be seen in the light in their eyes; it could be seen in their bearing as they walked and moved about; it could be caught in their conversation . . .

'The second great contributing factor was the physical fact of parachuting. The training through which these volunteers had to go was vigorous and intensive. It had to be. When the parachutist jumps he knows that when he hits the ground he will hit it hard. The force of impact is equivalent to a free drop from a height of approximately twelve feet. As the parachute descends there is considerable oscillation and the man swings in a great arc like a weight at the end of a pendulum. If he is on a downward swing backwards as he touches down he hits the ground at twenty miles an hour, and only by rolling like a ball will he save himself from injury. If the ground is soft he is lucky. If the ground is hard and boulder-ridden he is unlucky. He may hit a house, a tree, a chimney or fall into water . . .

'He is aware, too, that once on the ground his future lies in his own skill. The gun which he carried down in his drop and the small supply of ammunition on his person are his only weapons for support in either attack or defence. His water and food are what he can carry when he jumps. His sense of direction, his skill in field-craft and in map-reading, and his physical strength must all be of a high order. He may be alone for hours, he may be injured, he may be dazed from his fall. But it is his battle and he knows it.'

I don't recall much of those two weeks at Hardwick. We had splendid squad instructors who urged us on through a rather repetitive daily grind. I found it no worse than the battle school in Kent, and in due course I moved on to Ringway, which was a large airfield nowadays better known as Manchester Airport.

We were made very welcome and comfortable by our RAF hosts and tended by a smart and attractive bevy of WAAFs, and their quiet confidence made us actually *want* to jump out of aeroplanes without further delay.

All the same, nobody can really claim that he has had no apprehension at the prospect of that first dreaded leap into space, and in those days our equipment was much less sophisticated than that used today. In particular, we had no reserve 'chutes in the event of failure, so absolute confidence

A Hollywood studio still, taken in 1950

Wartime snaps: CSM John Lord at Sandhurst, 1940   With Tony Bowler at pre-D-Day training camp in Wales   Irene, with whom I was billetted   Her three children – the friendlier face of Germany in 1945   Oyston, my batman – possibly about to ransack a knocked-out enemy tank   The Ardennes Château, our HQ over Christmas 1944

Ranville a week after D-Day. Gliders cluster, just as they landed (*top left*); the church tower, separated from the church; 6th Airborne Div. HQ – the château for the senior officers, the stables for the rest!; Orne River bridge, with Pegasus Bridge our main objective. The whole area is well pock-marked with shell holes

With Kitty, my first
leading lady on my
comeback to the theatre
after the war. We were
Claudia and David in
Rose Franken's play. By
the end of the run we
had decided to marry

My first film, *For Them
That Trespass*. I played
a bit of a wide-boy –
obviously trying to
persuade a doubting
Patricia Plunkett

in our parachutes had to be instilled in us from the beginning.

We were taken to the packing hangar where we watched the 'chutes being packed by specialist WAAFs, and the working of the canopy was minutely explained to us. There was no doubt left in our minds that any mishap would certainly not be due to the manufacturers or the packers.

Our first week was spent entirely on lectures and ground exercises designed to perfect our jumping and landing technique, mostly carried out in a vast hangar known as Kilkenny's Circus, after the RAF senior instructor who had designed the apparatus we used. It was like an enormous gymnasium, with all the usual paraphernalia of landing mats, wall bars, parallel bars and beams.

Two pieces of equipment were, however, unique to Kilkenny's Circus: the fan tower and the landing wire.

The tower was a steel girder construction, about forty or fifty feet high, with a platform reached by a metal ladder. The jumper sat on the edge of the platform wearing a simplified parachute harness which was hooked up to a steel wire wound round a drum. When the jumper projected himself into space the wire played out above him, spinning the drum which in turn activated internal fans which slowed down the speed of descent to about that of a normal parachute drop so that a simulated landing was made on the mats below.

The only deficiency in this simulation was its perfectly perpendicular descent, a luxury very rarely enjoyed on a real parachute landing. But this treat was compensated for by the other piece of apparatus, the dreaded landing wire – at least, I dreaded it. I had never quelled my fear of heights, and this device gave me some very testing moments.

At one end of the hangar a metal ladder went straight up the wall to a tiny platform at a height of perhaps sixty feet. From above the little platform a steel wire ran the length of the hangar, ending over landing mats, and diminishing quite sharply in height. On this wire was a small pulley from which two hand-rings dangled. The idea was that one gripped these rings, took off hanging on to them, and whizzed down the wire until the mats were reached, by which time one was swooping along at maybe twenty miles an hour, letting go on a bellowed 'Go!' from the instructor and landing in the approved folding banana position, feet and knees locked firmly together and elbows tucked into the sides, feet turned at a slight angle to avoid pitching.

Fine! It enabled us to put into practice all that we were being taught about safe landing drill: the only trouble was that I had to get hold of the hand rings in the first place, and by the time I had clambered gingerly from the ladder to that bloody little platform I was already quaking, not daring to look down, my hands fumbling sweatily. As I gained the platform and stood there, my back pressed rigidly against the wall, I then had to look up for the rings on the pulley. The whole device had been designed for tallish men – while other trainees simply reached up and took a firm hold before launching off, I had to make a despairing leap and hope that my wet fingers would take a good grip before I sped downwards and outwards.

Obviously they did, or I would have been wearing a different set of wings shortly afterwards.

Finally, in the second week, came the great day when we made our first actual parachute jump. Qualification for the coveted Para wings was seven jumps, five from captive balloons and two from aircraft, one of which was a night drop.

The dropping zone was in Tatton Park, a few miles from the airfield. Every British paratrooper of those days will remember this place, not least for the little wooden hut on its perimeter where lovely, welcome cups of tea were dispensed by kindly volunteer ladies. That sugary, steaming cuppa after the first successful landing meant more to us than any subsequent champagne toast.

The balloons had little square, railed baskets designed to take five jumpers and one dispatcher. In the middle of each floor was a hole approximately two-and-a-half feet in diameter, the same size as the exit hole in the Whitley aircraft which was our transport in those days. A metal bar across the basket was the strongpoint to which our statichutes were clamped.

Statichutes were so called because the opening of the canopy was not activated by a ripcord after the exit but by a

static line, attached to the balloon or aircraft, which pulled
the chute out of its bag.

The parachute itself was a simple, umbrella-shaped
canopy, but the material of the umbrella stopped short of
the actual apex, leaving a circular hole at the top which
allowed the air to escape, thus ensuring a regulated speed of
descent. From the base of the canopy rigging-lines converged
together, half of them on each side, to meet at four metal
rings which in turn were at the end of four webbing strops,
known as lift-webs, which went up from the jumper's
shoulder-harness in a V-shape, two going up forward of the
jumper and two behind.

By reaching up and pulling down on these strops the
jumper could steer his 'chute by spilling air from the
canopy. The 'chute was packed into a large canvas bag worn
on the back and was attached to a webbing harness which
criss-crossed the body and went between the legs to meet at
a quick-release box worn on the midriff and opened by a
twist and a blow from the hand.

From the strongpoint in the aircraft or balloon ran a heavy
webbing strop some twenty feet long, the static line. This
was attached to the apex of the parachute by a cord with a
one-hundred-pound breaking strain. As the jumper launched
himself into space the strongpoint strop extended to its
maximum length and then pulled the bag from the 'chute,
allowing the canopy and rigging-lines to unfold to their full
length, whereupon the cord snapped and the 'chute was free
to open with the force of air. From then on it was up to the
jumper to steer himself to a safe landing.

All very easy – when you knew how!

The snags that could occur were numerous, and most of
us were to experience them at some time or other.

For one thing, somersaulting nearly always occurred during jumps from the Whitley aircraft which was a converted,
antiquated bomber. All our training was done from Whitleys.
The belly-turret had been removed, leaving an aperture in
the centre of the aircraft from which we jumped. The 'hole'
itself was about two-and-a-half feet in diameter and formed
a tube about two feet deep between the floor and the outer
skin.

A stick of Whitley jumpers consisted of ten men seated in a knees-up crouch on the floor of the narrow fuselage, five each end of the hole, even numbers to the rear and odd numbers forward. On approaching the DZ the first man would sit ready on the edge of the aperture, his legs dangling in the hole, hands by his sides on the lip, ready to launch himself in a chin-back, arms-to-the-sides position of attention, fingers gripping the sides of his trousers, feet and knees together.

The odd-numbered jumpers from the forward section usually had a nice soft exit, sitting on the slip-stream of the aircraft, but the even numbers, facing the other way, were not so fortunate. When they exited, the slip-stream caught their legs and whipped them backwards, causing almost inevitable somersaults. Providing the jumper's legs and arms were locked close, there was no danger: one simply somersaulted a few times through the shoulder-strops until the canopy opened. But an untidy, uncontrolled exit could have dire results – at best a dislocated shoulder if an arm was allowed to foul the rigging-lines, and at worst a failure to open if the lines got rolled up by flailing limbs.

Another minor problem with the Whitley exit was 'ringing the bell', a euphemism for getting a broken nose. If the jumper did not, in his excitement (or panic), push off hard enough to project himself well forward, his pack would foul the edge of the hole, tipping him forward so that his face smashed against the opposite side of the hole. The object was to hit the chest against the tube; hence the chin-back position of attention on exiting.

And there was 'twisting', which only occurred on exits from side-door aircraft like the Dakota. As the man jumped from the door the slip-stream tended to spin him, causing his rigging-lines to be twisted and the canopy to open only partially. This was corrected by going through the motions of 'running' like mad in the opposite direction to the twists and unfurling them.

This little list of potential obituary notices would not be complete without mention of the ever-present oscillations. With the type of statichute that we used, the forward speed of the aircraft caused the canopy to billow out initially at an angle almost horizontal to the ground, with the result that the jumper then swung in huge arcs like a pendulum. This movement had to be corrected before landing because the speed of the pendulum-movement, added to the speed of descent plus any wind speed, meant that the jumper smashed onto the ground with considerable force. Oscillations were corrected by the jumper pulling hard down on his lift-webs and spilling air from the canopy, causing the 'chute to glide.

All these corrective measures had to be applied pretty swiftly by the jumper as soon as he realised that things were not going right. Training jumps were from seven hundred feet and in action the sticks were unloaded at heights as low as four hundred feet, so not much time was spent in the air, when a paratrooper is completely vulnerable to fire from the ground.

Having been told about all these possibilities it would not have been surprising if most of us had viewed our future with something less than equanimity. All the same, our detailed training and the calibre of our instructors gave us total confidence in our ability to cope, and there were, we knew, very few accidents.

My stick was under the guidance of Sergeant Husband, who had himself, like the other RAF instructors, made several hundred parachute descents. One felt that nothing could possibly go wrong so long as he was in charge.

At the DZ Sergeant Husband checked that we had properly adjusted our harnesses to a firm and comfortable fit. Then we were told what the jumping order was to be. I was actually pleased to find that I was to be No. 1 from the first balloon. At least I wouldn't have to hang around.

Harnessed up to my 'chute, I clambered aboard the basket with the other four trainees and the RAF dispatcher. Once we were all safely aboard the dispatcher shouted to the winchman, 'Up seven hundred. Five dropping,' and we began to rise.

It is an eerie feeling, being in the basket of a captive balloon. It rocks gently and, even on a still day, there is a plaintive rustle and faint whistle of wind in the rigging.

As the ground receded I was gratified to find that I had no

feeling at all of being at a height, and was able to look down at the panorama below with none of my usual giddiness – that is, until I made the fatal mistake of looking down the hawser to the winch on the ground. Then I immediately felt the blood drain from my head and my hands break into sweat. I looked back into the basket, and the feeling passed. It seems that my form of fear of heights has something to do with being connected to the ground below, and the perspective of the receding link, even if only a cable, affecting the balance nerves in the brain.

There was a slight bounce as we reached the end of our ascent at seven hundred feet, and at once the dispatcher rapped out, 'Number One. Feet in the hole!' We had already clipped our strops to the strongpoint.

My mouth dry, I sat down on the edge of the exit, and tried to remember all I had been taught.

'Number One. Go!'

I launched myself outwards and downwards in the approved fashion: chin back, feet and knees firmly clamped together, hands gripping the sides of my trousers, body rigidly at attention.

For what seemed an eternity nothing happened. I just felt myself falling. Then there was a glorious jerk on my harness and a loud, sharp rustle above me. I looked up and there was that lovely mushroom between me and the sky.

Now I had to think about the landing. I reached up and pulled slightly on my forward lift-webs. The ground was coming up much faster than I had expected but I had a nice forward glide with my descent. Angle the feet, knees together. I heard Sergeant Husband on his loud-hailer saying, 'Nice exit, Number One. Take it steady.'

Then, thump, roll – and I was on the ground intact.

I released myself from the harness, bundled my 'chute into the truck and scuttled over to the tea hut. Never had a brew of tea tasted so good! I won't say I felt like a king amongst men – there were too many others doing the same as I had done – but I was pretty thrilled.

Balloon drops soon became routine, and one even had time to appreciate the marvellous view of the countryside before preparing for the landing. Then came the two aircraft jumps, which were surprisingly easy. The worst part was the discomfort of sitting hunched up in the narrow fuselage of the Whitley, hoping that no-one would be airsick. The Whitley bomber was no airliner and was incredibly noisy, with everything vibrating and adding a harsh jangling to the roar of the engines. Otherwise I found my aircraft drops in many ways much less daunting than jumping from a balloon.

Our final qualifying jump was the second one from an aircraft and done at night. This was the easiest of all for me. I jumped from the forward section and had a very smooth exit. As I floated down I was surprised to see that I was drifting towards the river that skirted Tatton Park, so I pulled down on my rear lift-webs and checked the glide, landing very softly close to the bank.

On our last day at the Parachute Training School there was a little ceremony as we were all presented with our wings and badges given by the makers of the parachutes. The event was rounded off by a lusty communal rendering of the jumper's song:

> When first I came to PTS my CO he
>   advised
> 'Bring lots and lots of underwear, you'll
>   need it I surmise,'
> But I replied, 'By Gad, sir! You're
>   wrong, upon my soul,
> For I shall keep my trousers clean when
>   jumping through the hole.'
> Oh, jumping through the hole,
> Jumping through the hole, etc. . .

My underwear was immaculate.

At Salisbury Station I was met by a 7 Para Battalion driver and taken the few miles to Bulford Camp, the centre of 6th Airborne Division's area. The camp was an unlovely, congested sprawl of military buildings ancient and modern, on the fringe of Salisbury Plain.

The battalion was quartered in a hutted camp built during the First World War, with a large officers' mess bungalow and a fairly modern headquarters building on the edge of the barrack square.

My room was a spartan little wooden box in one of the old huts, with a plain boarded floor and the regulation iron bedstead, chest of drawers and wardrobe. Waiting in the mess I met some of my fellow junior officers. They were a charming, friendly bunch, most of them in PT kit, and I was struck by the way most of them rushed in, gulped down their tea or coffee, and rushed out again. All very different from my palmy days with 42nd Armoured Division.

The motto General Gale had chosen for the division was 'Go To It' – these chaps certainly seemed to be in a hell of a hurry to get there. I just hoped I would be able to keep up with them.

As soon as I met him, I knew that I was very fortunate to be in a battalion commanded by Lieutenant-Colonel Geoffrey Pine-Coffin, DSO, MC. Tall, lean and tough, with long-nosed, humorous features and quizzical, crinkled eyes, he was the quintessential military leader. A Devonian (a Pine-Coffin had been with me at my prep school in Exeter), he had been one of the earliest officers to volunteer for parachute duties, and was a man of extraordinary bravery, but still a caring, wise commander whose planning always took in the welfare of his men. Quiet-spoken and almost gentle in his manner, there was no tough-guy swagger about Geoffrey Pine-Coffin.

He allotted me a rifle platoon, but told me that, because of my specialist training, I would also act as reserve signals officer, and might eventually also take over as 2 i/c of the mortar and MMG platoons after I had done the required courses of instruction.

So it looked as though I was going to be a sort of jack-of-all-trades, as well as training as a conventional platoon officer. I didn't mind what I did, now that I was at last a part of a group preparing for a role in the imminent Second Front. That there was soon to be an assault into Europe no one doubted. Americans, Canadians and others were pouring in; Britain was bulging at the seams with military might.

I went through a three-inch Mortar course at Netheravon,

and having passed that I joined Tony Bowler as 2 i/c of the mortar and MMG platoon, while Malcolm Hill commanded the MMG platoon.

The combined mortar and MMG platoon was unique to para battalions, and consisted of eighty men, the physical pick of the battalion because of the hefty loads of weaponry and ammunition that each man would have to carry into action.

But none of them matched Malcolm Hill in strength or physique. 'Garth', as he was called after a comic-strip hero of the day, a sort of Superman, was a tremendous lad, massively built and enormously powerful. Good-natured and smiling, he was a perfect foil for his senior, Tony Bowler, a smallish, wiry Somerset man of my age with a sharp sense of humour and a tremendous zest for living.

The months sped by at Bulford, crammed with a busy training schedule. The old Whitley had by now been phased out and we were using Dakotas, Albemarles and Stirlings and had to learn and practise the techniques for exits from these planes. We also now had to allow for containers and learn to cope with kit-bags.

The containers were metal tubes about six or seven feet long which could be filled with supplies and weapons, with their own parachute attachments, which were loaded into the bomb-bays of the aircraft and dropped by the bomb-release switches.

The kit-bag was a canvas bag slightly larger than a soldier's conventional kit-bag, filled with all sorts of extra supplies, grooved to fit onto a man's leg, and reaching from foot to thigh. The jumper released the bag from his leg as soon as he was floating earthwards, and lowered it hand-over-hand to the end of a twenty-foot rope, so that it dangled below him and hit the ground first. This dangling bag often gave a stand-up landing since its weight disappeared on impact and arrested the speed of descent.

By the end of 1943 our battalion had been developed into a crack unit, even by airborne standards, and was ready for any task we might be called upon to carry out.

What we did not know was that, in the middle of February 1944, General Gale had been briefed on the whole plan for the invasion of Europe, and had been given his orders for the part that 6th Airborne Division would play.

Our training now began to be even more concentrated and on a larger scale. Our field exercises and schemes were at brigade and division level, and our field-firing practice was intensive.

It was at about this time that I acquired Oyston – or rather, he acquired me . . .

I had recommended my batman for promotion, as I felt that he was too good a soldier to be held back as an officer's runner, so I needed to find another man willing to take on the task of looking after me – not an easy quest in a parachute unit.

It was the company sergeant-major who had the foresight and good sense to suggest Oyston for the job.

I have to admit that at first I was rather less than enthusiastic about the idea. Oyston, while certainly not a trouble-maker, had always been a problem in the company. A big, red-headed Geordie, he had a fiery temper and a surly manner that came close to dumb insolence. Yet he never went too far and had an immaculate conduct sheet. A loner, he had no particular pal in the battalion and appeared to be something of a misanthrope. His conversation was not exactly academic, his barrack-room language was sulphurous, his appearance off parade left a lot to be desired also: he invariably looked scruffy and his natural gait was a lurching shamble. On parade, however, his drill and turn-out were smart and precise – small wonder, since he came to us from the Coldstream Guards.

This, then, was the man that the company sergeant-major suggested I should consider as my batman. The prospect seemed to me akin to trying to make a pet of a rhinoceros. I acknowledged that the CSM had had years of experience with soldiers. If he reckoned, therefore, that all Oyston needed was for somebody to take an interest in him and give him some special responsibility, I respected his judgement.

'You won't find a more loyal man, sir,' he said.

When Oyston faced me in the company office, standing stiffly to attention, there was a stony-faced pause after I had explained what I wanted and offered him the job. Then, grudgingly: 'All right, I'll have a go.'

Our first few days were not propitious. Oyston would come crashing into my room within minutes of reveille, bang a mug of tea on the table, shake me with a loud 'Come on, then, rise and shine!' and then ask me sullenly what he was to do next. He seemed to regard me with deep suspicion, and went about his tasks in silence.

But gradually he got into the routine of the job, and began to thaw. The metamorphosis in him was remarkable. He became positively jovial, and not only were my clothing and kit kept immaculately, but he too became as smart and cheerful as any man in the unit. He was expert in 'winning' anything I lacked, and I soon learned never to ask where it came from. The answer would be a huge, gap-toothed grin, but no explanation.

For many months Oyston watched over me devotedly both in training and in action, and no man ever had a more loyal minder. As he once said, 'By heck! I look after you like a mother.'

The early months of 1944 were particularly busy times for us, as our large-scale exercises took on new intensity of purpose. We had two exercises, involving the whole division, which entailed mass night drops with containers and kit-bags. The first of these was my thirteenth aircraft jump, and, superstitious as I am, I was glad to get it behind me.

One particular concept of Airborne thinking and Airborne morale was constantly dinned into us: conventional infantry normally fights on an identifiable front line but parachute troops and glider-borne troops know that they will probably operate in groups and pockets behind the enemy lines. Objectives captured by surprise assault then have to be held, and the Germans were good at counter-attack. So Airborne men learn to waste no time in digging in deep and setting up fields of fire surrounding their newly won positions. They know that their defences will probably be infiltrated, but they also know that this can be to their advantage. They are dug in, they know the ground, they are concealed. But the counter-attacking enemy is in the open, uncovered, vulnerable. He may find a gap and get through, but while he is behind you it is equally true that you are behind him and in a much better position. He, too, feels cut off, but not in a place of his own choosing.

These were the tricks we were taught, and our confidence was boundless. We were quite sure that we could take and hold anything required of us.

Our months of preparation were unfortunately not without accidents and tragedy. In one supply-drop exercise with massed aircraft a plane had been hit by a container and had crashed, killing all the occupants. A few paratroopers had died in jumping accidents, and there had been many minor mishaps and broken bones. Still, this was only to be expected, and the proportion of mishaps to safe landings had been very low.

In May, two special events occurred. The first was when the Commander-in-Chief, General Montgomery, arrived to inspect the division. We knew by now that he was to command all the Allied forces in the invasion of Europe, and we were naturally curious to see and hear our leader. He was accompanied by General Browning, the very handsome and fabled commander of all our British Airborne Forces.

Montgomery inspected us in three enormous brigade groups on Salisbury Plain. Then he spoke to each brigade group in turn, standing on a jeep while the men crowded around. He harangued us in his familiar, clipped tones, making sure that we shared his confidence in the outcome of the great exploit before us. This was no mere pep-talk: he spoke with passion and sincerity, and a dry sense of humour that made his words far more convincing than any high-flown rhetoric would have.

The next memorable event was a visit from the King and Queen, accompanied by the then Princess Elizabeth, who spent the whole day inspecting the division, and watched a mass glider landing and a drop by the Canadian Parachute Battalion.

My own personal moment to remember came when, being a member of the regiment, the K.O.Y.L.I., of which she was Colonel in Chief. I was introduced to the Queen. With the marvellous warmth and choice of phrase that is unique to her, Her Majesty made me almost feel as if I were an old friend. In my subsequent brief meetings with her over the years she somehow has always conveyed that same sense of cordiality. A very special person, the Queen Mother.

On our return to Bulford towards the end of May it was clear that our long wait was nearly over. General Gale spoke to all the officers of the division, leaving us in no doubt that we were soon to spearhead a mighty assault into Europe. I had been appointed Assistant Adjutant, and had already been helping to fill in the complicated load-tables for our aircraft, which included the men to be carried, the containers and kit-bags to be used, and even the details of their contents, but even I still had no idea what, or where, our task would be. Only the CO and the adjutant knew this, together with the intelligence officer, and they weren't telling.

About 1 June 7 Para Bn moved into its concentration camp on Salisbury Plain. These camps had been prepared at various points for elements of 6th Airborne Division and were usually as near as possible to the embarkation airfields. They were wired-in enclosures with tents and a briefing-hut, totally cut off from the surrounding countryside. Even the daily arrivals of rations and mail were dumped outside the guarded entrance gate, and collected only when the delivery truck had departed. The inmates of these camps had no contact at all with the outside world.

There was good reason for this rigid security: on our first afternoon in the camp Colonel Pine-Coffin briefed his officers on the 6th Airborne task in general, and on the role of 7 Para in particular. So we now knew exactly when, where and how the invasion of Europe would take place.

Just before the briefing he had told me that I would be included in the party as assistant adjutant, but that I was to be prepared to take over the mortar platoon or the signals platoon if necessary, so that I would need to attend the briefing with this in mind.

The briefing hut was hung with aerial photos and maps of our objective and the divisional area in Normandy, and the centre of the room was taken up by a large sand-table model of the bridgehead we would form. It was in great detail, down to individual trees, houses and tracks, and had been

splendidly made by Bertie Mills, our intelligence officer, and
his section. Another model showed our particular DZ and
objective in large scale.

D-Day was to be 5 June, an invasion over the beaches of
some fifty miles of Normandy, stretching from Ouistreham
in the east to the base of the Cotentin Peninsula in the west.
On the night 4/5 June, some four or five hours before first
light, two airborne operations inland would secure the flanks
of the bridgehead and weaken the beach defences by attacks
from the rear: these airborne assaults were to be carried out
by 82nd and 101st American Airborne Divisions on the right,
at the base of the Cotentin, and by 6th British Airborne
Division on the left, in the Orne Valley.

The overall commander of the entire invasion force was
General Montgomery, as C-in-C 21st Army Group. His
Group consisted of 1st US Army under General Bradley,
and 2nd British Army under General Dempsey.

The British beach assaults were to be to the left, or
east, of the invasion front over some twenty miles between
Ouistreham and Arromanches, and the seaborne landings
nearest to 6th Airborne would be made by 1st SS Brigade
and 3rd British Division. They should link up with us by the
late morning of D-Day.

It was hoped that Caen should be taken by the end of
D-Day.

The entire operation code-named Overlord has been written about too often to warrant description here, but this is
the part that affected us: 6th Airborne was to capture and
hold a vital bridgehead that would secure the east flank of the
entire invasion. From Ouistreham to Caen ran two parallel
waterways, the River Orne and the Canal de Caen, forming
a natural obstacle, roughly north to south, against any attack
from the east. The only crossing places were two bridges,
one near Benouville over the canal and one over the Orne
near Ranville. These bridges were linked by a narrow causeway road that traversed the four hundred yards of wet,
marshy ground between.

The 6th Airborne bridgehead would be bounded to the
west by the river and the canal, with an additional small
bridgehead to be held west of the canal in the area of Le

Port and Benouville; to the south by a line of villages and orchards running from Longueval to Herouvillette and including the main village, Ranville, and Le Bas de Ranville, Le Mariquet and Escoville; to the east by a heavily wooded ridge running from Salanelles to Troarn; and to the north by the coast.

As the Orne and canal bridges were strongly defended and certainly prepared for demolition, surprise was an essential element of their capture. Therefore, a *coup de main* force in six gliders would land, three to each bridge, on or near the bridges, half an hour after midnight and thirty minutes before the main parachute troops landed concurrently with the pathfinders of the Independent Para Company. This hazardous glider-borne operation was to be carried out by a company of the 52nd Oxfordshire and Buckinghamshire Light Infantry, and a party of Royal Engineers, under the command of Major John Howard.

The 1st SS Brigade was expected to fight their way from the beaches to arrive before noon on their way across the bridges to take up their positions beyond, and during the afternoon elements of 3rd British Division were expected to reach the small western bridgehead and to relieve the Airborne troops there, while throughout the operation some support might be given by the guns of HMS Warspite and other big ships of the covering Royal Navy fleet.

In all this, we of the 7th Para had been allotted the crucial task of relieving the *coup de main* party on the Orne and canal bridges, and establishing the western bridgehead, which would protect 6th Airborne's west flank and prevent counter-attacking German forces from moving out of the Caen area to meet our seaborne troops, and so contain their drive southwards from the beaches.

In the event that Major Howard's *coup de main* party did not succeed in capturing the bridges, we would capture them, either directly along the line of the road, or by attacks across the waterways in inflatable rubber dinghies.

At all costs, our western bridgehead in the Le Port and Benouville area was to hold firm until relieved by forward elements of 3rd Division, late on D-Day afternoon.

Apart from the German troops already in our bridgehead

area, we could expect immediate counter-attacks from the south and west, almost certainly led by armoured Panzer units, against which our only defence would be our PIATs (a form of hand-held bazooka), and the Gammon bombs that every man would carry (a hand-thrown ball of plasticine-like plastic explosive which, with luck and a good aim from about twenty yards, could blow the tracks off an armoured vehicle).

So now we knew.

Colonel Pine-Coffin then went on to explain his personal plan for the battalion's operation, and to give us his orders.

Our DZ was to be a flat area of arable and grass land north of Ranville, bounded to the east by woodland and to the west by a ragged escarpment that bordered the River Orne. It was a very open plain with no trees, few hedges and no buildings, ideal for a parachute drop. The only snag was that aerial reconnaissance photos showed that in recent weeks the Germans had been erecting thousands of poles on all the likely landing and dropping zones along the Normandy coastal hinterland. It was not yet known whether the poles had been connected together by wires that would detonate explosive charges. That was a chance we had to take.

Speed was essential. Every man, after landing, was to collect what he could in the way of dinghy-filled kit-bags and make for the rendezvous at the top of the escarpment. Bugle calls would help us locate the RV. Once we were collected we were to move with all speed to the bridges about half a mile away. A rear party would recover the rest of the kit-bags and the mortar and MMG platoons would gather up their weapons from the containers.

The CO then gave his order of march to the company commanders and specialist officers, and a short period of question and answer ensued before the gathering of officers broke up into groups for a more detailed study of the sand-table models and the aerial photos.

I don't remember the atmosphere of that briefing session being unusually taut, nor do I recall my own thoughts or feelings. Perhaps I tried not to have any. Now that the task had been revealed, one's only thought was of how best to go about it.

The next three or four days were filled with activity, and there was an air of exuberance over the whole camp.

We were all issued with certain items peculiar to airborne soldiers. Perhaps the most intriguing of these was the escape pack and the map packet, designed for use by a man cut off from his own forces and consisting of a plastic bag for carrying water, a tiny compass, some dried vitaminised food tablets, some French currency and ten Benzadrine tablets to help keep the man awake for movement by night, and a little wad of maps of France and neighbouring countries printed on silk. I still have my escape kit somewhere intact – except for the Benzadrine tablets, which I think I used from time to time years later during a heavy night-clubbing period.

We were also each given an ordinary looking button to sew onto our battledress. It was, in fact, magnetised, and could be used as a compass if balanced on the point of a pin!

To carry these things about the person, in addition to all the webbing equipment, ammunition, weapons and spare clothing which a paratrooper needed to have with him, required special clothing and a good deal of ingenuity on the part of the wearer.

Our helmets were simple domes without rims, lined with sponge rubber and with straps with a cup which fitted over the chin. These helmets were covered with a net into which we wove lengths of camouflage scrim.

Our battledress trousers had two extra pockets, one on each buttock. Into these we stuffed our shell dressings, which considerably distended the shape of our backsides, but which acted as useful padding for the base of the spine in the event of a backward landing.

In addition we were given camouflage netting squares, which most of us wore round our necks as mufflers, and we had the now-familiar camouflage smocks in mottled greens and browns, with a tail-piece which went between the legs and snap-buttoned in front. The smock had four capacious pockets, and I carried, amongst other things for both personal and military uses, a signals message pad in my top left pocket and a ball of plastic explosive for the Gammon bomb in the bottom right.

We transformed our smocks in several ways. Nearly all of

us had lengths of the thick container lining-felt stitched into the shoulders, from the collar to the arm-seam, covering the collar-bone in front and the shoulder-blade at the back. This prevented the straps of the heavy loads we carried from cutting into the bones. It also gave us a frighteningly burly appearance; even a slender chap looked very broad-shouldered, and, with my short and stocky build, I must have seemed as wide as I was long. In addition, we found that the deep double-lining at the back made a useful receptacle. When the top seam of this lining was unpicked it formed a huge poacher's pocket into which we stuffed spare soft clothing such as sweaters, underwear and socks, another protection against landing bumps.

For the actual jump only the parachute pack was carried on the back, so everything else was worn in the front until after the landing. Before we climbed into the parachute harness we donned a jumping-smock, an armless, legless sack zipped up the front, to cover all the equipment and prevent it fouling the rigging lines of the 'chute. Once in his jumping-smock a paratrooper waddled about like an over-ripe pear.

All officers were armed with 9mm pistols using the same bullets as the Sten gun, but many elected to carry a Sten as well. Everybody carried ammunition pouches with spare Sten magazines, whether or not they actually used a Sten. Altogether, each man must have hefted about eighty pounds of arms and equipment into battle.

During those few days in the concentration camp the weather was fine and sunny and we spent a lot of time stripped to the waist in the sun, quietly checking weapons and daubing our webbing equipment with camouflage paint. I did my own brushwork, because the faithful Oyston was not with me. He had developed foot trouble and was not allowed to jump, but would be following up to Normandy a few days later with the seaborne reinforcements.

Sunday 4 June dawned fine but a bit blustery. This was to be our day. By nightfall we would be heading for perhaps the most consequential moment of our lives. What were my thoughts that morning? I have no idea. Did I eat my breakfast wondering if it would be my last? I don't think so. Certainly we airborne men were no more stressed or taut (hyped-up would be the modern phrase) than those in more conventional units.

By mid-morning our convoy of three-ton lorries, all formation and identification markings obliterated and canopies closed up, was lined up outside the camp. We loaded our equipment, and embarked in our stick order. I was to be in aircraft No. 33, so I led my stick into the appropriately numbered truck. Once inside, the canopy was closed up again and laced tightly. There was no sign that this fleet of lorries had anything to do with Airborne Forces. Then we bumped and swayed for an hour or more en route to Fairford, which was to be our departure airfield. It was gloomy there in the dark interior of the vehicle, and pretty uncomfortable. At least we had our bottom-padding to sit on.

Our laager near Fairford was a lush grass field, screened from the road by a belt of trees and not near any houses. A field kitchen had been set up and hot stew was the first thing on the programme.

As we arrived and clambered out of our transport, the CO called the officers together:

D-Day had been postponed for one day, due to unsuitable weather conditions. We were to have our meal, and then return to our camp and repeat the process next day.

Most of the reaction to this news was unprintable. We had got all dressed up for the ball, but the band had got lost in a fog.

The stew did not taste as good as usual. Some of us even remembered to be sorry for the people cooped up in the assault craft and landing ships. They would be feeling sicker than us.

By early evening we were back in the concentration camp, on Salisbury Plain. Our great day had dawned, brightened – and fizzled out in gloom. For most of us it was a frustrating postponement; for many it was a twenty-four hour extension to their lives.

13

BY AIR TO BATTLE

Next morning, Monday 5 June, we repeated the previous day's short journey to Fairford. Again, all our lorries were closed down, their canvas canopies lashed tight, but this time I sat up front with the driver in shirt-sleeve order, wearing no red beret. It was a beautiful morning and we were passing through some of England's loveliest scenery, so I enjoyed the drive a great deal more than I had the first gloomy trip.

Once at our laager the entire battalion tucked into another hearty meal of stew and rice pudding. There could not have been a more tranquil pastoral setting for an alfresco picnic. Even the cattle in our field seemed to accept our presence without question. Most of them cooled their shins in the shallows of the stream bordering the field, while a few wandered across through the buttercups and daisies to snuffle curiously at the food containers.

After the meal everybody relaxed for a while, dozing in the sunshine. Later, men formed into section and platoon groups for final checks of weapons, and tea and 'wads' were served out, followed by another short period of rest.

Then, as the shadows lengthened and the midges began their close-of-day offensive, the stand-to order was given. The last ceremony of that day was a drum-head service conducted by our much-loved padre, Captain Parry. Known to us all irreverently as Pissy Percy the Parachuting Parson, Percy Parry was a wiry little chap with a nature as fiery as his crinkly red hair, and a heart and courage to match. His puckish sense of humour endeared him to us and he was a friend to every man in the battalion.

Six hundred and ten men were drawn up in a hollow circle, facing inwards towards the padre who stood on an ammunition box. A more unlikely or piratical congregation could not be imagined; every man abristle with the weapons of war, his face and hands crudely besmirched with black cream, his helmet on the ground before him, his rifle or Sten gun laid across it.

Prayers were brief and extempore, the responses equally short. His sermon contained a heartfelt message of courage and belief. Percy was a Welshman, and words came easily to him with moving sincerity.

Hymn-sheets had been handed out and the unaccompanied singing was lusty if tuneless. *Onward Christian Soldiers* went well, but *Abide With Me* was rather more ragged. It was not easy to sing that in such a setting and at such a moment, without swallowing a lump or two. But sentiment comes rather easily to me, so perhaps I was more affected than others by those last minutes in that peaceful setting.

Immediately after the service, we embussed in our lorries. This time the canopies of the trucks had been removed, and the villagers of Fairford obviously knew what was afoot. Every doorstep, every cottage garden, rose-embowered, had its group of well-wishers to cheer us on. That pretty little town, its Cotswold stone walls a warm yellow in the last light, gave us a wonderful send-off. V-signs, thumbs-up signals and blown kisses were answered by cheerful waves from the men.

Once on the airfield our convoy halted, we dismounted from our lorries, and mugs of hot cocoa were handed out by WAAF girls. Finally, just after nightfall, at about 2300 hours, we remounted our vehicles, and slowly rumbled round the perimeter track to our waiting aircraft, the massive Stirlings silhouetted ominously in the airfield arclights. As we reached No. 33, we scrambled out of the lorries, clutching our kit-bags and arms, and formed up in a line in our stick order, with me at the head, as I was jumping first.

Our pilot appeared to be a rather senior officer, judging by what I could see of his rank badges. He wished us all luck, then told me he would be the senior officer flying that night with our group, and he intended to go in first. I tried to look pleased and clambered aboard.

'Gawd,' I thought, 'I'm going to be the first man on the ground, apart from Major Howard's glider troops and the Independent Company Pathfinders.' I fervently hoped that their missions, timed for half-an-hour before our arrival on the scene, would be one hundred per cent successful.

In the cramped, spartan interior of the fuselage we sorted ourselves and our equipment into some sort of order, and sat in two rows on the floor facing each other, foot to foot. I had with me two kit-bags, one of which, filled with mattocks and shovels, I was to jettison as soon as the jumping signal was given, and the other, containing a rubber inflatable dinghy, I would take down with me, suspended by rope from my belt. Next to me, jumping No. 2, was the soldier who was taking Oyston's place temporarily as my batman.

It was now after nightfall and the interior lights, hard and bright, illuminated the scene. With camouflage cream obliterating our faces and hands, and all swaddled in our smocks and scrimmed helmets, only eyes, teeth and bare metal glinted from the cluttered, matt background.

Within minutes of our emplaning the engines started their wheezy turn-over and then, one by one, roared to life. Presently the pitch of our engine-tone lifted, and we were rolling. At the end of the runway our interior lights dimmed, the aircraft bellowed and bumped down the runway, and was airborne, leading its straggling aerial fleet.

We knew that we would be stooging about over England for half-an-hour or so as the aerial armada marshalled and took station before we approached the Channel, and that the flight to the French coast would then take about forty-five minutes. So for about an hour we had nothing to do but sit there and wait – wait to hook up and prepare to jump.

We must all have had our own very different thoughts. Personally, I fell asleep. A useful ability, like an ostrich, when in trouble, when feeling threatened, to stick the head in the sand, and blot things out.

It must have been about 0030 hours when I was awakened by the dispatcher: 'All right, sir. Time to get ready.'

I heaved myself to my feet and began to prepare for the jump, lacing on my kit-bag and buckling my harness. There was no need to check on the others – they knew the drill and were checked by the dispatcher.

For about ten minutes we jostled and swayed while the aircraft yawed from side to side in its search for the exact line of flight. Finally, we hooked up to our static lines and shuffled to our jumping positions. The dispatcher had opened the doors of the aperture and I waddled to the hole, my right leg clamped to a kit-bag, my right hand clutching it firmly to my leg and my left hand prepared to jettison a second bag.

Oyston's stand-in was behind me, himself straddling the hole, holding on to my smock at the back and helping me not to fall out. As the aircraft jinked from side to side it was difficult to maintain balance, especially with no hands free.

For what seemed to me an age we flew like this. Looking down, I could see the white-etched crests of the sea's waves. With the aperture doors open, the combination of wind and engine noise was shattering. Then the scene below me changed; the lines of coastal rollers gave way to a blur of land features. The red warning light had already come on, and now I saw yellowy orange dots of light begin to float up towards us. Like little, leisurely shooting stars the tracer bullets criss-crossed my field of vision, framed by the shape of the aperture. They didn't seem to be coming very near us but, as the normal loading of tracer was one in every five bullets, I realised that there must be a lot of lead spraying about.

About one minute after we crossed the coastline the green light came on. I heaved the dinghy kit-bag into the hole, brought my legs together, and was out after it almost simultaneously.

There is only so much that the brain can register and the memory retain, but I remember a hell of a lot of what went on in the next few moments.

My exit had been good and I knew I had less than ten seconds before I hit the ground. The moment I felt my canopy snap open I pulled the rip-cord to release the leg-bag, holding on to its rope with my other hand. I should have let the bag down hand-over-hand, but in my flurry to do things quickly, I let it slip through my right hand, and felt it skin my palm and fingers.

'Bugger!' I shouted, to no one in particular.

With the kit-bag dangling twenty feet below me, I reached up to my lift-webs and had a few seconds to look around. The sky seemed full of other paratroopers beginning their descents, their canopies silhouetted against the moonlight and the flashes of explosions – probably anti-aircraft guns, I thought.

The din was almost mind-numbing: aircraft, chattering machine-guns and the thudding of shells or mortars. And still the night sparkled with tracer bullets.

I seemed to be drifting quite fast to my left and tried to turn myself that way, although I knew that the impact of my kit-bag hitting the ground and releasing its weight would soften my landing.

At about 0040 hours on Tuesday, 6 June 1944, I thumped onto a cornfield in Normandy, an illegal immigrant without a passport but nevertheless welcome, I hoped, at least to the locals.

I discarded my parachute harness and fumbled to untie the kit-bag cord from my belt. I realised that my right hand was a bit messy.

Then I crouched down and took stock of things. Aircraft were still coming in and I got my bearings by noting their flight path. There was no one near me, but I could dimly pick out figures moving about in the distance. Not knowing whose side they were on, I kept low, and looked for a landmark. South of me I could not see the separate tower of Ranville Church, so I reckoned I must be rather further north than I had expected. That was probably because I had jumped No. 1, and was therefore at the extreme end of the stick. About two hundred yards to the east I saw the dark line of a wood, and concluded that I was a good half-mile from the battalion rendezvous. Meanwhile, the DZ was being raked with small-arms fire, so I decided to get into that wood. I put my Sten gun together and loaded it, then wound the cord of my kitbagged dinghy round my left wrist. I was suddenly aware of an aircraft in flames to the north-east, and saw that the planes were now flying through heavy fire from the ground. Clearly we ourselves had got in before things really opened up, and the later aircraft were having a rough time. Perhaps the switch of my Stirling to No. 1 had been providential.

I set off at the double, still crouching, and was soon in the cover of the wood. I heard voices and, realising that they were speaking English, I moved towards them. In a little clearing, there stood Colonel Pine-Coffin and about a dozen others.

The CO said there was no way of knowing if John Howard's glider-borne attack on the bridges had been successful and we must get to the RV as quickly as possible.

We broke out from the woodland and set off at the double. I still had the boat in tow.

Things were quieter now. Some planes were still coming in but there was not so much anti-aircraft fire.

We came across a farm track and were able to move pretty fast along it. Now we knew where we were. This track led right to the RV. Scurrying figures were everywhere, many of them moving westwards, as we were.

By about 0100 hours our group, numbering by then some fifty men, was at the RV at the top of the escarpment leading down to the river. A bugler repeatedly blew our rallying signal, and men came stumbling towards us, shadowy, bulky figures in the moonlight, some singly, some in small groups.

But still no mortars, no machine-guns and no wireless.

Time was ticking by.

From what we could see and hear from the ridge, the bridges were intact, but there was still fighting going on around them, especially at the canal bridge. And anyway, even if the *coup de main* party had taken the bridges, they would not be strong enough to withstand counter-attacks. So at about 0130, when we mustered some one hundred and fifty men out of the six hundred and ten who had set out from Fairford two hours before, the CO gave the order to move off to the bridges.

I was glad to shed my rubber dinghy. We moved fast down the slope through the scrub to where the road curved in its approach to the bridge spanning the River Orne.

All seemed quiet as we reached this bridge and trotted over it. Men of Major Howard's force were in defensive positions around the east end, and the glider men were using the former German trenches and wire. As we crossed the bridge and started along the causeway road I got my first close-up sight of a war casualty: a legless German lay on the edge of the road, a groaning sound coming weirdly from him.

Internal gasses, I supposed. Normally, the sight of blood on others turns my stomach, yet I felt nothing, only mild curiosity.

A few yards further on we passed a small, shot-up German staff car. This had apparently belonged to the officer commanding the bridge defences. He and his driver had come racing in from the direction of Ranville when the firing started, heading for his HQ on the canal bridge, but hadn't got very far.

As we doubled along the causeway towards the canal bridge, a large iron structure that could be opened for river craft, it was clear that Major Howard's men were being attacked. Suddenly all hell erupted on the road ahead. Heavy explosions, flashes and tracer bullets rent the night like a spectacular firework display. We speeded up our jog-trot.

Then, as quickly as it had started, so the tumult died down. An old tank which had been probing the bridgehead had been hit and set on fire, and this was its ammunition exploding.

We reached the little café-bar at the west end of the bridge and I was directed by the CO to set up Battalion HQ on the reverse slope of a conical hill to the north-west of the bridgehead, just below the tiny hamlet of Le Port, whose church could be seen on the crest.

Here our HQ party began furiously to dig in.

The sound of intermittent fighting was all around the perimeter, especially from Le Port and Benouville to the south.

So far, so good. Phase one of our task had been accomplished. The bridges had been captured intact and the bridgehead established.

Now we had to hang on until some time the next day.

The soft light of dawn glimmered unnoticed by us. Long before then the night sky had been continuously seared by brilliant parachute flares and the incessant flashes of explosions in and around the bridgehead. In our little toe-hold on the west bank of the Caen Canal very few seconds went by without the flickered illumination of shell-bursts or mortar bombs. And then, minutes before first light, a shattering cacophony erupted, with a glare that would have made full daylight seem pale in comparison, as some three miles north of us the softening-up bombardment of the German coastal defences began. For about half-an-hour the din, the vibration of air and ground, the magnitude of that destructive assault, was far beyond anything I could have imagined.

Hundreds of aircraft, American and British, rained thousands of bombs along that concrete strip of gun-positions, trenches and pill-boxes that menaced the landing of our seaborne invasion force.

Artillery and batteries of rocket-launchers firing from special craft at sea poured a continuous hail of shells across the water, while naval guns, including the big ones of HMS Warspite, helped to pulverise the defences.

From our grandstand position on the slope of the knoll at Le Port, the sights and sounds were literally breathtaking. The ground shook beneath us, and I felt sorry for the poor sods I could visualise cowering in those German bunkers. How could they possibly emerge and fight back? How could they even survive? But they did, and retaliated with impressive vigour. The effect on their morale must have been shattering, but they recovered and continued to fight.

Whilst the mighty invasion from the sea was being fought out, quite a lot, on a smaller but no less deadly scale, was going on in our little area. There was no cessation in the Germans' probing with patrols and counter-attacks, some led by tanks, and the regimental aid post was overrun by an enemy group in the early hours. The wounded being tended there were all killed where they lay. So too was Padre Parry, who had evidently fought like a tiger to defend them.

A Company in Benouville, with all its officers killed or wounded, was to hold out for seventeen hours, even though reduced to a strength of less than twenty. From time to time we could hear an officer's voice rallying his troops with shouts of encouragement. What we did not know till later was that he was lying wounded by the window of a house in the village, one leg blown away.

One of his men, Private McGee, fed up with being shot at by a tank as he ducked down in his fox hole, leaped up and charged down the street, firing from the hip. The tank crew closed up the shutters and were temporarily blinded, whereupon McGee threw a Gammon bomb from a few yards and crippled the vehicle, which slewed across the road and effectively blocked any further tank movement.

B Company, in and around Le Port, repelled repeated attacks, one of their worst problems being the large number of snipers making movement difficult as they picked off men from cottage windows, roof-tops and especially from the church tower.

That stout little Norman tower was right in the centre of B Company's area, and very difficult to deal with. The church was surrounded by open ground and was virtually impossible to attack with the few paratroopers available.

Finally, early in the morning, Corporal Killeen, of the anti-tank platoon, found a solution. With his Piat, he crept from cottage to cottage until he found a position with cover from view, and within range of his bombs. His first bomb blew a sizeable hole in the tower and succeeding ones practically shattered it. He stood up, and no shot was fired at him. He then rushed across the grass to the church doorway, determined to finish off any snipers who still lurked inside, but he had no need. His bombs had killed all the occupants.

Later in the day Corporal Killeen recorded an interview with Chester Wilmot, the Australian BBC war correspondent, who had flown in by glider with Advance Div. HQ. Chester, one of the few people actually presented with a red beret to wear, was always to be found where things were at their stickiest, puffing at his large-bowled pipe, and lugging along his heavy and cumbersome recording equipment. I was present when he spoke to the embarrassed Killeen, a good Irish Catholic lad. I remember how Chester carefully drew out from him a hesitant description of his brave exploit, but it was the corporal's last sentence that I shall never forget: 'When I got to the church door I looked up, and, och! I was sorry to see what I had done to a wee house of God – but I did take off my tin hat when I went inside!'

C Company, dug into positions in the grounds of a chateau to the south, was also heavily attacked throughout the day and, down to about platoon strength, still repulsed continuous attacks, and destroyed several tanks, with Piats and hand-thrown Gammon bombs.

Meanwhile, Battalion HQ and Headquarters Company, a skeleton of our normal strength, mustered a few more men as the day wore on and paratroopers who had been dropped wide managed to get through to us. Sadly, we had no idea what had happened to Tony Bowler, 'Garth' Hill and the rest of the mortar and machine-gun platoons – and many others. Several mortarmen did find their way to us, and these the CO told me to organise into a small reserve force of riflemen, equipped with rifles or Stens gathered from casualties.

We still had no mortars or machine-guns and no wireless. The lack of radio communication within the battalion was one of the colonel's greatest problems. At times it was impossible to know exactly what was happening in the outlying positions. It was difficult for runners to get through, as the areas between our HQ and the forward troops were frequently infested with enemy patrols or infiltrators and snipers. All we knew most of the time was that our hard-pressed units were still fighting.

At one point during the morning the CO told me to take four or five of the mortarmen and to find out what had happened to part of a platoon in an outpost position that had been sent about five hundred yards northwards up the canal to guard our flank nearest to the sea and the invasion beach. Nothing had been heard from them since our arrival at Le Port.

We set out along the line of the canal, moving cautiously through the low scrub and reeds of the water meadows. I was not sure where the platoon, which probably numbered only a dozen or so men, had sited itself, although I knew that its task was to cover the Ouistreham road which ran parallel to the canal, and to stop any enemy movement along that axis.

We had gone only a few hundred yards when I spotted a glint of metal right ahead of us. Then I saw that this came from a well-hidden figure crouching behind a hummock in a perfect firing position. Motioning the others to get down, I crept off to my right and slipped along below the canal bank

until I reckoned I was about abreast of the enemy sniper. I
carefully peered over the bank – and realised that it was one
of our own lads lying there. I walked over to him and saw
that he was dead. He was a teenager that I knew well by
sight, with a little hole in his forehead, no blood or anything,
his chin resting on his rifle.

So much for my daring outflanking ploy . . .

At least I was able to contact the platoon commander and
find that all was well in his outpost.

From my shallow slit-trench on the slope at Le Port, poorly
dug due to my skinned right hand, I had a perfect view to
the east, over the bridges and into the divisional area. In the
distance, beyond the River Orne, the skyline was stippled
with flashes and puffs of smoke from explosions or air-burst
shells, while in the foreground, just below us, was the canal
bridge, so brilliantly captured a few hours before by John
Howard's glider party. The remains of three gliders lay there,
all of them within fifty yards of the ugly metal structure,
landed with pin-point accuracy by their pilots. Major Howard
and his men were now dug in close around the bridge and
were in reserve. By our end of the bridge stood the café
owned by the Gondrée family, a lonely building seemingly
miraculously still untouched by high explosive blast.

Georges Gondrée and his wife had already dispensed
ninety-seven bottles of champagne amongst all those of us
who had had time for a swig – mostly John Howard's men.
The sparkling cache had been hidden under the earth floor
of his cellar ever since the Germans had occupied the area
in 1940, so it had matured nicely.

Beyond the canal bridge stretched the raised causeway
road, now pockmarked along its length by the scars of mortar
bombs and shells.

I was contemplating this view when I suddenly noticed
emerging into sight from a screen of trees two boats apparently deserted and drifting slowly towards Caen. Remembering that there was no current on the canal I mentioned
my suspicions to the CO and although we could not see
anybody on deck, he ordered his HQ group to fire on them.
Our fusillade of shots was briefly answered by return fire
from below decks, and then all was quiet as two small parties

of Germans emerged from wheel-houses and holds with their hands up. They were taken prisoner, and the boats were left grounded.

Apparently they were small trawler-type patrol boats that had got away from the carnage in Ouistreham and were heading for the naval basin at Caen. So to add to our battle honours that day we were able to claim a naval victory.

At about ten o'clock in the morning two bulky figures hove into view calmly walking towards us along the causeway road between the bridges. Both wore red berets and were soon recognisable as General Gale and Brigadier Poett, our divisional and brigade commanders. Shells and mortar bombs were still falling on and around the road, yet these two strolled along as though out for a morning constitutional. It was a heartening sight.

They stayed with us for a while as Colonel Pine-Coffin gave as accurate a statement of affairs as he could, for our radio communications were still non-existent, and then they walked back again. Every man who had seen them must have felt the boost to his resolve.

By that hour we had expected the commando brigade to reach us from the beaches, but fighting must have been unexpectedly heavy in the Ouistreham area. We could hear the sounds of battle some three miles north of us, but no skirl of bagpipes to herald Lord Lovat's approach with his commandos.

Fortunately for us there was no enemy aerial activity, either because of our own control of the skies or because of the overcast weather. We would have been a prime target for bombers or strafing in our tight little island of ground. A new sound from above did now assail us: HMS Warspite was shelling inland targets, probably German armoured columns moving up from the Caen area, and the salvos from her big guns roared overhead like trains in a tunnel.

Finally, at about midday, the first respite for some of our hard-pressed men arrived, as the commandos passed through, clearing up the last of the enemy pockets in Le Port. It was a fine sight. Over a thousand men crossed our bridges, and there was great jubilation as red and green berets mingled momentarily on the road.

By about 1400 hours the last of the commandos had passed through, and the rest of the afternoon and evening ground wearily and hazardously on.

The D-Day programme appeared to be running behind time. Later we learned that a stiff wind and choppy seas had delayed the arrival of some troops and armour on the beaches and that a traffic jam of vehicles and tanks had taken some time to sort out. Chester Wilmot's *The Struggle for Europe* observes an absence of drive on the part of two of the three leading battalions. Be that as it may, there was still no sign of the seaborne infantry or armour reaching our area.

Some time during the middle of the afternoon the CO sent me to check on the B Company positions in and north of Le Port and to get a situation report from the company commander. Having done this, I walked up the road northwards a few hundred yards to see if anything appeared to be heading in our direction from the coast. To my utter amazement, a convoy of three-ton lorries came trundling into view. The leading truck stopped, and a florid-faced, ginger-moustached RE Major jumped out. He was in charge of a Royal Engineers bridging party, and had simply collected his vehicles together off the beach and driven the three miles down the main road towards Caen, totally unaware that only the commando brigade had gone before him. He asked me if the Orne bridges were intact and if the road from there to Caen was clear. I put him in the picture and advised him to hang on where he was and to have his men take up defensive positions. If a bunch of soft-skinned vehicles could have reached this far intact, where the hell were the expected forward invasion troops, I wondered?

The CO was relieved to know that B Company was now totally in control of their area. Our A and C Company positions were still being probed by German infantry and armour, but were holding. A captured German anti-tank gun was used to good effect and blew a gaping hole in the Benouville water-tower, eradicating a group of snipers who were using it.

All that day our numbers were swelled by men who got back to us from the scattered night-drop, some of them having found their way through enemy lines. One sergeant-

At the beginning of *The Hasty Heart*, persuading John Gregson (*right*) to
look after my bagpipes. At which he said his one word in the entire film – 'Aye!'

The same film: Ronald Reagan rubs it in

Backs to the wall: as pictured with Ruth Roman in *Lightning Strikes Twice* (1950),

and again, with Eva Bartok two years later, in Venice

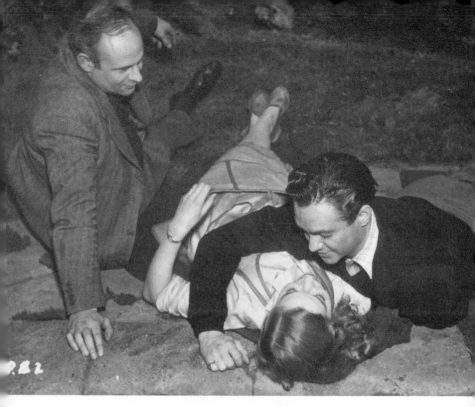

Taking advice from my director on how to get down to things with Valerie Hobson in *Interrupted Journey*. The film was originally called *The Cord*, while in the States it had yet another title, *Journey Into Darkness*

Further directorial advice – perhaps on the dangers of smoking? – from Alfred Hitchcock during *Stagefright*

Collecting awards for *The Hasty Heart* from the Hollywood Foreign Correspondents Association (Golden Globes)

With Jean Simmons, Anna Neagle and Michael Wilding during rehearsals at Elstree

major was led to the bridges by a French girl. He was dressed in her brother's civilian clothes and riding her brother's bike, and the pair of them had cycled some miles through German-occupied territory. By the end of the day we mustered about two hundred and fifty men, having lost some sixty killed and wounded from the original hundred and fifty that had established the bridgehead.

At around 2100 hours the leading troops of 3rd British Division reached us and soon afterwards the sky was darkened by the arrival of one hundred and forty-five huge gliders and their tug aircraft. Within minutes two reinforcing battalions of 6th Airlanding Brigade were on the ground, plus more guns.

When the relieving infantry of 3 Division finally reached us in semi-darkness, the mopping-up operation in the Benouville area still took some time, but by midnight our two companies were extricated from their doggedly held positions, and the casualties evacuated. Then we assembled as a battalion on the road by the canal bridge, and began our march to an area just north of Ranville, where we were to go into brigade reserve.

The Gondrée family was there, smiling and waving as the men passed by. All day they had helped to tend the wounded who had been brought to their house after the aid post had been overrun, and many of us owed a great debt of gratitude to these kindly, brave people.

Already fastened to the girders of the canal bridge was a crudely-painted sign: 'PEGASUS BRIDGE', a name derived from the badge worn by British Airborne Forces, the winged horse of mythology. It had been a day to remember.

> And gentlemen in England now a-bed
> Shall think themselves accurs'd they were not here.

So General Gale is reported to have quoted aloud as he returned to his HQ after his visit to the bridges on the morning of D-Day.

And I believe that every man who survived that first day of the re-conquest of Europe would echo that sentiment. For the victor in any conflict, there must always be a brief period of elation before more sober reaction sets in: thoughts of the cost to others in lives and injuries, and an awareness of the struggle ahead.

As we headed through the darkness for our new positions on the north-eastern fringe of Ranville, less than two miles from Pegasus Bridge, the pace was that of light infantry-men, brisk and buoyant, tired and laden though the men were.

It was clear that we could not expect a restful night. The sounds and flickering lights of battle came from the entire southern and eastern perimeter of the divisional area, some three miles square.

Guns banged, shells and bombs exploded and small arms fire chattered away. And Ranville, in the heart of the div-isional area, was constantly being shelled and mortared. As we passed close to the little chateau that was the general's HQ we saw that it was taking a pounding from German artillery.

An hour or so after we had left the bridges we dug into our new temporary battalion HQ in a field two or three hundred yards north of Ranville Church, whilst the CO disposed his companies to the south-east.

Then most of us slept for a few hours, oblivious of the noise.

D-Day plus one, 7 June, dawned brightly and noisily for us in our position near the Ranville Church. Sporadic mortaring and shelling started up at first light and continued intermittently throughout the day. Shells and bombs explod-ing in the trees caused a particularly nasty air-burst effect, and the area around Div. HQ, about half a mile to the west of us, seemed to attract the brunt of the fire.

Approximately fifty per cent of the battalion had been killed, wounded or were missing since we had landed some thirty hours previously, and the final tally of casualties twelve weeks later, when the unit was withdrawn from Normandy, was sombre:

> Killed   – 6 Officers
>   – 84 Other Ranks

Wounded– 12 Officers
       – 236 Other Ranks
Missing – 2 Officers
       – 112 Other Ranks

A total loss to the fighting force of 452 out of the original strength of 610, even allowing for reinforcements after D-Day, was a heavy toll. Nevertheless, I believe that only an airborne force could have achieved what 6th Airborne Division succeeded in doing during the vital first day of the invasion of Europe.

The division had captured and held, or destroyed, all its objectives. Its successes had been gained partly by the surprise of its landings, which no conventional land force could have emulated, partly by General Gale's brilliant planning and by the leadership of his commanders, and above all by the individual skills and resolute bravery of the troops. To quote from the official account of the British Airborne Forces, 'They attacked with that spirit of genial ferocity which is the hallmark of airborne troops.'

6th Airborne Division had safeguarded the eastern flank of the entire invasion force, had stemmed and disrupted movement by enemy troops and armour from the Caen area against the seaborne landings, and had caused havoc to German communications and intelligence.

General Gale's use of parachute and glider troops had been almost text-book in its accuracy and planning. First, he dropped parachute infantry and Royal Engineers to infest areas, destroy bridges and hold ground against the first waves of counter-attacks. Then he brought in his guns by glider, followed by his more heavily-armed airlanding battalions to thicken up his forces and secure ground already won but thinly held, and even to push on in some areas. The gliders had come in almost unmolested, their landing-zones already held and cleared.

For the capture and holding of Pegasus Bridge he had devised a plan totally the reverse. The Orne and the canal bridges not only had to be captured, but it was also crucial that they should remain intact, although almost certainly prepared for demolition in the event of attack. Paratroopers, because of the noise of their approach, and their need to rendezvous after their scattered landing, could never have got to those bridges before they had been destroyed. Thus it was that gliders, coming in silently in the night and delivering a concentration of troops right on the spot, achieved an almost bloodless capture, while paratroopers came within about an hour and a half to take over the defence and form the western bridgehead.

All this we began to realise as we took stock of our situation early on the morning of 7 June, and as information began to trickle in to us later that day. Fighting was still noisily going on all around, especially to the south-east and south, where anti-tank guns, German self-propelled guns, tank guns, artillery and mortars were all busily banging away.

Our first priority was to dig deeper into our positions. My own entrenching efforts were greatly speeded up by the bursting of a shell about twenty yards away in a hedgerow. My skinned hand hampered my spadework, but the battalion provost sergeant, a huge man, came to my aid with some hefty blows from his pick.

The CO had meanwhile been to Brigade HQ, and had then visited our three company positions. He came back to tell us that he had been warned to expect enemy infiltration through Ranville and a possible counter-attack from the east. The Germans still held Bréville, right in the middle of the high ground to the east. They were believed to be massing there ready to attack, and it was clear that Bréville was the weak point in our perimeter.

During the morning our battalion positions were feebly attacked by infiltrating patrols, but these were quite easily dealt with. At one time German patrols were seen to be moving towards us from the Bréville direction, using the crashed gliders as cover. These, too, were beaten off, but some snipers remained active from the trees below the Bréville Gap.

My first waking memory just after dawn that day had been the sight of two elderly, black-garbed Norman women unhurriedly milking a small herd of cows at the far end of our field. Even though they had passed a terrifying day and two nights since our landings, even though their homes might have been scarred and battered and even though the air was full of danger, still nothing deterred them from tending their animals. Their buckets filled and their task completed, they trudged towards us and smilingly offered milk to all who wanted it. Throughout the Normandy campaign our army rations were liberally supplemented by milk, cream and marvellous cheese.

They bore us no grudge, those people, but welcomed us as liberators and friends, and were kind and hospitable – even those who lost relations, homes and livestock. To this day, the Airborne and Commando Cemetery at Ranville is a hallowed place, where many of the graves with their regulation crosses have little footstones added by the locals.

Although I was relieved to be still in one piece, and thought of those who had gone or were hurt, one didn't dwell on those things. No one mentioned the losses, certainly not amongst my little group of mortarless mortarmen, some fourteen out of the original eighty.

All in all, D + 1 was a fairly edgy but not very active day for 7th Para.

Then, on Thursday, D + 2, we were ordered to move east to new positions close to the Le Mesnil crossroads, about a mile south of the Bréville Gap. On the way, a distance of about two miles, we were to mop up scattered enemy positions in the orchards and hedgerows, left-overs from the previous day's fighting and the German infiltrating patrols.

7th Para was soon in its new area west of Le Mesnil. Battalion HQ was set up in a small farmhouse beside the road between Le Mesnil and Ranville. Our prisoners were herded into outhouses and fed. The farmer and his family welcomed us warmly and seemed not the least concerned about their precarious position.

Our new positions were in bocage country, an area of dense cider orchards and woodland. Although technically in reserve, we were backing up a very thinly held series of outposts and less than a mile from us was the German-held Bréville Gap where the gallant but decimated 9th Para were grimly holding on.

By now 6th Airborne Division and the Commando Brigade, already severely weakened by casualties, were containing three much stronger German divisions, and on Friday, 9 June, our eastern perimeter, some five thousand yards long, in very enclosed country, and held by a total of only some fifteen hundred commandos and paratroopers, was heavily attacked. But the Germans were beaten off and another attack that same evening, preceded by very heavy shell and mortar fire, was also repulsed.

By Saturday, D + 4, it was obvious that something was going to happen around Bréville, since the Germans were obviously massing for a breakthrough in the area.

At 8 a.m. the German 346 Division put in a heavy attack and began moving in strength towards our old positions north of Ranville, that were now held by 13th Para. The Germans were still using the masses of wrecked gliders as cover.

Their movement was carefully watched by 13th Para, well dug in on the south perimeter of the open plain, but fire was held until the last second. Finally, at only fifty yards range, the paras opened up their fire with devastating effect. Over four hundred Germans were killed, one hundred and fifty captured, and the remainder fled.

That morning I saw lines of British infantrymen moving along the road past our battalion HQ on their way up towards the Le Mesnil crossroads to attack Bréville and to close the gap. I recognised them as being part of 51st Highland Div. and felt sorry for them as they trudged along in the sunshine. Most of them had yet to see any action, and I knew what they were heading for. Few of them had any battle experience (like me a few days ago) and those that had were used to the desert fighting of North Africa. They must have felt uneasy in this enclosed, heavily wooded terrain.

We watched them go by, and expected at any moment to be pitched into the coming fight ourselves.

About mid-morning, Colonel Pine-Coffin returned from a Brigade HQ briefing and sent for me. He told me that casualties at Div. HQ had been heavy and that General Gale had asked for me to be posted to his HQ staff as GSO III (Ops) – General Staff Officer Grade III (Operations), to give the job its full title. I was to move that afternoon and to be promoted to captain immediately. All this was because I had had some experience of staff work when a liaison officer.

Sunday, 11 June, was my twenty-fifth birthday, a fact which seemed to go unheeded by the combatants. Certainly, there was no pause for celebration. But, unknown to me, a little party had been arranged by our jovial 2 i/c, Major Eric Steele-Baume (popularly known as 'Tin-Ass'). In that pretty little Normandy farmhouse, set in a very active battlefield, seven or eight of us sat down to a convivial luncheon of army rations augmented by fruit, Camembert and cider provided by our genial French host.

After lunch I climbed with all my kit into a jeep, and set off back to Ranville and Div. HQ, stopping briefly at the field ambulance centre on the way to get my sticky right hand re-dressed.

Div. HQ in its little château a few hundred yards west of Ranville showed its scars plainly, and I could well understand how casualties had been so severe there. Every tree was shattered and riven by shell and mortar fire, buildings and roofs were pockmarked and the surrounding ground heavily pitted. General Gale and his senior officers had their offices and quarters in the house itself, while the rest of us worked and slept in the nearby stables and farm buildings.

The operations centre was in a cider storeroom, part of which was taken up by a row of enormous barrels resting on hefty timber supports giving a clearance of two feet above the stone floor. Reckoning that, if we got a direct hit, the building might collapse but not these barrels, I had my bed-roll laid out under one of them. I might drown, but I wouldn't be hurt.

I was briefed on my duties by the GSO I, Colonel Bobby Bray, a charming and intelligent man whom I was lucky to be called on to serve. My work was mainly to keep the divisional battle map in the operations centre up to date, and to take my stint in controlling the wireless network to brigades, supporting arms and flanking formations. My information was gleaned from intelligence reports, from direct wireless communication and from the liaison officers. I also kept up a corps battle map and, so far as possible, a picture of the Second British Army situation. At least I had some idea of what to do from my old days as an LO with

42nd Armoured Div., and my signals training was a decided
advantage.

The atmosphere at Divisional HQ was electric. The
Bréville situation had become ominous. A British attack
along the ridge towards Bréville had failed, with heavy
casualties. The Germans had heavily reinforced their troops
there, obviously hoping to exploit the gap. We all knew that
here was a potential make-or-break emergency.

Our radio links crackled away all that day and through the
night, and grave-faced officers kept watch on swiftly changing
events.

Next day, 12 June, at 5 p.m. the general returned from
a visit to Le Mesnil, immediately called for all available
information, and prepared his plan to liquidate the threat to
our bridgehead.

His reasoning was this:

The Germans had been fighting hard for three days and
their losses had been severe. They had the initiative and
would scarcely credit us with the ability to stage a counter-
attack, at least until the following day. If we waited, they
would be rested and would have time to organise their
Bréville positions.

General Gale decided to attack that night.

Our assault force was to consist of the half-strength 12
Para, some sixty men of the Independent Para Company, a
Company of the Devons, and a squadron of Sherman tanks
of the 13/18 Hussars. They would have plenty of artillery
support.

So we would have some five hundred foot soldiers attacking, twelve or so tanks, and massive artillery fire.

The enemy strength was considerable and could rely on
the build-up of almost an entire division.

At 7 p.m. the general issued his orders. The attack would
go in at 10 p.m.

12th Para led the assault, supported by Sherman tanks on
the flanks. The battle raged nearly all night. The Germans
opened up with all the fire-power they had. Le Plein and
Amfreville were towns in inferno. Soon Bréville too was
alight.

But the gallant 12th, with their supporting troops, suc-

ceeded, against great odds and with grievous casualties. Their
CO, Colonel Johnston, was killed, along with eight officers
and one hundred and thirty-three men. Lord Lovat and
Brigadier Kindersley, the Commander of 6th Airlanding
Brigade, were both seriously wounded. Bréville was captured, and this was the turning point in the battle for the
bridgehead. Never again was the division ever heavily attacked. The troops suffered weeks of shelling and mortaring,
rain and mud, discomfort and mosquitoes; many acts of
individual gallantry were performed in patrolling and in
defence – but no major actions took place involving 6th
Airborne until August.

During the Bréville battle, sitting with my head-set
clamped to my ears, it would be less than honest to suggest
that I did not have some sense of relief to be sheltered in a
stable and not charging into the holocaust. But such are the
fortunes of war: you go where you are sent.

After Bréville, although our task became primarily defensive, the atmosphere was by no means tranquil. Most nights
the odd German bomber dropped its noisy load somewhere
in our area, and shelling and mortaring was more or less
incessant.

In the first month in Normandy the division had lost, in
the paras and airlanding troops alone, two hundred and
fifteen officers and two thousand seven hundred and fifty
other ranks, with proportionate losses amongst commandos,
gunners, engineers, signallers, medical units and the headquarters staff.

Our weekly losses during the subsequent ten weeks aver-
aged over three hundred. We were given reinforcements of
six hundred infantry from Second Army, of whom over four
hundred volunteered to become parachutists. And later still
our bridgehead force was further strengthened by the Belgian
Brigade and the Royal Netherlands Brigade.

Early on we were visited by the Commander-in-Chief,
General Montgomery. Monty arrived wearing his Airborne
red beret and seemed in great spirits. Within minutes of his
arrival at Div. HQ he had made accurate alterations to my
battle maps. He seemed to have an astoundingly detailed
knowledge of our own and enemy positions, right down to

the exact number of dug-in Mark IV German tanks on our southern boundary.

The C-in-C congratulated us all on the achievements of the division, and then proceeded to give us a résumé of his strategy and future plans. Some of his forecasts seemed optimistic, to say the least. But everything he predicted turned out to be exactly what eventually happened, almost to the day.

He likened the whole Allied front to the action of an opening door. The Orne area was to be the hinge or fulcrum on which the rest of the door would swing. His plan had been to draw the main might of German armour onto this eastern front, leaving the Americans further west with a softer skin to break through once Cherbourg had been captured.

I know that subsequently there has been criticism of Montgomery's planning and doubts cast on his intentions, but nobody who had listened to him in that Normandy cider-store in June 1944 would have hesitated to believe exactly what was, and always had been, in his mind for the conduct of the Normandy campaign, however optimistic it may have seemed at a time when we were fighting to maintain even a toe-hold.

Monty told us that there was soon to be a major onslaught on Caen and a great armoured drive southwards from our area. Caen eventually fell, and later in July came the slugging tank fight of the Falaise Gap, where the British to the north and the Americans to the south tried to close the pincers on the bulk of the German forces in the area, and almost succeeded. The slaughter here was dreadful.

And so it came to pass . . . By early August the door swung open, led at a gallop by General Patton's Third Army.

We in 6th Airborne Division saw some of this but took no part. We now simply faced east towards the Seine, holding our line and waiting for the break-out.

During July and early August my job had entailed a fair amount of moving around, visiting units to gather information or taking messages and situation reports to other formations. Some of my more distant trips gave me the chance to see more of the ravaging effects the war had had on Normandy. Whole villages smeared by massed bombing to close roads; scarcely a farm or a house in the beautiful countryside that was not smashed or scarred; thousands of cattle and horses rotten and bloated in the fields; shattered tanks and vehicles lying in the ditches; and everywhere the stench of death, especially in the ruins of Caen. That smell seemed to cling to me for months. And all the time there was the distant rumble of gun-fire.

At the beginning of August, after the battle for Caen and just as the great battle around Falaise was starting, we had another of the Commander-in-Chief's unheralded visits. Monty was obviously in good form and well-pleased with progress. He stressed his appreciation of 6th Airborne, and acknowledged our frustration at being bogged down in an infantry defensive role. Then the C-in-C positively twinkled for a moment.

'But you will soon be on the move,' he said. 'We shall take Paris and Brussels within the month.'

To those of us listening to him, after two months of stagnation, this was a staggering promise. After all, Paris was about one hundred and twenty miles away, and Brussels about two hundred. It seemed impossible.

But there was no doubting his terse, clipped tones as he finger-pointed the situation south of Caen in the Falaise area, on my army map, and then enthused how the Americans would sweep through with a right hook to Paris and the British Second Army and First Canadian Army would punch across the Seine and on to Belgium.

He was right, of course. On 25 August, French and American armoured columns entered Paris, and on 3 September the Guards Armoured Division drove into Brussels.

We all felt jubilant as the C-in-C left us and set off down the road in his staff car, chucking packs of cigarettes to troops as he passed them. Monty was in the great tradition of flamboyant actor-managers. I would have joined his company any time.

On 7 August, General Gale received orders to prepare to take advantage of any signs of German withdrawal on our front. It was not anticipated that we could move fast or far due to our lack of transport and armour and our depleted strength.

This understandably cautious approach was like a red rag to 'Windy' Gale's bullish nature. He was determined that no mere infantry division would head his airborne lads in the forthcoming fifty-mile dash for the Seine. 6th Airborne and the commandos had shown what they could do in attack and defence: now they would show what they could do in pursuit, with or without transport. We had by now been reinforced by the Belgian Brigade and the Dutch Royal Netherlands Brigade, each with full-scale transport and some reconnaissance light armoured vehicles. In addition we had a fantastic array of artillery: our own light regiment of mountain 75mm howitzers, two field regiments of 25-pounders, one medium battery and a heavy anti-aircraft regiment firing air-burst shells in the ground role to a range of sixteen thousand yards.

In brief, the plan therefore was to keep close contact with the retreating Germans on a ten-mile front, never letting the enemy draw breath to re-form and never losing the advantage of aggressive harrying. The terrain was very difficult, with steep hills, rivers, swampy areas and roads made almost unusable by our own shelling during previous weeks. But, with tremendous energy, we pushed on.

I will not attempt to give a blow-by-blow description of the break-out and the thrust to the Seine, our ultimate objective. I saw little of it at first-hand, as I spent nearly all my time cooped up in the armoured command vehicle that had been allotted to General Gale, never far behind the leading troops, because he always wanted to be in the van.

My training as a signals officer was really put to the test as I controlled the constantly active Div. Command wireless net, while the air fairly crackled with orders, information and reports.

Despite fierce fighting with a well prepared and stubborn enemy rearguard, and despite the obstacles, the impetus of the attack never waned, night or day. Those tired paratroopers, and their comrades, had been in action constantly for three months in debilitatingly damp and unhealthy conditions, but they never faltered. Five or six days after the first break-out it was clear that nothing would stop us. The division rolled on at a steady average of some six miles per day; against stiff opposition, in difficult territory, with pretty heavy casualties to both sides and using all manner of improvisations to keep moving and cross obstacles. On the coastal road, at one point, an airlanding battalion commandeered a fire engine and a milk float, one voluntarily driven by a brass-helmeted fireman and the other by its owner.

Only casualties and the terrible consequences to the local population, many of whose pretty little towns such as Dozulé, Beuzeville and Pont Lévèque were burned to the ground by the retreating Germans, marred the cock-a-hoop spirits of the soldiers.

Then, on 27 August, we were ordered to halt our advance and concentrate in the area between Honfleur and Pont Audemer, ready to be taken from there back to England.

I am sure that I was not the only one to feel relieved. These had been a wearing three months.

14

PRAISE THE LORD AND PASS THE AMMUNITION

I suppose that my two main reactions as we sailed from Normandy back to England were relief and pride, and I am sure that every man left in 6th Airborne Division felt much as I did. We had all lost friends, we had all seen dreadful things, but we had accomplished every task that had been set for us. We knew that there would soon be more for us to do, but we also knew that the end of the war was in sight.

I must have matured a great deal during those three months in Normandy. For the first time in my life I had been at moments completely unselfish, putting other things and other people before my own personal safety or convenience, without hesitation and without balancing the consequences to myself. This is an experience shared by all servicemen engaged in an armed conflict. What they do is done partly from instinct, partly from a well-drilled sense of duty. Great fear there may be, but there is no thought of material personal gain.

We all realised how lucky we were back at home and going on leave, whilst others were still slogging it out in France, and we determined to make the most of our break.

First, I decided to spend a few days in London. Feeling quite wealthy, with my bank account swollen by three months' accrued pay and allowances, I booked in at the Mayfair Hotel, where they let me have a small suite for the price of a single room.

I then set off to Ireland once more to stay with my Fitz-Patrick uncle and aunt – and visit Granny Todd, who was still going strong.

My whimsical Uncle Fintan was as jovial and resourceful as ever. He had served in the British Army in the First World War and was a confirmed Anglophile. But above all he was a great Irishman, with an irrepressible sense of humour. For example, one day I asked him what would happen if the Germans invaded the coast of Ireland.

'We'd fight them,' said he.

'But the British would have to come to your aid, so what would you do then?'

'Half of us would turn round and fight you,' he replied.

On this particular evening he asked me if I would like to accompany him to a rather formal cocktail party in Dublin, without specifying where it was to be. I said that of course I'd like to go with him. So we drove down to one of the areas of fine Georgian mansions in Dublin, parked the car, and proceeded to walk to our destination. We had just gone a few yards when he grabbed my arm.

'Take off your hat and show your respect,' he ordered.

Surprised and clueless, I did so.

'Now look up,' he said.

And there above the house we faced fluttered the German flag.

Beaming with glee, Uncle then told me that this was where we were going. I was not too sure that it was a good idea, but Uncle Fintan propelled me to the door. Once inside, he had pleasure in introducing me to the German Ambassador.

'May I present my nephew, Captain Todd of the British Army,' said he with becoming gravity.

After a very quick drink, we left that rather strained atmosphere, Uncle Fintan chuckling all the way home.

With that, and a few days spent at the FitzPatricks' beach chalet, it was an enjoyable change from Normandy.

I and about seven other staff officers of 6th Airborne Div. HQ were now billeted in an enchanting thatched house whose garden was edged by the River Avon two or three miles from headquarters, a big, secluded house set amongst trees not far from Netheravon.

My job was pretty tedious, office work pure and simple, involving a steady stream of bumph – letters, notes, inter-

office memoranda, directives and piles of pamphlets. I had
to learn the various forms of address to other units and
formations and the formal jargon of missives to the people
I had to deal with, being careful to word things tactfully,
especially to senior officers.

We had been briefed to prepare for an airborne attack on
the Ruhr, with Cologne as the probable primary target. So
our infantry practised street-fighting, with bombed-out areas
of Birmingham and Manchester as training grounds, using
up large quantities of grenades and Sten ammunition needed
for close-quarter fighting.

We had lost our splendid G I (Ops), Colonel Bray, who had
been promoted to brigadier. His replacement was Colonel
Michael Roberts, KOYLI (my parent regiment). I found
him rather humourless and stuffy and I don't think he was
over-impressed with my lack of formal staff training.

I began to look forward to our next operation, or even a
return to 7th Para.

I got both sooner than I expected.

On 16 December 1944, Hitler's forces mounted a massive
attack on the Ardennes area of Belgium in an attempt to
break through to the Belgian and Dutch ports, especially
Antwerp. The Battle of the Bulge had begun, and 6th Airborne Div. was put on stand-by as the main strategic British
reserve.

Immediately, the well-oiled, experienced machinery of the
division began to buzz. The nucleus of the division had all
seen action in Normandy, and the replacements by now were
thoroughly integrated and trained.

To my great sadness, General Gale had, a week or so
earlier, been promoted to take over the British Airborne
Corps and replaced by Major-General Bols. Since Normandy, I had come to know Richard Gale pretty well and
my admiration for him was enormous. I was lucky enough
to keep in contact with him up to his death in 1982, and I
shall never forget the tremendous turn-out of be-medalled
veterans at his memorial service in Westminster Abbey.

Since the end of September 1944 the Ardennes front, a
sector roughly seventy-five miles long between Aachen in the
north and Luxembourg in the south, had been comparatively

quiet, and by mid-December the US Army had only five divisions in the area, most of them new to battle.

Hitler, meanwhile, had concentrated twenty-eight divisions against this force, five of them armoured. This build-up had gone on almost unnoticed until December, and even then, due to lack of information, it was not thought that any immediate danger of attack existed. The territory was heavily wooded, hilly country, criss-crossed by steep, narrow valleys and with poor roads winding through the forests – not, it was thought, ideal for tank formations in the wet, snowy weather of that winter.

Hitler, despite the reservations of his senior generals, thought otherwise. At dawn on 16 December, fourteen German infantry divisions, supported by five panzer divisions and thousands of guns, crashed through the thinly held American line. The 28th US Division, stretched out over almost thirty miles, was assaulted by five German divisions and overwhelmed in the River Our sector. The 106th US Division was outflanked and encircled within twenty-four hours, though they bravely held their ground.

The American fighting troops did everything possible to hold out against vastly superior numbers, fought stubbornly and bravely, and nowhere on that first day did the Germans gain all their objectives. During the ensuing days, however, the Germans battered their way forward and their reconnaissance elements actually reached almost to the Meuse in the Namur-Dinant area. They left behind them pockets of individual resistance where American troops continued to hang on. Still remembered today is the gallant defence of Bastogne by the 101st US Airborne Division and a combat group from 10th US Armoured Division, as well as the defence of St Vith by 7th US Armoured Division and the remnants of the troops who had taken the initial battering there.

On 20 December, General Eisenhower appointed General Montgomery to command all the Allied forces north of the Bulge, a decision that was not popular with the other senior American commanders, but a wise one that was forced by urgent operational need. Montgomery had the reserves required and the intact organisation to deal with the situation.

He had already moved XXX British Corps near to the Meuse between Liège and Dinant, where he was convinced the Germans planned their main crossings of the Meuse, and where the American defences were almost non-existent.

On the north of the Bulge salient the Germans threw twelve divisions against the US First Army's stretched front. They gained little ground at first, but a second attack took St Vith and by-passed Bastogne, and a third drove to within a few miles of Dinant, having travelled over sixty miles.

It seems that General Montgomery was not unduly worried about these setbacks. He was tidying his line, and the enemy meanwhile was having increasing difficulty in maintaining supplies to its leading troops, especially of tank fuel.

By Christmas Day Patton's armour had broken through to relieve Bastogne, and General Collins' 2nd US Armoured Division assaulted the forward German troops from the north. This latter battle raged for two days, culminating in the destruction of 2nd SS Panzer Division.

From then on the Battle of the Bulge became effectively a mopping-up exercise. By 27 December the Germans had begun their retreat from the River Meuse. Hitler's last great offensive had been broken, and with it a great part of the attacking power of his armies.

It was into this situation that we made our appearance in Belgium around Christmas-time. We had been on stand-by for over a week, and on 24 December the order to move was received. I was ordered to leave at once with a small Div. HQ party, my task being to establish advanced Div. HQ near the Meuse at Dinant and to prepare for the arrival of the rest of Div. HQ.

Within a few hours I was on board ship with my little group en route for Ostend. We docked in the early hours of Christmas Day and set off towards Dinant, just over one hundred miles inland.

Some aspects of that journey I remember vividly. We were passing through country that had, in one generation, been a major battleground in two world wars. No wonder every village, every town, every roadside was lined by groups of anxious-faced Belgians. Standing in my armoured scout car at the head of our little convoy I felt something of a celluloid hero as we were greeted by hand-waving, V signs and blown kisses. But thank God we were heading in the right direction for them. Motoring eastwards we could only be new reinforcements going to the front.

By the evening of Christmas Day 1944, we were in the house that was to serve as advanced Div. HQ just west of the Meuse. We knew that the battle was raging just the other side of the river, with German armour and infantry still trying to break through, and our lads were soon engaged in a ploy they knew only too well: giving the impression of greater force by buzzing about in patrols in the woods, and mounting bren-guns in jeeps that scoured the side-roads, letting fly an occasional burst of fire to discourage enemy infantry patrols.

After 27 December, the German attacks virtually ground to a halt, partly due to lack of supplies of fuel, and partly because of determined new counter-attacks from the north and south by the United States forces. From then on, at least on our front, operations were mostly local skirmishes whilst pockets of resistance were mopped up. The Allied ground forces were greatly helped when the murky winter weather cleared for a few days, allowing the British and American Air Forces to bomb and strafe German tanks and supply convoys cluttering the narrow roads.

On 3 January Montgomery ordered a large-scale counter-attack by Americans in the north and by British troops, including ours, in the west. This move coincided with worsening weather and heavy falls of snow. The air attacks were halted and the Germans fought hard to hold their positions, well dug-in on the forest slopes, and now camouflaged by snow. During this time, I and the two liaison officers were kept busy jeeping around collecting information from our leading units, which were not always easy to locate in this sort of fluid battle and enclosed country.

On New Year's Day, our HQ was sited in a pinnacled, towered fairy-tale castle set on a rise amidst the snowy pine forests. I seem to remember its name was Le Château de Nef, and it was the home of a Prince and Princess whose names I do not recall. All our units, including Div. HQ, had brought the ingredients for Christmas dinner with them, and, as things were comparatively quiet on that day, it was decided to celebrate with our Yule-tide fare.

There could not have been a more perfect setting for our feast. Here we were, in this great Disney-esque castle, girt by snowy forest, and using as our officers' mess dining-room the great hall, a vast chamber of Victorian Gothic taste, with its huge open fire, massive refectory table and scattering of heavy carved chairs.

And then early that month I returned to 7th Para. My feelings were mixed. Certainly I had missed the family feeling that General Gale had always created around him, so I was glad to be back with my old unit. Nevertheless, I had never got on with Colonel Roberts, and had in effect been sacked, which did not exactly thrill me.

I was put in charge of motor transport, and as MTO was responsible for seeing that the battalion vehicles were restored to reasonable condition.

The battalion's main preoccupation at that time was to keep fit in the snow and bitter cold in the forest, so at long last my Iceland training came in useful. But then, within a week or two, we were moved north to hold the line of the River Maas in Holland. This was a dreary and unpleasant area of waterlogged slit trenches and weapon pits, and I was one of the lucky ones to be billeted in a house.

The citizens of that area were stodgy, and did not particularly go out of their way to welcome the British soldiery. They were great church-goers, and Sunday mornings saw a steady stream of black-clad burghers on their way past my house to their devotions, all very solemn and staid.

By mid-February it was known that 6th Airborne Div. was to be withdrawn to the UK to prepare for another operation. Colonel Pine-Coffin told me I, as motor transport officer, was to remain in Europe with the transport, drivers and mechanics, ready to rejoin the battalion whenever and wherever it was to drop.

The brigade left on 22 February, and I set off with my group to a small town near Arras, in northern France, where we were billeted in a farming village, busy only in bringing our vehicles into good working order, and feeling pretty cut off and clueless.

In fact a lot was happening during those weeks, in particular some very successful battles in the Rhineland, led mostly by Patton's army.

Finally, in late March, I received my orders to move my team of vehicles and stores up to an area just east of the Rhine and on German soil. We were to stop that night in Belgium, and I was briefed to have my men and vehicles at a certain spot by the riverside at dawn the next morning, where we would then embark on rafts for the river-crossing, just behind the first assault troops.

On landing on the east bank, I was to get my convoy through as quickly as possible to join up with 7th Para. on high ground topping the wooded slopes of the Diersfordt Forest. It was to capture this high ground and the bridges crossing the River Issel, leaving the way clear into Western Germany, that the airborne assault was directed. And it so happened that the area to be taken by 6th Airborne Div. was held by the German 6th Parachute Division, a crack force that fought stubbornly and well.

As we approached our riverside area at first light on 24 March, the skies erupted and the earth trembled under a huge artillery bombardment. From where we stopped to await our embarkation, we could see the assault troops surging over the huge river in a fleet of boats, rafts and amphibious tanks and vehicles. There was some enemy artillery fire, but nothing like as intense as our own, and the landings on the far bank seemed to be going well.

Quite early that morning my convoy crossed the river and motored eastwards a few miles to join up with 7th Para., which had landed accurately, and with few casualties. Whilst I was searching for Battalion HQ I saw something that epitomised the high spirit of our men:

Careering along the road came a pair of horses drawing an ornate glass-sided hearse in which was piled a load of ammunition boxes. Outside, on the driving seat, were two paratroopers, Sten guns slung on their backs and silk top hats replacing their helmets, lashing on their normally sedate chargers. As they passed me they grinned and sang out at the tops of their considerable voices, 'Praise the Lord and pass the ammunition!' Some local funeral parlour had obviously been pressed into service to re-supply advance units.

Colonel Pine-Coffin was in great spirits. Casualties had been light and all objectives had been taken. The CO had a furrow grooved in his cheek and the tip of his nose had been shot off, but he delighted in telling me that the first thing he had done on landing was to piss on German soil, something he had wanted to do for a long while.

From that day until the end of April I had one main task: to keep the battalion on wheels of some sort so that the spectacular advances of 6th Airborne Division and the rest of the Allied army could be maintained. Airborne troops are very short of transport compared with their infantry and armoured comrades. So it was that, apart from our own few jeeps, trucks and lorries, we assembled a weird collection of local vehicles. The hearse served us well for a couple of days, then was replaced by all manner of cars, motor cycles, bicycles, vans, lorries, a fire engine and even a steam roller (used to great effect to overrun an anti-tank gun).

Those were exciting days; we no longer had merely the scent of victory in our nostrils – we *knew* that the Allies had won, and that nothing but politics could stop our advance.

Once the break-out from the Rhine bridgehead had been accomplished my memories are mostly of constant movement forward; of light skirmishes with the German rearguards; of endless lines of German prisoners shuffling westwards; of shattered, over-bombed towns through which roads had to be bulldozed; of sullen, terrified and dazed civilians all vehemently denying that they were Nazis or that they had ever heard of the Jewish extermination camps.

The dreadful aftermath of war was visible everywhere. Only the stoniest of hearts could have felt no pity for some of these confused, defeated people.

And still 6th Airborne kept rolling on, abreast or even ahead of their neighbouring formations. We reckoned, when we finally came to rest just short of the Elbe River, that we had covered some three hundred and forty miles in thirty-six days. Not bad for a unit that was basically supposed to be foot-borne!

When rest was possible, we billeted ourselves in any suitable buildings, though these were hard to find in the rubble of the bigger towns. One night, unable to use any light, Oyston and I found an intact building with a large room well supplied with tables but no chairs, so we each stretched out on a rather cold table to get a few hours sleep. When day dawned we woke to the realisation that we had occupied a morgue. Never have two stiffs beaten a more hurried retreat!

Oyston had now acquired an assistant. The Allied advance had overrun a number of prisoner-of-war camps and some of these had contained a few Russians. One such was Boris, who somehow attached himself to us, pleading not to be sent back with the other Russians. Since Boris proved to have some culinary skills and was quite happy to cook for us, the great, shaggy Oyston, who had a massive appetite but very little ability to cater for it, was only too happy to take charge of the plump Ukrainian.

Then, somewhere in north Germany I, too, acquired a companion. 7th Para. had captured a forested area after some quite stiff resistance. A railway line ran through the woods and a train of several coaches was found parked there in a deep cutting, camouflaged from aerial view by trees that had been felled across its top. I was ordered to take charge of a patrol to capture any enemy troops who might still be lurking in the train. We had no difficulty in rounding up a few dejected prisoners who offered no resistance, and, so far as I know, none escaped. The train itself, which transpired to be a brigade headquarters, was obviously something special. It consisted of three or four carriages of considerable splendour, linked to a few freight cars. The latter we later found to be filled with an amazing variety of goods, including boxes of medals, crates of tinned sauerkraut and other comestibles, and piles of uniforms, weaponry and ammunition. The passenger carriages were very ornate and included a small dining-car and kitchen, and a pantry stacked with excellent china and glass. The train had, in fact, been the Greek Royal Train moved up to Germany by some commander who evidently liked to travel in comfort.

When we had checked all the coaches, and I had detailed a party to march our batch of prisoners back to battalion HQ, I returned to my jeep. And there, on the back seat, was the biggest, ugliest dog I had ever seen. It was an enormous, cropped-eared brindle great dane, who growled menacingly as soon as I got near. He had obviously taken possession and was guarding his place.

Now, I had lived with confidence among a variety of canine types all my life, but I had never encountered a situation like this. Obviously, I wanted my jeep back, but I didn't want to be mangled in the process. So I went back and questioned the prisoners, and an English-speaking German told me that this was a trained patrol dog whose handler had been killed. The dog's name was Ajax.

I knew enough about trained dogs to know that they will only answer the bidding of one person, their handler. Armed with this knowledge I went back towards the jeep and tried again, hoping that the monster might have the sense to adopt me as his handler.

'Ajax,' I rapped. *'Raus!'* But he showed no inclination at all to get *raus*. I strained my scant German vocabulary to its limits, but got no reaction, apart from some awful rumblings and a warning curl of the lips.

Then I thought that perhaps all he wanted was to retain his majestic seat in the back of the jeep, which he seemed to have made his territory, so I advanced firmly, sweat breaking out on my forehead, and spoke soothingly in what I hoped must be an international dog language. 'Good boy,' I said. 'Go-o-o-d boy.' I clambered into the driving seat, expecting my neck to be savaged at any moment, and started up. Before moving off, I risked looking round and caught his eye. I swear he grinned at me.

Ajax had adopted me, and became my constant companion for the rest of his short life, with Boris taking charge of his care and feeding.

Towards the end of April, we came to a halt near Schwerin, and were ordered to prepare for a final airborne operation to cross the Elbe. Our battalion companies were billeted in a group of rural villages somewhere west of the Elbe, and on our arrival I designated a large farmhouse as our HQ, and ordered the ground floor German residents to move into the barns, whilst my men had the comfort of the house. I felt they deserved this in their weary and dishevelled state. After all, they had not let up for some five weeks of constant action and movement. The kitchen was to be left entirely to the civilian residents, and the top floor of the house was to be left undisturbed, because I was told that there was a young German woman there with a maid and three small children, renting the rooms.

That evening, having gone round the other billets to ensure that all our men were well housed, I reported to the CO that all was in order, then returned to the farmhouse.

Oyston told me that he had moved the maid out of her room on the top floor and had moved my things in there, as there was no other suitable room in the house which was not already filled with soldiers.

I was finishing my supper when I answered a knock on the door. It was the maid, saying that Frau Lang asked if I would take coffee with her.

I had seen the children, two charming little girls and a baby boy, but had not seen Frau Lang herself, and in any case I was dreadfully tired and we were not supposed to fraternise with Germans. However, it seemed churlish to refuse. After all, I was occupying her premises.

So in a few minutes, Ajax and I presented ourselves at the sitting-room door.

Frau Lang was slender, very pretty and blonde. She also spoke quite good English. She was obviously worried. Her home had been bombed in some industrial city and she had fled with her three children to this quiet area. Her husband had been missing for two years on the Russian front and now suddenly the war had overtaken her and her family yet again.

I assured her that she and her children were quite safe. The war was nearly over and then things would return to normal. I felt really sorry for her, vulnerable and alone in such a ghastly area.

Before I nodded off from sheer tiredness, I excused myself and prepared to leave. When I went to shake her hand she simply put her hands on my shoulders and kissed me very gently, saying nothing.

I don't know how long I had been asleep when I awoke, instinctively sure that there was somebody in the room apart from the noisily slumbering Ajax. Alarm bells rang in my mind, but I suppose I was not fully conscious, otherwise I would have sat up. Presently, I felt the bedclothes being quietly drawn back. I think I must have known all along who it was. A warm, soft body crept in behind me, an arm went round my shoulders, and I drifted back into sleep.

In the morning, when I woke up, she had gone, and I wondered if I had been dreaming. I never mentioned that night to Frau Lang during the next four or five days of our stay in that house. It had been a very human moment, and it would have called its spontaneity into question if I had queried it.

We kept in touch for some years after the war, and I still receive an annual Christmas card, forty years on.

After a few days of preparations for the forthcoming airborne operation, events occurred that changed not only our planning but the whole state of the war in Europe. On 30 April, Hitler and his bride of one day, Eva Braun, committed suicide. Admiral Doenitz was proclaimed President of the Reich.

The day before, Montgomery's troops had crossed the Elbe and had driven north to meet the Russians at Wismar, on the Baltic, and thus prevented them from driving into north-west Germany and Denmark.

On 2 May the Russians finally captured Berlin, a target that could well have been within our grasp, and on 4 May Montgomery, at his headquarters on Luneburg Heath, received the signed capitulation of all German forces in north-west Germany, Denmark, Holland and Dunkirk.

That same day, Eisenhower halted his American forces on the line just inside Czechoslovakia which had been agreed with Stalin, at a time when Patton's Third Army could easily have advanced to Prague. In honouring this agreement, the Allies had inevitably left Russia to occupy the Czech capital. Thus was the future political map of Europe established.

On 7 May, at Eisenhower's HQ in Rheims, the two senior German commanders, on behalf of Doenitz, signed a treaty of unconditional surrender of all German forces on all fronts.

The war in Europe ended at midnight 8/9 May 1945.

Meanwhile, our orders to refit were rescinded and we were to await our return to the UK. No words can describe our relief and exultation. All that remained now was patiently but excitedly to prepare for normal civilian life and the rebuilding of the ruins.

By mid-May, I had been deputed to get the transport and battalion stores and equipment home by road via Calais, a trip which lasted several cheerful days. Ajax went with me. Regulations were easier in those days, and from the port officer in Calais I obtained a certificate that he was a war dog and could therefore be taken into England. My ugly friend seemed quite content as he curled up amongst piles of stores in a three-ton truck, ready for embarkation.

At Dover we arrived to a quite clamorous reception. After a night spent in the Dover transit camp, we set off to drive to Bulford, which I calculated would take four hours at convoy speed. I told everybody we would have a 20-minute halt about half-way.

The moment for this break occurred somewhere near East Grinstead, in Sussex. Seeing a large modern pub by the roadside I gave the order to halt. My lads wasted no time in parking, leaving a few men to watch the vehicles, and piling into the big lounge bar. A line of exuberant paratroopers called their orders and swigged down the first gulps of beer before taking in the scene. It was a typical lounge, with little groups of people, quietly talking and drinking. Some were civilians and some were in uniform, mostly that of the RAF. Every single serviceman already there bore pathetic signs of injury: maimed faces, hands and bodies. We had happened upon a meeting place for relatives visiting patients at Sir Archibald McIndoe's famed plastic surgery unit at East Grinstead Hospital. The difference between their state and ours was salutary. Within minutes we airborne men had sunk our pints and filed quietly out of the place.

We were indeed the lucky ones.

Once back at Bulford we had a few weeks to sort ourselves out and bring the various units back up to establishment in men and equipment. The contrast between those summer weeks in England and the year before was immense, both for serviceman and civilian. A year ago I had been in Normandy, and Londoners were being smashed by doodlebugs and V2 rockets. Now families were reunited, street lighting was restored and the black-out ended. Rationing of food and

clothing, and many shortages, still existed, but they were
cheerfully borne.

   And I still had Ajax, who clearly enjoyed barrack life and,
with his war now over too, was showing the usual gentleness
and good nature of his breed.

15

PALESTINE

During the next month or two it was assumed that our next task would be some sort of airborne operation in the Far East, the only theatre of war still in existence. Singapore seemed to us the most likely place.

In fact, however, when my own posting came through, I was to join HQ 3rd Para. Brigade as camp commandant prior to the move of the re-formed 6th Airborne Division to Palestine.

I spent my brief embarkation leave with the Lawson family, friends who lived near Newcastle, the reason being that they had agreed to look after Ajax for me. During the few days that I was there the great dog settled in very happily, and was particularly gentle with the Lawsons' two little boys.

Our shipment to Palestine was a veritable pleasure cruise. The troop ship was a former P&O liner, and, although packed with servicemen, very comfortable by army standards. As we sailed through the Mediterranean we spent most of the time lolling about on deck sunning ourselves, with only a few routine duties and parades to interrupt our life of leisure, secure in the knowledge that for the first time in years we ran no risk of being bombed, strafed or torpedoed.

As we passed Gibraltar I received sad news. A telegram from the Lawsons told me that Ajax had died and that a letter would follow. I later read that a few days after I had left him with the Lawson family the poor dog had become very listless and refused his food. A vet was called but could find nothing wrong with him. Within a week he quietly passed away. The vet's opinion was that he had just given up wanting to live. Perhaps the loss of two masters within a few months had been too much for the faithful Dane.

On arrival in Palestine we were quartered in a sprawling temporary tented camp near Gaza, and I took up my duties

as camp commandant. My sergeant-major, CSMI Tommy
Evans, was one of the finest I had ever known. A man
with a twinkling sense of humour allied with tremendous
efficiency, humanity and loyalty, he was a short, powerfully-
built ex-boxer, formerly welterweight champion of the British Army. During the war he had become a senior NCO in
the Army Physical Training Corps, and had then joined the
Parachute Regiment. I was lucky to have Tommy Evans as
my friend, adviser and right-hand-man throughout my year
in Palestine.

Although we had a defence platoon of some thirty men,
it was soon evident that these were inadequate to cope with
the security and guard duties required in that area, and it
was later augmented to become a company over one hundred
strong. Meanwhile, our security was in the hands of a
company of Basuto soldiers from South Africa. These were
fine, enthusiastic men whose smart bearing, crashingly-
zealous drilling and love of snappy saluting on every possible
occasion compensated for their rather wild shooting accuracy.

Movement after dark became quite hazardous with our
Basuto sentries. Their knowledge of English was limited,
and when challenged by one of them at night it was prudent
to stop very still or go to ground. Otherwise, 'Halt! Who goes
there?' Bang! was the likely outcome of such an encounter.

We needed all the security force we could get. In 1946 we
had to contend with terrorist activity, but during our entire
stay we faced the constant attentions of Arab pilferers.
They were magnificent, cunning thieves, those Arabs. Even
despite our Basuto guards we lost all manner of stores and
equipment in that Gaza camp. The highlight was one occasion
when ten soldiers awoke to find that their bell-tent was no
longer there.

Within a week of settling in at the camp, a minor disaster
struck me.

Brigadier Lathbury asked me one morning to go into Gaza
to make contact with the local British Palestine Police force.
I took with me CSMI Evans and we arrived by mid-morning
at the police fort. After a brief meeting with the police chief,
I went to the officers' mess for coffee while Tommy Evans

went to the sergeants' mess. What neither of us had anticipated was that our coffee was to be accompanied by stiff
tots of Cyprus brandy, a regular habit with those hardened
policemen.

I had never drunk brandy in the morning, and quickly
became extremely unsteady. So, while I could still walk
reasonably straight, I clambered into my jeep in the courtyard. Within moments I saw that Tommy Evans had fared no
better as he tottered out of the sergeants' mess, beaming
vacantly. Once aboard, with the sergeant-major beside me,
I started up and set off.

For some reason or other, I seemed to have difficulty in
getting the jeep out of its steering lock and circled round the
inner court of the square-built fort several times before
successfully heading for the gate entrance, which I cleared
in great style.

After that, we roared through Gaza at a tremendous lick
until, a mile or two out of town, our progress came to an
abrupt stop.

The police report said we had been driven off the road by
an Arab truck, but I have my doubts about that. All I can
remember is that my front wheel went off the hard shoulder of
the desert road, dug into the sand, and the jeep somersaulted.

I woke up in military hospital three days later. I still have
my medical report, which says,

'Day I: Unconscious. Unfit for theatre.

'Day II: Unconscious. Unfit for theatre.

'Day III: Semi-conscious. Occasionally obstreperous.'

It seems that I had a fractured skull and a broken shoulder,
together with some lacerations.

I spent several miserable weeks in that Gaza military
hospital, my right arm strapped up in a suspensory sling. I
asked about Sergeant-Major Evans and was told that he
had landed on his hands and broken some fingers but was
otherwise all right.

By the time I was discharged from hospital my unit had
moved to Sarafand, a large, permanent army camp south of
Tel Aviv, and it was here that I rejoined.

I was fairly fit again, but still having physiotherapy on my
shoulder, which never really knitted properly. Indeed, there

was no question of my parachuting again during the rest of my service, but I still wanted to stay with my unit, and my camp commandant's office gradually settled down to a normal routine again.

One of my fellow officer's little japes caught me out around April 1946. I was passing brigade HQ one day when Andy Cattanach beckoned to me from his office window, looking very concerned.

'Sweeney, do you know a girl called . . .?' and he mentioned someone I had known since my Conti era, who had spent a few days with me at an Amesbury hotel just before my leaving England some months earlier.

I said that I did indeed know her. What was the problem?

'Well, her father has written to the Brig. saying that she has had a baby and that you must be sent home to make an honest woman of her.'

'Christ! What do you think I should do?'

'If I were you I'd go in to see the Brig. right away. He's pretty furious.'

'Right. I'll do that.'

I went straight to the brigadier's office. He smiled benignly at me and asked what it was I wanted. Seeing that his mood did not appear to be at all frosty, I launched into a full account of the affair and my disbelief that there could possibly be any lasting outcome.

The brigadier listened gravely, his head gradually lowering in apparent deep thought. I feared that, by the way he appeared to be pursing his lips, while his face reddened, things were not going too well for me.

My anxious diatribe ended abruptly and rather lamely.

Eventually he looked up and, to my astonishment, burst into a roar of laughter.

'What letter are you talking about, Sweeney?'

'The one Cattanach said was in your mail this morning, sir.'

'I should go and ask Cattanach about it, if I were you. And remember the date – it's April Fool's Day.'

I headed for Andy's office. Delighted that his scheme had worked so perfectly, Andy produced a letter for me sent by the girl in question, her name and address written on the

In *Stagefright* with the family: Jane Wyman, Alistair Sim and Sybil Thorndike

Stagefright again: Alfred Hitchcock advising Marlene Dietrich on how to be glamorous

Elton Hayes (Allan-A-Dale) and myself, disguised in the livery of the Sheriff of Nottingham's men, let Walt Disney feel the weight of our helmets. The 'solid' dungeon wall behind us is pure wood and plaster, the 'metal' ring papier maché

With James Hayter as Friar Tuck. The 'solid' belly between us is mostly padding. Mine was natural!

Dropping from the tree for the umpteenth time on to that bloody horse. The dangers of miscalculating a landing on that high wooden pommel can well be imagined

RH·Prod2

Baron, greeting me at the entrance to Wayside House

back of the envelope. It was merely a friendly note saying that she was fine and hoped that all was well with me.

It was weeks before I lived down that story.

Up till about the end of 1945 our tour of duty in Palestine was relatively peaceful, and most of us managed to see a lot of that historic land. Nearly every weekend I was able to take my jeep and with a Bible in one hand and a map in the other, scour around fascinating places of interest, many of them seemingly unchanged since the beginning of Christianity. Jerusalem, Bethlehem, the Dead Sea, Jericho, the Sea of Galilee, the Inn of the Good Samaritan – my knowledge of the Scriptures improved considerably.

But our stay in Palestine was not one that many of us would recall with any pleasure. We were in the unenviable position of being a peace-keeping force in a land that was far from peaceful at that time – not a happy task for any soldier.

We merely carried out our orders as decisions were made in world politics as to the fate of Palestine and the future of Israel. But our efforts to control the flood of illegal refugees made us heartily disliked by much of the Jewish population, and the rate of killings of British soldiers by terrorist organisations gradually increased, culminating in the murder by the Stern Gang of seven men who were guarding the airborne vehicle park in Tel Aviv one night. So that by the next year, 1946, it was no longer wise to roam around Palestine singly.

Early that summer, while I was awaiting my demob, I acquired an enterprising volunteer helper, rather like Boris the Russian. Zaki, an Arab employed as odd-job man, was squat, powerful, and rather evil-looking, who seemed to attach himself to me particularly, and was always tidying, sweeping and dusting round our camp HQ. I particularly noticed a vase of flowers that he kept replenished in the office. No flowers grew in our camp, so I asked him one day where he found them. Zaki grinned sheepishly and said, 'Yehudi cemetery at Gat Rimon. Yehudi he sleep, Zaki take flowers.'

At last the day approached, in July 1946, when I was due to be shipped home to England. Had my damaged shoulder not put an end to my parachute training I might have decided to stay in the army. With reservations, I had enjoyed army service. I had no ties of any sort, and had found the mess almost a substitute for a family home. But as more and more of my old friends left to rejoin civilian life, or were transferred, a lot of the old wartime camaraderie went with them.

I suppose I was also apprehensive about my return to civilian life. I had no idea what I would do or where I would go, and there was no close family for me to shelter with while I sorted something out. Nevertheless, when the time came, I was glad to get away, and the last good thing I managed to do was to recommend Tommy Evans for a commission, which he soon received.

In late July I sailed to Toulon in France, where I spent a few enjoyable days before taking train to Calais, and a ship to England.

16

CAUGHT IN THE ACT AGAIN

At Aldershot demobilisation centre I completed all the form-filling required to return me to civilian life. Among other things I attested that I suffered no disability as the result of army service, which was not exactly true, but I felt that it would seem rather feeble to note that I still could not pour tea from a pot single-handed because of my shoulder injury. After all, in every other way I was intact, thank goodness.

Then I lined up with dozens of others in a large clothing store to collect my free hand-out of civilian clothes. I took a quite respectable dark suit, an overcoat, a shirt and a pair of shoes, but declined the hat, which was quite dreadful.

I also collected my demob pay (gratuity). I can no longer remember how much it was, but I reckoned I would need every penny of it during the weeks to come. I had only a minute amount left in my current bank account and I had no idea what I was going to do next. I was not sure that I wanted to return to being an actor. Six years of army service, during which time I had never even mentioned that I had been on the stage, had not been the best preparation for attending juvenile lead auditions in some 1940s light comedy.

I had been considering my options for weeks. Perhaps I could indeed get work in the theatre. Alternatively, there had been an offer from an old friend of a start as a trainee in a large firm of estate agents of which he was a partner. With my country background and interest in architecture, this was the option that I favoured most.

But there was also the offer of a job from my chief instructor at the School of Signals in Catterick, working under him in the personnel management department of J. Lyons, the huge food conglomerate. Perhaps this was not a bad idea either.

Anyway, I had a few weeks' leave to enjoy before I started to worry about my future, so I decided to make the most of my return to the peaceful life. There had been worse worries during the previous years.

I took a train to London and booked into the Mayfair Hotel. I had no specific programme ahead of me. I no longer had a home to go to, or parents or close relatives to visit in England. In fact, I suppose I felt pretty lonely: most of my boyhood and wartime friends no longer existed, and I realised that I had now to make a completely new life for myself.

Of course, I would at some stage go and visit the Fitz-Patricks and Granny Todd in Ireland. But first I reckoned that while I was in London I should sort out my immediate future. My funds were not going to last very long.

That first morning at the Mayfair Hotel I felt all dressed up with nowhere to go. I desperately wanted someone to talk to – not necessarily about myself and my problems, but just to have companionship of some sort. For years I had led a communal existence, and now, suddenly, I was solitary.

I phoned my estate agent friend's office, but he was out.

Then I tried another call, one that was to influence and establish the rest of my life. I phoned Robert Lennard.

Bob had briefly been my theatrical agent before the war, and a couple of months before I was due to leave Palestine, he had written to me. He explained that he was now casting director of the Associated British Picture Corporation, about equal to the Rank Organisation as a big film production, distribution and exhibition group in Britain, and he wanted to know if I could get home at once to test for a leading part in the film *Quiet Weekend*, which was due to start soon.

I had replied that I could not advance my demob, and that, in any case, I was not sure if I wanted to return to acting.

His response was very understanding, and he hoped that I would contact him when I got back to the UK.

Suddenly that morning I remembered Bob and phoned to ask him if he would care to have lunch with me. Fortunately, he was free, and agreed to meet me at the Berkeley Buttery.

I had always considered Bob Lennard one of the nicest and kindest people in the entertainment industry, a man who truly cared for those actors whose careers he was able to influence and assist. They formed an imposing list: Audrey Hepburn, Richard Harris, Robert Shaw, Janette Scott, Maggie Smith and Laurence Harvey were just a few of those who owed something to his perceptive casting and guidance.

While we talked, Bob made no attempt to persuade or pressure me about my future. He accepted that I had severe doubts that I would be able to fit happily once more into the theatre.

He asked me what I planned to do with my period of demob leave, and when he realised that I was pretty vague about that he made a suggestion which I thought made a lot of sense.

'Why don't you spend a couple of weeks in Dundee? After all, it's almost home to you, and you have a lot of friends up there.'

'You're right, Bob. That's what I'll do.'

I am pretty sure now that he had a good idea of what the outcome of that visit would be.

On my first evening in Dundee, having taken a room in the classy Royal British Hotel, I decided that I might as well book a seat for that night's show at the theatre.

The company had obviously improved since my time there, for it had become one of the foremost provincial theatre companies in the land, particularly since coming under the direction of a Mr Whatmore, whom I had never met.

I cannot remember the play being performed that night, and can only assume that it did not exactly rivet my attention. I never saw the second act. The reason for my defection was not, however, the play or the players; it was caused by an enchanting girl at the theatre bar.

I met her whilst talking to a group of theatre-goers who remembered me and who introduced us. When the others went back to their seats, I stayed at the bar, chatting to my new acquaintance.

She was Catherine Bogle, a Scottish-born young actress,

who had just arrived to start rehearsals next day for the
forthcoming production, a light comedy called *Claudia*. Just
nineteen years old, she had previously worked with the
Dundee Repertory Company, but had been at home for
nearly a year as the result of a nervous breakdown. Now
recovered, but still not totally well, she had been invited by
Mr Whatmore to play the leading part, Claudia, in Rose
Franken's comedy.

Kitty, as I was always to call her, was ideally cast as the
capricious child-wife in the story. She was tiny and quite
beautifully-formed, with long, natural blonde hair dressed in
the page-boy style fashionable at that time and the most
lovely, shy, greeny-blue eyes. She had delicate hands and
tapered fingers, and her skin was as flawless and smooth as
any china.

Her shyness and reserve made me the more determined
to gain her confidence. Even though I was not likely to
see her again, and despite the fact that she gave me no
encouragement whatsoever, I was very taken. Hers was not
a type that I had frequently encountered during the previous
six years.

I did manage to find out that she was very nervous about
taking on her first leading role, especially after her year's
absence from the theatre. She was also apprehensive about
working with her leading man, a very good actor, whom she
had never met, Geoffrey Lumsden, due to arrive next day
from London.

Plainly she needed reassurance, so I did my best to convince her that Mr Whatmore would not have offered her the
role if he had not been sure that she could cope with it, and
that I was sure that Lumsden would be very nice and helpful.
She had really nothing to worry about, I told her.

My good deed for the day was soon interrupted by Mr
Whatmore when he came to introduce himself, having heard
that I was in the theatre that evening. He invited me to join
him for a drink in his office. I would have preferred to stay
talking with Kitty, but she was leaving anyway, so I found
myself being regaled in the director's extremely comfortable
and orderly little den.

I liked him immediately. A tall, handsome man, greymoustached and impeccably dressed, he had a curiously military bearing which was accentuated by his brusque manner. There was nothing of the flamboyant theatrical impresario about him, and I could see why he had gained a reputation for no-nonsense efficiency and disciplined hard work with his previous theatre company in Aberdeen, where Stewart Granger had been among the young hopefuls.

We chatted briefly about my early pre-war days in Dundee, and then Whatty asked me what my plans were. I told him I didn't really have any.

Then he asked me if I would like to rejoin the Dundee Repertory Company. I would still have quite a following among their local supporters, he said.

So, here I was, faced with a decision that I had hoped to put off until I had had time to be sure what I wanted to do with my life. I still had reservations about picking up the threads of a career that I had deliberately renounced for so many years. Perhaps, like Kitty, I too had doubts about my ability.

'Just do one play,' Whatty said. 'I'll find a good one for you, and I'm sure the rep will do great business with it. Then you can make up your mind.' For all his keenness, I was pretty sure that he was not a man to hang around waiting for my decision.

Suddenly, I had an idea. Pretty Kitty and her problems had come to my mind.

'Right, sir,' I said. 'I'll do one play for you. I'll play Geoffrey Lumsden's part in your next production.'

It was Whatty's turn to make a decision.

He picked up the phone and asked for a London number.

'Geoffrey, I've had to make a change of plan. Could you delay coming up to Dundee for a few weeks?'

Miraculously this suited Lumsden, and the deal was done.

Without more ado, Whatty handed me a play script and said, 'Rehearsals start tomorrow morning, ten-thirty.'

I asked him not to tell Miss Bogle about the new casting until I arrived on stage in the morning, and he agreed. I then went back to the hotel and settled down to read the play.

Next morning I arrived in good time for rehearsal in the theatre I remembered so well from its opening in 1939. I was

still in uniform as I had not bothered to unpack all my
luggage, knowing that now I would need to find somewhere
more economical to stay, and I suppose I must have been an
incongruous sight among the rest of the company in their
very informal working clothes.

Whatty took me on stage to introduce me to the others,
and their surprise was only matched by Kitty's amazement,
and, I hoped, pleasure.

So here I was, once again sitting with a play script in my
hand at a first read-through.

There was nothing very demanding in the part, and all
went well for me. Later that day I was lucky to find comfortable rooms in a pleasant house on the western outskirts of
Dundee with a marvellous view right across the Tay estuary
to Fife. The play was to run for three weeks, after three
weeks of rehearsals, so I would have plenty of time to get to
know Kitty, the company and my way about the city again.

And I did get to know Kitty. I spent every possible minute
with her; I called at her digs in the morning on the way to
rehearsal, worked with her, lunched with her, and then spent
hours going through lines with her in the evening. She was
tiny and rather frail, and still not properly recovered from
an anaemic disorder which caused her to suffer occasional
dizziness. I soon began to recognise the onset of one of these
spells and was often able to support her without anybody
else realising. But as her confidence grew she began to regain
her normal health and spirits, and by the opening night of
the play she was nearly back to her real self: always tending
to be shy, but equally ready to laugh with others; a quick-
moving, mercurial little person, nevertheless imbued with
plenty of Scottish practicality.

I knew myself well enough to realise that my interest in
her was not based on purely professional considerations. She
was an exceedingly attractive girl and in ordinary circumstances I would probably have set out to win her favour on
that account alone. But the fact that I was actually able to
help her, and that she appreciated my support, added an
extra dimension to our relationship.

I had not been close to anybody in this way before.
Since my mother's death I had never felt any real sense of

responsibility or permanence towards any woman friend, nor had I any sister or near relative. I enjoyed this new situation. At last I had someone to care for. Not surprisingly, I began to think of Kitty as part of my life.

As opening night approached I knew one other thing: I was caught in the act. All the old excitement of the theatre had gripped me again. Whatever it was – the smell of the greasepaint, the anticipation of an audience, the close world of an acting company – I was part of it once more.

All the insecurity of the actor's profession, the uncertain future, the hard work and the poor living conditions, I decided to take a chance on. After all, in the army I had become quite used to not knowing what the next day would bring.

I consulted with Bob Lennard and then signed a six-month contract with the Dundee Repertory Company.

Claudia opened on a Monday. The dress rehearsal was on the Sunday evening, and that afternoon, when I arrived at the theatre, carrying my newly acquired make-up box and all the bits and pieces that I would need in the dressing-room, I found the stage staff busy rigging the set and finishing last-minute scenery-painting, so I gave them a hand. One of them said it was the first time she had seen the leading man work as a scene-shifter, but I suppose for me it was simply a way of keeping my mind off my coming ordeal.

Kitty's parents travelled to Dundee for the opening performance, which was a great success. They stayed a couple of days, and were extremely nice to me. The family name was Grant-Bogle, and her father turned out to be a very affable, kindly man, a Glasgow industrialist who had inherited a brass foundry from an uncle. Margaret Grant-Bogle was a charming, pretty woman whose family had prospered in business and farming round Rothesay on the Isle of Bute.

During the run of *Claudia* I had inevitably started rehearsing for the next production, so I only saw Kitty during lunchtimes and after the show in the evening.

She had already been engaged by the Liverpool Repertory Theatre as a leading juvenile, and would be joining John Fernald's company there immediately after our play ended. I was delighted for her, as Liverpool Rep was perhaps the most prestigious provincial company in Britain at that time.

During *Claudia* Kitty celebrated her twentieth birthday and Whatty gave a little champagne party for her after the show. During that evening, Ethel Ramsay, a lovely, wise old actress who was playing Kitty's mother in the play, said to me quietly, 'Be kind to her, Richard. Don't hurt her.'

Certainly as the day of our parting approached we both knew that we would miss each other sorely. I think we realised that we wanted eventually to be together, but any talk of serious engagement was totally ruled out by my current salary of £12 per week – just enough to get by alone in Dundee. So Kitty went off to forge her own career.

But every single evening for months I phoned her or she called me.

In October my discharge from the army became absolute. By then I had in any case become fully integrated into the theatre company and had even claimed the special 'tools of the trade' allowance granted to ex-servicemen to help them start up again in their work. In my case, the tools were a couple of good suits which I had tailored for me locally.

Play followed play, and I extended my contract for a further year, partly because I felt safe there, partly because I needed more experience, but mostly because I was trying to put together enough reserve funds to risk a long 'rest' looking for work in London, the Mecca of all actors. At the end of my first six months I was given the company's top salary, £15 per week. At least more than I had been getting in the army.

We were basically a fortnightly rep, with two weeks to rehearse each show – luxury for me, after the weekly rep of pre-war days. Every three months we performed a Shakespeare piece or a classic such as a Restoration comedy or an Oscar Wilde play. Before these we did a pot-boiler, like an Agatha Christie who-dun-it, which ran for three weeks, giving us an extra week for rehearsal. So we presented some twenty shows each year.

I thoroughly enjoyed my stay in Dundee. I had a nice flat where I was given breakfast and a late meal, lots of friends and plenty of social activity besides the hard-working hours we all put in at the theatre. My shoulder injury hampered my golf, but I took some coaching and eventually developed a flattish swing which enabled me to play fairly respectably. Often, before rehearsals, I would nip up to the municipal course at Caird Park, where I could play a round alone for a shilling.

I cannot remember many of the plays that we performed, but a few of them stick in my memory. First, there was my first leading role in a Shakespeare play, in which I played Orlando to Pauline Jameson's Rosalind in *As You Like It*. I had understudied the role in the Open Air Theatre years before.

Of the modern pieces, two stick in my memory: the first was *Of Mice and Men*, a stunning play which even brought tears to the gruff Whatty's eyes at one final rehearsal; and the second was John Patrick's *The Hasty Heart*, a most moving play set in an army hospital in Burma. In this production Joseph Greig, a Shetlander by birth, was brilliant as the recalcitrant little Scottish corporal, Lachlan McLachlan. I played the Yank.

The high spot of 1947 for us came when we were invited to perform for the Royal Family at Balmoral. The Countess of Airlie, a lady-in-waiting to the Queen, was a regular supporter of the rep. She had found that I had been an officer in the regiment of which the Queen was Colonel-in-Chief, and wrote to me asking if I could go to Balmoral Castle one weekend to see if I thought a full-scale performance there would be feasible.

I determined to arrive in style. As I had no car then, I hired a local Rolls Royce that I had seen about the town in various wedding and funeral processions. When I explained the purpose to its owner, I got it for a very moderate sum for the day – a Sunday.

As I drew up outside the great castle itself I wondered what door I should head for – was I a tradesman relegated to the kitchen entrance or a visitor entitled to go in by the front door? I got out and dithered for a few moments, and it was then that I noticed for the first time the large plate on the back of the car bearing the sign 'HACKNEY CARRIAGE'.

Before I could do anything about it the front door opened
and a man came to greet me. He was a household official
who had been expecting me, and was polite enough not
to notice the fallen status of my vehicle. I was taken to
look at the ballroom and some adjacent rooms that
would be usable as dressing-rooms, and I gave my opinion
that a fully staged play could be done in the ballroom.
Even if I had had any doubts, I would not have voiced
them.

Soon after, we received a formal invitation and Barbara
Borrow, our scenic designer, went to the castle to draw up
her plans.

The play was to be *At Mrs Beams*, a rather awful boarding-
house comedy, so far as I can remember.

When the day came, we were all taken by coach to Balmoral. Soon after we arrived the Queen herself very char-
mingly thanked us for coming and said she was greatly
looking forward to the evening.

After the performance, which seemed to go down quite
well, we were led to a meal that had been prepared for us,
and then invited to join the Royals in the drawing-room for
drinks.

There was quite a gathering there: all our own Royal
Family (am I right in remembering that Princess Elizabeth
had just become engaged to Prince Philip of Greece?) were
present and several other foreign Royals also. It says much
for their charm and easy grace that we felt quite at home and
chattered away happily.

Then came my moment of utter confusion.

With all the excitement, I had neglected to attend to the
needs of nature. Fuelled by generous quantities of wine with
supper and a massive whisky now in my hand, I suddenly
reckoned there was not a moment to lose. Aware that one
should not leave the room without some sort of royal assent,
I edged over to Peter Townsend, who was then the equerry
on duty, and confided my problem. Mercifully, he was a
quick thinker.

He said it would be perfectly all right to slip out and
indicated a door at the end of the room. 'Go out there,' he
said. 'Right across the hall you will see a door. That's usually

only used by the King himself, but it leads to a cloakroom.
Be quick, and you'll be OK.'

I scurried into the hallowed royal loo in the nick of time,
and stood in shuddering relief at a urinal. (That seems hardly
the right nomenclature for the plumbing facilities in such
august premises.)

Many seconds later I was still in full spate when, to my
absolute horror, the monarch himself hurried in. Now, to
my knowledge, there is no manual of etiquette or protocol
that deals with this particular situation. All sorts of solutions
raced through my head. Should I bow politely and carry on
unperturbed, or should I hurriedly apologise and retreat?
What on earth was I to do?

As he stood beside me, I thought I detected a slight flicker
in the King's jaw muscles, often the prelude to conversation
made difficult by his speech impediment. After what seemed
an eternity, however, he said nothing and I eventually managed to cut off my water supply. Fumbling with shaking
fingers at my buttons (we had no zips in those days) I backed
away, still in silence. Anxious to retreat as quickly as I could,
I nevertheless took a few moments to swill my hands at
the wash-basin, not wishing to seem ignorant of personal
hygiene.

Then, remembering what I had seen of court behaviour in
various Hollywood films, I proceeded to back out of the
cloakroom, bowing as I reached the door, and then fled,
sweating with embarrassment, back to the drawing-room.

In March 1948, a telegram arrived from Robert Lennard,
asking if I could travel to London in two weeks' time to take
a screen test for a film about to start in April. I was to phone
him without delay.

I went to Whatty, wondering if he would release me from
my contract. I had been in Dundee for nearly eighteen
months, and my engagement then still had several weeks to
run.

'Of course you must go,' said he. 'I'll get somebody to
replace you in the next play. Can't think why you stayed
here so long. You should have gone to London months ago.
And good luck.'

The following days were spent sorting out my few bits of
business in Dundee, saying goodbye to friends, and on 15
March 1948, I travelled to London.

The film was to be *For Them That Trespass*, a rather
down-beat story of a young man imprisoned for a crime
committed by another man. After serving a long sentence he
leaves prison, considerably aged, and bitterly dedicated to
proving his innocence and exposing the real culprit. Not the
most original or cheerful of stories!

I was tested for the leading role at the Associated British
Picture Corporation studios in Welwyn Garden City, and
Robert Lennard had told me that a decision would not be
made for at least a couple of weeks. Since I realised that, if
I got the part, the director would be taking a big chance on
a complete unknown with no screen experience, I kept my
fingers crossed, but felt that really it was all too good to be
true.

Eventually, I was called to Bob Lennard's office. He was
jubilant.

'You've got the part, and the Corporation is going to put
you under long-term contract!'

Strangely, considering my previous doubts, I was not all
that greatly surprised – delighted, yes, but not stunned.
Certainly, fortune had smiled on me. Here I was, an unknown
repertory actor, about to star in my first feature film, my
screen career assured by a seven-year agreement with
Associated British – even if the contract's terms were not
exactly going to put me in the Croesus class. But I had been
through a long and exacting apprenticeship, so I was simply
happy now to get on with the job. It never occurred to me
to question that, during my first two pictures, I would be
earning just seven pounds a week more than my stand-in.

My salary for the next seven years was to increase thus:
Year One: £25 per week; Year Two: £35 p.w.; Year Three:
£50 p.w.; Year Four: £75 p.w.; Year Five: £100 p.w.; Year
Six: £150 p.w.; Year Seven: £200 p.w. This was in 1948, so,
allowing for inflation to increase the sums, say, ten-fold, the
later figures were quite impressive. In addition I was to earn
fifty per cent of the average on any loan-outs to other
production companies. This meant that once my ABPC

salary had been deducted, I split the profit with the corporation. In fact, during that seven years, Associated British never had to pay me my annual salary, as loan-out revenue more than covered the basic yearly wage.

So both parties were happy – especially me!

Of course, I phoned Granny Todd, Kitty and everybody I could think of with the good news. I had last seen Kitty when I had taken a short holiday from Dundee to visit Granny Todd in Ireland, and had spent a night en route in Liverpool. Now I told her that we could marry within a year or so, if that was what she still wanted. She said it was.

I was introduced to the chiefs of Associated British and embarked on a course of PR and press meetings, all arranged by the Corporation's head of publicity and public relations, the exuberant and very astute Leslie Frewin, who was to mastermind my public image and appearances for years to come.

One of my first public duties was to present the cups and awards at a goat show somewhere in Surrey. Never mind – it was a beginning for a beginner!

It was an exciting new world for me. To be picked up and escorted everywhere by PROs; to be ferried around in chauffeur-driven limousines; to lunch and dine in the most famous and expensive restaurants with journalists; to have endless still-photo sessions – Sausage or Sweeney Todd had never had it so good!

On top of all this activity there were the preparations for *For Them That Trespass*. Victor Skudetski the producer, and Cavalcanti the director, were enormously helpful, and Cav in particular spent many hours going through the script with me. He was a quiet-spoken, crop-haired South American, academic in manner and artistic in taste. Realising that I had a lot to learn about film technique, he decided that all the people to be tested for leading roles in the picture would work on scenes with me, so that I could gain some camera experience. This was a wise move, and I gradually became adept at hitting my marks, finding my key-light, cheating my eyelines, and adjusting my playing to the differences between long shots, medium shots and close-ups.

With my new-found wealth, I gave up my Chelsea digs
and took a room at the Comet Hotel, in Hatfield, only a few
miles from the Welwyn Studios. Being still car-less, I bought
a bicycle, and pedalled to and from the studios each day. It
wasn't quite up to the standard of the Rolls Royce or Cadillac
of today's leading film actors, but it was economical and got
me there without fuss.

Finally, the great day arrived when I recorded my first
cinematic efforts for posterity. We started with a couple of
days in a scruffy little public park somewhere in a run-down
area of London. Any dreams I had of romantic locations
were soon dispelled. Apart from those first few days my only
other exterior shots were confined to the acrid interior of a
railway tunnel at night.

In those days nearly everything was filmed in the studios,
with street scenes laboriously and expensively built in the
sound stages. Even a short sequence in a corridor of a
block of flats used a constructed set with sharply-tapering
perspective to give length to the view, while dwarfs were
hired to enhance the sense of distance at the far end of the
corridor.

I think I coped fairly well, thanks to Cavalcanti's quiet
help. Every day after filming finished he insisted that I sat
with him at the rushes – the developed and unedited film
shot the previous day. At these sessions he would point out
all my mistakes and weaknesses and lecture me on ways to
eradicate them. Over-acting in medium and close-up shots
was my earliest fault. I also had a tendency to blink my eyes,
a habit which, magnified enormously in close-up, produced
an effect like an exaggerated twitch.

Watching myself and the others day after day in rushes, I
gradually began to learn the rudiments of film technique,
and to understand why the good takes were printed, and
others discarded. It also helped me to become aware of
continuity, so that, on returning to the same scene perhaps
days later, I had a pretty good idea of the mood, pace, dress
and setting of the previous takes.

Some actors claim that they never go to rushes. God knows
how they learn – or maybe they don't.

The atmosphere of a film studio was in stark contrast to

the live theatre. It seemed to me that, from the moment I arrived at the studio, usually at about 7.30 a.m., I was required to do almost nothing except get on with my work. My make-up was done for me, and on stage there was always a make-up artist ready to rush in with a dab of powder, an ice-cooled, cologne-scented leather to freshen up the sticky face, or a deft comb to smooth a wayward lock. My clothes were laid out for me by a dresser who was in attendance all day, flicking away imaginary specks of fluff.

You could say that I was happy in my work.

Through Cav, I learned another facet of filming that was to stand me in good stead: I suffer mildly from duck's disease. I can just reach five feet eight inches if I stand very erect. I am not the only actor with this slight drawback – Alan Ladd was the same height – but it can at times create difficulties. It is not easy to dominate tall actresses or to hold one's own with giant actors. I was always aware of this, but Cav taught me not to be self-conscious about it. Camera angles can control the imbalance – to be nearest to a low-angle camera helps – but when all else fails, to be literally jacked up is the answer. Cav had the carpenters make two or three little ramps for me, of varying lengths and height, so that, for example, as I walked into a two-shot, I would gradually loom taller and taller. Subsequently, at my request, every studio I worked in in Britain or America had a supply of these gadgets. I had no false modesty about it. On exterior locations I would have them dig a trench for the other actors, if need be!

But then, a few weeks later, while keeping in training at a sports field near the studios, I broke my Achilles tendon! I phoned the local doctor and told him what I had done. He arrived a few minutes later, strapped me up, told me to stay in bed, made some phone calls, and arranged for a specialist from London to visit me first thing next morning. I also made some calls and broke the news to a horrified producer.

By now the full misery had hit me. Here I was, in the middle of my first film, crippled and facing an operation and hospital for God knows how long. Bang goes the film, my contract and my career, I groaned!

In theatrical circles, 'Break a leg!' is meant as a good luck wish. God knows why . . .

While the surgeon examined me next morning, Skudetski and Cavalcanti stood anxiously by. Within moments the surgeon announced that I must have an immediate operation to join the tendon together again, and at this my two film bosses really showed their anguish.

I sympathised with them. It was a Tuesday morning, and on the previous day, when I had the accident, we had just started to work on my film trial at a court in the Old Bailey. The sequence would need the whole week to shoot, and the massive set took up the whole of our biggest sound stage. Until the scenes had been finished and the courtroom demolished no further sets could be built and the film would grind to a halt.

No wonder Cav and Victor were frantic!

I felt a bloody stupid nuisance.

They explained all this to the surgeon, and after brief thought he said that, providing I was willing to put up with the pain, he could delay the operation until the Saturday morning. Meanwhile, he would strap my leg very tightly. He insisted that I should be carried everywhere and he also laid down that a doctor or trained nurse should be in attendance at all times.

Naturally, I agreed to all this. I would have done anything to make up for the trouble I was causing and to salvage my all-too-brief film career.

So, after an early lunch in my room, I was duly carried to a car and taken to the studios. Once again, the kindness and solicitude of everybody was remarkable.

Fortunately, throughout the courtroom scene I was standing in the prisoner's dock and did not have to move about. Neither was the lower part of my body visible, so from the knee down my injured leg was resting behind me on a cushioned stool, and I managed perfectly well.

We finished the sequence on schedule on the Friday afternoon and that evening I moved into hospital. After the operation I was interned there for two weeks, during which time the film schedule was easily altered to shoot around me, doing all the bits in which I did not appear.

Luckily I healed very quickly and in due course a so-called walking plaster encased my lower leg. It was an unwieldy affair, with a bulbous foot. I spent the entire weekend practising walking, but on Sunday night I still clumped around very clumsily. And I would have to do better than that, because I was filming on the Monday.

Then I had an idea: I procured a desk blotter (one of those large, round-bottomed affairs) and first thing on the Monday morning I went to the plasterers' shop at the studios and got them to fix this to the underside of my foot. It worked like a dream. Soon I was walking with no perceptible limp, but with, I suppose, a slightly rolling gait.

Filming continued without any great problems. As most of the work was on interior scenes, the cameraman had no difficulty in keeping my sock-covered foot in shadow or behind various pieces of furniture, and I was able to move about quite naturally, with no perceptible peg-leg stumping.

Finally came the last day of shooting on *For Them That Trespass*, and there was great jubilation at Welwyn Studios. Somehow I had completed my first starring role, and my contract was intact. That same evening I had to attend a reception at the new ABPC Studios at Elstree. The party was in honour of Jack Warner Junior and Vincent Sherman, producer and director of the forthcoming *The Hasty Heart*, the first Anglo-American co-production to be made under a recently formed tie-up between Warner Brothers of America and Associated British.

Apparently, Vincent Sherman was going to test a number of actors for the leading role of the dour Scot, Lachlan McLachlan, and was still making his list of possible candidates. He caught sight of me, and turning to Robert Clark, one of the board members of ABPC, he said, 'You see that guy over there? He's exactly the type I'm looking for. Right size, right age – everything.'

Mr Clark told him that in fact I was an Associated British contract artiste.

'Right,' said Sherman. 'I want to meet him.'

I was led across the room, introduced to the two Americans, and Sherman asked me if I knew *The Hasty Heart*. I said I did, and that I had recently played the Yank in the play in Dundee.

'How would you like to test for the Scot, Lachie?'

I told him that there would be no point. I was not a Scot, and anyway, I was certain that I was not right for the role. Never could an actor have tried harder to talk himself out of a marvellous opportunity. I was that stupid even then.

Fortunately for me, Vincent Sherman was an infinitely patient man.

'Well, anyhow,' he said, 'I want to do a test on you.'

Very soon after I left, having had a script thrust into my hand, and a few days later I reported to Elstree. I was made up, dressed in Burma uniform, and played the scene in which the little Scottish corporal proposes to the nurse in an army hospital. The ordeal was over in less than an hour. Other actors were tested for the rest of the day.

The following week I was called to Bob Lennard's office. I'd got the part!

17

STAGE FRIGHT

Before starting filming on *The Hasty Heart* I had moved with
all my worldly possessions (just over a trunk-full) into a
delightful mews house off Belgrave Square. I was to share it
for about a year with two close friends, Bobby Temple and
Tim Reeve.

We had perfect quarters; three bedrooms, a large sitting-
room, dining-room, bathroom and kitchen, and a huge
ground floor garage, in which I proudly parked my latest
acquisition, a massive green open sports-tourer Railton,
pre-war and powered by a Hudson straight-eight engine.
Such a car had been my dream for years.

Belle, our daily housekeeper, was fiercely protective of
her three young gentlemen, and ran the place scrupulously,
turning a blind eye to the littered aftermath of our evening
parties.

We were a contrasting trio in some ways. Bobby and Tim
would set off each morning in the traditional uniform of City
gents: dark suits, bowler hats and neatly-furled umbrellas,
whilst I, the actor, would scramble out in whatever I could
hastily don to get me to the film studios on time.

Still, we had a lot in common. Bobby, like me, had
been an officer in the Parachute Regiment and had fought
outstandingly at Arnhem, where he had been wounded.

Tim, an Old Etonian, had served in the RAF during the
war, and was a tall, deceptively languid man with a great
sense of humour and a ready, chortling laugh.

Both of them had bedroom mantelpieces regularly be-
decked with a never-dwindling array of invitation cards to
London society functions, and thoroughly enjoyed their lives.

Our shared establishment was a lively place.

One of the features of Belgrave Mews West was the Star
Tavern, perhaps the most popular pub in those days with the

young set. On sunny Sunday mornings visitors to the Star spilled out into the street itself, and there was a colourful fashion parade of pretty girls and glossy sports cars. One snag of our proximity to the Star was that many of our acquaintances seemed to regard our house, three doors away, as an annexe to the pub and would arrive, glasses in hand, on the doorstep at closing time.

Whilst preparing to start work on my second film, I persuaded Kitty to come to London. My departure from Dundee had brought such fortunate results that I felt she too should take the plunge. So she arrived and shared a flat with a friend in Charlotte Street. Sadly, her career did not prosper with any great speed, and I felt very responsible for perhaps having given her the wrong advice.

We spent a great deal of time together and Bobby and Tim took to her greatly, especially when she came to our house and prepared delicious dinners for us, despite the rationing still in force.

She was a lovely person, and I felt as protective towards her as I had during our first rehearsals together. With my career prospects looking bright, I reckoned it would not be long before we could marry.

With some weeks to go before shooting started on *The Hasty Heart*, Associated British kept me busy and started grooming me as a fully fledged contract artiste of the Corporation. I was given an allowance to kit myself out with West End tailoring, and had some suits made by Cyril Castle, who has remained my tailor over all the years since then.

I also acquired an agent, Al Parker, who was regarded as being the foremost representative of film actors at that time. A short, forceful American, his bark was more effective than his bite, and most of my day-to-day problems, slight though they were, were handled by Monti Mackey, one of his assistants, and by Robert Lennard.

A couple of weeks before filming started in Elstree Studios that autumn I had daily sessions with a real Scot who attempted to provide me with an authentic Scottish accent, and also with an ex-army pipe-major, who taught me how to set up and handle a set of bagpipes, and even to finger *Hieland Laddie* on a chanter.

So I was ready to start on my first international movie. The final hurdle that I had to clear was the initial meeting with my two distinguished co-stars, Ronald Reagan and Patricia Neal.

The two of them had every reason to need assurance that I would adequately perform the role of Lachlan McLachlan, round whose character and problems the picture would revolve. If they were to size me up quizzically I could not have blamed them.

I need have had no such qualms.

We met over a specially arranged luncheon at Elstree, and it could not have been a more friendly or relaxed encounter. Ronnie, tall, lean and humorous, beautifully mannered and courteous, seemed to be genuinely as pleased as I was about the chance I had been given, and Pat, lovely and statuesque, was equally warm and amiable.

We knew we would enjoy working together.

The Hasty Heart was a story set entirely in an army hospital in Burma during World War II, with very little movement and a small cast of characters – ideal material for a cheap-to-make movie. But in addition to our American stars we had two major bonuses: Vincent Sherman, an enormously experienced American director whose credits had included some of the great Bette Davis and Joan Crawford pictures, and a beautifully written script little changed from the already successful theatre play.

He was the sweetest, most patient and kindly of men, from whom I never heard a sharp or irritable word, and his good humour and tolerance permeated the entire unit while we were filming. A man of great sensitivity, one always knew when some particularly moving scene had touched him by the tear-blotched front of his suede tunic.

Whilst Vince always knew exactly what he wanted from each scene, and never wasted a foot of film by indecision or the sort of incompetence one has seen so often since then, he did not so much direct his actors as coax and cajole the performances he needed. As an ex-actor himself, he could talk one into the mood of the scene before shooting even started.

To aid him he had two supremely skilful helpers: Terence

Verity, the art director, and Wilkie Cooper, the lighting cameraman. Terence had designed the entire setting of the film on one sound stage; a sandy compound fringed with bashas (bamboo and wood huts) and sprinkled with a few palm trees. The basha in which all the action took place was mounted on a revolving turntable which could be swung so that the key lighting never had to be changed for different camera angles. Wilkie, quick and confident, went quietly and unobtrusively about his work, seldom causing any of the hold-ups so often associated with lighting.

One of the advantages of *The Hasty Heart* was that the whole picture could be shot indoors in the studios, with none of the frustrations of bad weather, changing light, extraneous noises or crowd control that can so often plague a unit on location. It was Terence Verity's skill and Wilkie Cooper's lighting that gave the impression that we were working in a clearing in the jungle.

Due to Vincent Sherman's patient guidance, and the friendly acceptance of me by Ronald Reagan and Patricia Neal, I was not in the least overawed by my responsibility in having the leading part in my first international film. I worked conscientiously, always knew my lines, and seemed to have a rapport with the character of the lonely, defensive little Scot that I was playing. It was a very happy, close-knit unit, and we were all on excellent terms. The two jokesters who mainly kept us in good spirits were the ebullient Howard Marion-Crawford, who played the Cockney, and the genial Ronald Reagan, with his endless fund of amusing stories and reminiscences.

As our schedule moved into winter, the weather was dreadful. The proverbial London pea-soup fogs shrouded us, even penetrating the studio stage, and it was bitterly cold and utterly miserable. I was driving myself daily to Elstree in my open Railton, but even with the top up and the side screens flapping it was not the ideal all-weather conveyance.

It was then that Ronnie Reagan offered to give me a lift each day. His chauffeur-driven car picked him up every morning at the Savoy Hotel and he reckoned it could easily come down to Belgravia and my mews home, dropping me off again in the evening.

It was during these daily trips that Ronnie and I got to know each other pretty well. I soon realised that, for all his good-natured manner, he was not a particularly happy man. For one thing, he had not really wanted to come to Britain to make the picture, but had been persuaded to do so by Warners' promise of a forthcoming film subject bought especially for him. Had he not told me this, I would never have guessed from his demeanour that he had arrived in England in something of a sulk.

Then, too, he was lonely. This was his first trip abroad and he had no friends here, except for Patricia Neal. He had arrived in a bleak, war-scarred London still struggling to free itself from food rationing, still ill-lit and gloomy, and he was clearly not impressed with our weather, our food or our living conditions – not surprisingly, because only a Briton or a European would realise that even this state of affairs was luxury compared with what had been endured a few short years before.

But his principal personal sadness at that time was caused by the recent breakdown of his marriage to Jane Wyman, and his worry about the effect it might have on their children. He, who had been so close to his own parents, was born to be a family man.

All these things, and many more, we chatted about during our daily journeys together.

Another of his reasons for fretting about his absence from America was that, as President of the Screen Actors' Guild, he knew he should be in California guiding his union through the trauma of change that the film industry was experiencing. For some years he had been a dedicated, hard-working officer of the Guild and was a skilled and respected negotiator. He took his responsibilities deeply seriously – perhaps too seriously for the good of his career and private relationships. He never spoke to me of his family problems at any length, but I sensed he was hurting.

We discovered we had a lot in common. We had both been keen games-players and were avid followers of sport; we had both overcome physical defects – his being poor eye-sight – to fiddle our way into the wartime services; and we were both farmers at heart. I have never met an American who so profoundly believed in the greatness of his nation. His views then were perhaps a little myopic and insular, but in those days he had little knowledge and no experience of the rest of the world. Ronnie literally warmed to London and England as he adjusted to the climate, and found time to explore London and take car trips into the countryside. Certainly, he was happy in his relationship with a small band of British film-makers, and extremely well liked by us all.

If I discourse at some length about just one person of my acquaintance, it is perhaps not surprising. Since he first announced his intention to compete for the Presidency of the United States, I have quite naturally tried to equate the Ronald Reagan that I knew back in 1948 with the man of destiny that he has since become. And I would say that he is still, and always has been, a man of real sincerity of purpose and deed. He cares profoundly for the good of his country and its people. One thing I was sure he would give to his compatriots, if he were to be elected President, was pride: pride in themselves and the country.

He is probably the most articulate, moving and understandable public speaker that I have seen or heard since Winston Churchill. And so he should be! A man who had been a successful radio commentator and a skilled actor – not by any means the B picture cowboy he is sometimes vilified as – should be capable of delivering his speeches with some panache.

For me, one of his most endearing qualities is that he does not forget his old friends. Now, nearly four decades on, I still receive birthday greetings from him and his wife.

My own future was being worked out there at Elstree, though to what extent I had no idea at the time. As *The Hasty Heart* drew to its conclusion we all felt that we had made a very moving film. Many times at the rushes or when we saw rough-cuts of some of the more touching moments in the story, the lot of us would dissolve into tears.

I had loved working on the picture and we were all a little sad when the final shot was in the can. Apart from anything else, the film would not be premièred in London until late in 1949, and I had no immediate prospects of making another film. Still, I had my £25 per week contract, so I had no worries. Kitty was still in London, having put up with my total absorption with my work on *The Hasty Heart*, but we decided to bide our time.

1948 had been my year of opportunity. 1949 became another year of change for me. Professionally, it began quite tepidly. *For Them That Trespass* was shown with no great impact – except on me. For the first time I appeared in a full feature film, and, whatever the result, I could at least tell my grandchildren that I had once been the star of a moving picture.

The reviews for the film were unexceptional but one or two mentioned me as showing some prospect as a screen actor. The public did not exactly flock to see the picture.

In the spring I was offered my first loan-out film role playing the lead opposite Valerie Hobson in *Interrupted Journey*. I have no idea why I was chosen for the part, since I am sure that I was by no means everybody's idea of the ideal husband for the beautiful, sophisticated Valerie. However, it was an exciting script and I soon quelled any misgivings I might have had about my suitability and jumped at the chance.

Associated British were happy, too. Their part of the proceeds would cover my entire salary for the rest of the year.

We shot most of the picture at Riverside Studios in London, but at last I did have another location sequence: two nights' shooting a train crash at the Royal Engineers' Railway School in Hampshire!

Valerie and I got on well together and worked happily in our roles. My other romantic interest in the film (the *other woman*, in fact) was the effervescent, blonde and very engaging Christine Norden.

Meanwhile, Associated British were busy building my star image, under the able tutelage of Leslie Frewin and John Parsons, who was my PR companion and guide on most of my interviews and public appearances.

One embarrassing incident really put me in my place. It happened at the annual Film Garden Party, a money-spinning event which aided the Film Benevolent Fund and was attended by thousands of avid film-goers. The objects of the public admiration – as many British, Continental and American celebrities as could be herded in – were corralled in a central enclosure with the obligatory refreshment marquee, from which they were released at regular intervals to tour the grounds and side-shows.

One of these, the autograph tent, was the Mecca of the enthusiasts. Here, lined along the open front of a small marquee, were six tables, each occupied by a celebrity busily signing autographs at half a crown a time. The donors of these signatures were changed over every quarter of an hour, and my turn came at about 3.30 p.m., when I was scheduled to report to the tent.

For once John Parsons failed me, and I was left to fend for myself. First of all, I couldn't find the entrance to the tent, so I paid my half-crown and joined the queue as my only way of gaining admission. When I reached the first table I ducked under the restraining rope and mingled with the officials. But the person in charge didn't know me. I don't think I actually said, 'Please, sir, I'm Richard Todd and I was told to report here,' but that is what I felt like. He looked at me doubtfully, scanned his list, and asked me to wait until a table became vacant. When I realised who the busy signatories were, I almost wished I had stayed in the queue. Stewart Granger, Michael Wilding, Jean Kent, Glynis Johns – I, too, was quite a film fan!

Then the first table became vacant and I was plumped into the chair. Not a single person asked me for an autograph – they were all too keen to get to the luminaries beyond me. I just sat there, twiddling my pen and trying not to look envious. Eventually a motherly London lady shoved her book before me and said, 'Never mind, dear, I'm sure you'll be very famous one day.' I could have kissed her.

That summer my improved bank balance encouraged me to believe that Kitty's parents would not look unkindly on our official engagement, so I joined her and her family for a few days at her grandmother's house in Rothesay, Isle of Bute. They all knew the purpose of my visit and kept on tactfully leaving me alone with Kitty's father. Nevertheless, when I eventually sought his approval, he burst into tears, and it was left to the redoubtable Granny Crawford to say, 'What are you crying about? Where are the drinks?'

Kitty's father said we could have either a big wedding in Glasgow Cathedral or the gift of the lease of a flat in London, but not both. So we immediately set about flat-hunting, and the date was set for Saturday, 13 August.

Then came my most exciting career opportunity since *The Hasty Heart*.

Alfred Hitchcock wanted me to play a leading part in his forthcoming film, *Stage Fright*. This was to be a star-studded movie, with a cast including Marlene Dietrich, Jane Wyman, Michael Wilding, Alastair Sim, Sybil Thorndike and Kay Walsh. To be even considered as one of that illustrious group by the great Hitch was far beyond my wildest dreams.

I had not seen the script when I went to meet him at the Savoy Hotel – I didn't need to: I'd have happily worked for him even if he made the story up as he went along.

Hitch and his wife, Alma, who was still writing the script, were very warm and friendly. They told me about the story and my part, which was to be that of a psychopathic young man manipulated by his mistress, Marlene Dietrich, into murderous activities.

The portly, pink-faced Hitchcock described all this to me with boyish enthusiasm, not at all like a movie tycoon weighing up my capabilities, but rather like an avuncular fellow-conspirator hatching a bloodthirsty plot.

I left the Savoy in a euphoric daze, scarcely able to believe what was happening. Here was I, a year away from the Dundee Rep, having just had a two-hour audience with the greatest creator of thrillers in movie history – except that on this occasion I had been the audience and he had been the presenter!

My first contact with any of the cast of *Stage Fright* was with Marlene Dietrich at a luncheon arranged for our meeting at the Savoy. Dior-clad as always, the legendary lady was still as neatly-shaped as a young girl, and with her fine-boned features and slumbrous eyes. Only her hands gave me any idea of her age – but then at that time any woman over forty seemed to me positively ancient!

I suppose I might have been rather lost for topics with this very worldly star, but Marlene had a way of taking an apparently deep interest in whatever one said. She also told me a lot about her own career, and about her interest in astrology, which she took very seriously. Even her flight to London from Los Angeles had been dated according to the advice of her special star-reader. When she heard that I was engaged to be married, she asked me for details of my birth date and also Kitty's, saying that she would send for a horoscope for us. It was just as well that I did not share her obsession, because when the horoscope reached us, it was a terrible one, forecasting no good at all for Kitty and me.

Kitty and I were married in the bombed-out ruins of St Columba's Church of Scotland in Pont Street, Belgravia. Although our new flat in Park Street, Mayfair, was ready for us, we had not yet, of course, moved in, so my launching pad for the ceremony was still my shared flat in Belgravia. Bobby Temple was to be my best man, and Tim Reeve the usher. In the event Bobby, who had taken part as a crewman in the ocean-going Fastnet Rock yacht race, was becalmed at sea, but managed to get a wireless message through to me, and Tim took over as best man.

My stag night on the evening before had started quite properly as an all-male affair, but on our return to Belgrave Mews our numbers were considerably augmented by a roistering horde of regulars from the Star Tavern who insisted on celebrating with us, and I finished up in the small hours of Saturday ferrying various people back to their homes in my car, an enormous American convertible lent to me by Harry Meadows, one of the Star fraternity, who had decided that my Railton was too draughty for such an important weekend. It poured with rain during my short tour of London, and the dawn light when I finally returned home showed my glossy vehicle to be much bedraggled and weather-soiled.

Our gathering was a mere handful of close family, apart from my best man, Tim, and Kitty's maid-of-honour, Dorothy Primrose. My only relatives present were my Aunt Eileen and my FitzPatrick cousin, Jill Campbell, and her husband Bill.

St Columba's was still a war-gutted ruin, so the ceremony was held in the Church Hall which had survived the bombing.

But for the actual moment of blessing Kitty and I, and Tim and her father as witnesses, stood for a few minutes amongst the debris and fallen masonry of the actual church, a touching moment.

Our wedding reception was held in the Hyde Park Hotel. Leslie Frewin had arranged for only two press reporters to be present and for all the pictures to be done by our own studio photographer, so it was a thoroughly enjoyable, private affair. Kitty looked enchanting, and I was immensely proud of my new status as a married man.

We left the Hyde Park Hotel in our be-ribboned Rolls and headed back to collect my car and set off for our brief honeymoon. I had been a bit worried about explaining the filthy state of my borrowed barouche, but when we arrived, there it was, shining brighter than ever before! The entire lunch-time clientele of the Star Tavern had made their contribution to my wedding by setting to and washing and polishing the gleaming monster.

Because our honeymoon period had to be brief (I had been given no more than Monday off from the film), I had booked a room at the lovely Old Bell Hotel at Hurley, near Maidenhead. This had become our favourite venue outside London for summer-time suppers and Sunday lunches and we had been fairly regular visitors. When making the reservation I had never thought to tell the management that I was being married that weekend and had merely booked a double room in my name.

It was perhaps not surprising that we were welcomed with an air of coy discretion. 'Good afternoon, Mr Todd, good afternoon, Miss. Would you like to have your tea in your room or in the garden?'

It was next morning that the parade started. First, we were called with tea; then somebody brought us the newspapers, which all carried pictures from the wedding; then a waiter came to see if we wanted breakfast; then two or three people brought us our trays; then somebody else came to see if our breakfast was satisfactory.

Married bliss was a very public affair, I reckoned.

We spent a very leisurely Sunday roving around the gorgeous Thames valley countryside, with a special stop to gaze

longingly at a particular dream-house that we had discovered
some weeks previously. It was a lovely old half-timbered,
rose-bowered, rambling place with a pretty garden surrounded by the National Trust grassland and woodland of
Maidenhead Thicket. Perhaps, one of these days . . .

On the Monday evening we settled into our Park Street
flat, feeling as happy as all newly-weds must feel as they
move into a place of their very own. And the next day I was
back at work at Elstree.

Working with Hitchcock and a clutch of very experienced
stars on *Stage Fright* was marvellous experience. Hitch was
a different being on the set from the man who had been so
warm and fatherly at our first meeting. He was cold and
distant, and I personally found it hard to decide whether I
was pleasing him or not. As soon as a shot was in the can
and the next set-up ready to be prepared, Hitchcock's normal
practice was to hand a diagram of the moves he wanted to
his assistant director and then march off the set to his office.
The actors would then go through their lines and moves for
the benefit of the camera crew, lighting-man and sound-boom
operator, and then stand-ins would take over for the process
of lighting and laying camera tracks. Only when the scene
was completely rehearsed and ready would the great man be
sent for to give his final approval. Hitch never sat around on
the set or chatted with his actors. Only when he wanted a
particularly complicated shot would he stay on set to super-
vise the preparation.

Marlene and I worked happily together. She had formed
a very close, friendly relationship with Michael Wilding, and
became almost skittish in her off-screen moments. Mike
himself was a dear – elegant, humorous, easy-going to the
point of being lackadaisical, he wandered effortlessly through
the film.

The pair I loved to watch when they were working together
were Alastair Sim and Sybil Thorndike, as they niggled at
each other in their roles as a scratchy, eccentric pair of
parents. Here were two perfect performers, both beautifully
dotty but totally controlled in their work.

Dear Jane Wyman and I struck up a warm friendship, and

she was one of the nicest, prettiest actresses that I was ever to work with. She had recently won an Oscar for her portrayal of a blind girl in *Johnny Belinda*, but she was utterly without airs and graces, and patient and unselfish in her scenes with me. It was strange that I had recently worked with her ex-husband, Ronald Reagan, and she too was sad about the breakdown of their marriage, but perhaps she had needed a cosier, less politically involved partner.

I have read suggestions that she and Hitch quarrelled. Perhaps they did not always agree, but there was certainly no animosity between them that I noticed. Quite the contrary, in fact: the pair of them even came to supper with Kitty and me in our little Park Street flat. They were our first guests.

All in all, my weeks on *Stage Fright* were momentous. And then came the première of *The Hasty Heart*.

All of us connected with that little film were sure that we had made a good picture, but were in no way prepared for the impact it would have.

Probably the only one who had any idea of its potential was the astute Leslie Frewin. The film opened at the Warner Cinema in Leicester Square, and Associated British had organised a glossy occasion, with a huge guest-list of notabilities, presumably at his suggestion.

Thanks to Frewin's careful planning, Kitty and I were able to slip from our car into the theatre almost unnoticed, and to edge quietly to our allotted position with nearly all the audience already seated. We were both terribly nervous, and I realised that most of the attention, for good or ill, would be focused on me, since the big names would not be there. As we sat down I was handed telegrams from Vincent Sherman, Ronald Reagan and Patricia Neal, and their good wishes heartened me.

Within moments of our arrival the lights faded, and the programme started, beginning with the usual short preliminary features. Then the credits for *The Hasty Heart* began to roll. My hands were sweating and my heart was thumping. But as the film ran on, all the audience reactions seemed to be appreciative; there were laughs in the right places and apparently rapt silences during the more dramatic bits.

Now, as I have mentioned before, sentimentality comes rather easily to me, I'm afraid. I have the greatest difficulty in holding back my snuffles during moving scenes in a film, even one that I have been in myself, and this occasion was no exception. Mercifully, I began to notice that I was not the only viewer in this embarrassing state. All around me in the dim light I could see eyes being dabbed and hear noses being soggily blown.

As the film reached its tragi-comic finale, there was utter silence, except for the continuous nasal trumpeting throughout the cinema.

Then, as the film ended, Leslie Frewin's crafty machinations became apparent. Within seconds, Kitty and I found ourselves bathed in spot lights, and scrambled to our feet as the entire audience rose to their feet and began to applaud in our direction, cheering and clapping. I have never seen anything like this in any cinema.

Presently I became aware of Leslie Frewin beckoning to us from the side-aisle. We shuffled along our row of seats and were led up the steps to the rear exit. Nobody else moved until we had disappeared from the auditorium. Then, as we began our descent from the exit, we saw that the foyer was jammed. There was no way out through the main entrance doors, and even Frewin seemed at a loss to know how to get us to our car.

Apparently, even outside the Warner, word had got around that something unusual had happened, and crowds began to gather in Leicester Square, holding up traffic until extra police were called to sort things out.

Meanwhile, Kitty and I and various ABPC high-ups were crammed into an office. It was then that a jubilant Robert Clark suggested that we should all go and celebrate somewhere – but where, at that hour? I suggested a Jermyn Street night-club where I had membership. It was agreed that we should all meet up there, and the party was to be on Associated British.

Kitty and I were eventually escorted to our car and driven away. I mention this scene in detail not to impress, but because it happened, and was probably unique. I realise that attention was focused on me because I was the only leading member of the film's cast present, but it is still something to savour in my memory.

After a brief but very happy party in Jermyn Street some of my merriment was slightly doused when I realised that I would have to sign the bill, as the only member present. I never did recoup my outlay from the Corporation.

When I finished work on *Stage Fright*, Kitty and I went up to Scotland for a holiday with her parents. On our way back we stopped at a farm, near Catterick in Yorkshire, where a sign advertised golden retrievers for sale. As it happened there was none of that breed available, but we were shown a sweet little corgi bitch instead, already a year old but unsold. Wendy, the gentlest little dog I have ever known, became part of our lives.

Then, in November, came the next unexpected summons: I was to go to Hollywood to make a film for Warner Brothers. We were to travel to New York on the *Queen Elizabeth*, arriving there just after Christmas.

The next month or so was spent in a flurry of preparation. Kitty had been granted a very generous clothes allowance by Associated British, and I too had a few visits to Cyril Castle, my tailor. The only sorrowing member of the family was Wendy, who by some instinct seemed to divine that she was to be left behind. As we busily packed wardrobe trunks and cabin trunks, she sat around looking miserable. Kitty's parents came down to see us off and to take the little dog home to Scotland with them.

18

GO WEST, YOUNG MAN

Our five days on the *Queen Elizabeth* were sheer bliss. We had been allotted one of the principal staterooms, almost next, may I say, to the suite occupied by the Duke and Duchess of Windsor, the nearest either of us had ever been to sharing a habitat with a member of the Royal Family, apart from my previous experience in the Royal loo at Balmoral.

It was a thrilling trip, not least because there were no food-rationing strictures. For the first time in years we could wade into unrestricted dishfuls of luxury cuisine. We had been honoured by being seated at the captain's table, but after the first evening we dined alone in the very special night-club – the Starlight Room, I think it was called. Oh, the joys of an unlimited expense account. Apart from our attacks on the gourmet menus, Alka Seltzer was our staple diet!

On the day we docked in New York, I was asked if I would like to come up to the bridge to see the Statue of Liberty as we passed that venerable lady. The only other non-mariner on the bridge was the Duke of Windsor, muffled to the eyes in a heavy Ulster coat. Although he must have passed the Statue many times, he seemed as excited and impressed by the occasion as I was, his surprisingly powerful voice booming out happily.

After disembarking in New York we spent a few days there either exploring, mostly on foot, or wandering round the big stores on Fifth Avenue, goggling at the lavish displays of merchandise, in such contrast to the still austere shops of London. We both needed to buy extra luggage to accommodate our purchases.

The weather was crisp and cold, so we both dressed as we would have done in London, I in a dark suit and overcoat and topped with my bowler hat, a furled umbrella completing my winter wear. As we strolled on our first morning down Fifth Avenue I was disconcertedly aware of very curious stares from some of the passers-by. A few even turned round for a second look. I did not flatter myself that I was being recognised, and wondered what was wrong with me. The fact that we did not see in America another bowler hat, except worn with evening dress, did not sink in for some time.

With typical thoughtfulness, Warners had decided that we would like to see across America, so, instead of flying us to Los Angeles, they had arranged a 'Drawing-Room' for us on the Chief, a splendid train that took three days and nights to cross the continent, with a short break in Chicago.

On 31 December 1949, we were ushered aboard at Grand Central Station and ensconced in a large compartment which was a sofa-ed sitting-room by day and a double bedroom at night. The vast size of America made such luxuries quite routine for those who could afford them: we couldn't, but Warner Brothers could.

During the first few hours I found our compartment rather stuffy and overheated, so I opened the window to let in some air. Within minutes an irate attendant came in and banged it shut again, clearly taking a poor view of my ignorant stupidity. I had apparently upset the air-conditioning system of the entire train by lowering the temperature in our room, thus causing oven-like heat in the others. Obviously, we had a lot to learn about new-fangled gadgets!

As we passed through the flatlands of Ohio and later Illinois the outlook was pretty dreary and veiled in mist and rain. This was not the time of year to see the countryside at its best. After Chicago, however, our journey was far more interesting and scenically exciting. We went through the rugged terrain of Colorado, New Mexico and Arizona and climbed between the gorges and peaks of the Rocky Mountains, following the old Santa Fe trail.

During our second day on the Chief we were joined by a PR man who recorded an interview with me purporting to be a chat with Louella Parsons, the fabled Hollywood columnist. The PRO read her questions and remarks to me, and I replied. Later she filled in the tape with her own voice, and the interview was broadcast over radio networks the night before we arrived in LA as though it had been made by radio-telephone, complete with train noises. I was soon to meet the redoubtable Louella.

On 3 January we pulled in at Pasadena Station, about twenty miles from central LA, at 7.55 a.m. and were met by Carl Schaefer, a Warner Brothers representative. Our heavy luggage was trucked to our hotel, and Carl took us in a limousine for a short tour of the area. The Beverly Hills suburb was charming, with some splendid houses and beautifully kept gardens, few of them fenced in front, but with walled or hedged private area at the back, nearly all with the statutory swimming-pool. Hollywood itself was disappointingly scruffy and garish and the famous Boulevard was dreadfully unattractive. I was soon to realise that Hollywood was not any more the centre of the film industry, and certainly not where many of the film fraternity lived.

Our worst disappointment was the hotel into which we had been booked. It was a downtown (central) building, in an area that we did not like, and had the most depressing decor whose main motif seemed to be acres of green wallpaper depicting what I took to be banana leaves. However, we were given no time to mope about.

Our arrival at the hotel was the beginning of the most hectic three weeks I had ever experienced. We had no time to unpack, let alone relax, before a group of press photographers and reporters arrived. Then, at 11 o'clock, Carl Schaefer collected me again to drive me to the Warner Studios at Burbank, some miles away. At 11.30 I was to meet Jack L. Warner, the head of the company.

On the way to Burbank, I jotted down on a scrap of paper some of the points I wanted to make. Mainly, they were:

(1) I wanted us to be moved to the Beverly Hills Hotel, which I had heard was the nicest one in the region.

(2) I didn't want an expense account. Rather than sign for everything, I wanted a set sum of dollars per week so that I could handle my own budget.

(3) I did not want to be chauffeured everywhere, but

wanted to drive my own car, whether a hired one or a studio car.

Now, I had never met a real, live US movie mogul before, and had no idea what was in store for me. I was soon to find that the head of a major American film corporation was a sort of mini-Emperor, before whom strong men quailed, and who ruled his minions with a divine authority. At the studio I was introduced to various executives who were all extremely pleasant. I was then told that the Great Man himself was ready to see me, but nobody told me that this was a most unusual honour. I just concluded that this was the usual form, and thought how nice and friendly it was.

I was guided through a series of outer offices or ante-chambers before we eventually arrived at the Holy of Holies.

It was a large room with a dais at the far end, on which, behind a huge desk, sat Jack Warner, a smallish, neat man with a tanned face adorned by a narrow moustache, pencil-darkened. I have been told that one of the Hollywood Tsars (I believe, Louis B. Mayer) once had an audience with the Pope in Rome, and had been very impressed with the placement of the Papal throne on a raised platform. Since then, a similarly elevated position had become the norm for some of Hollywood's leading citizens. Ranged around the room were various executives.

Mr Warner could not have been nicer or more welcoming. He said he was glad to see me, that he had loved *The Hasty Heart* and that he hoped I would be happy working in California. If there was anything I wanted, I was only to ask.

I needed no further prompting. Pulling my crumpled piece of paper from my pocket, I ran through my list of requests, blissfully unaware of the shudder of horror that must have run around the room. This had certainly not been the intended purpose of my unusual interview: such impertinent trivialities should not have been aired in the inner sanctum.

But Jack Warner never for one moment lost his benevolent smile as he heard me out. Finally, he said, 'Sure, Dick,' and, turning to the studio head, Mr Trilling, he said, 'Fix it, will you, Steve.' And that was that!

Before the end of the day I had collected a brand-new Ford Mercury, been given one thousand dollars for my first week's expenses, and was told that we would move to the Beverly Hills Hotel at the weekend.

Late that afternoon I drove the Mercury from the studio garage back to join Kitty at the hotel, and finally managed to unpack and have a much-needed bath.

We had been invited to drinks with Jane Wyman at her house, and from there we all went on to Don The Beachcomber's Restaurant for a dinner at which we first tasted the delights of Hawaiian-style food and those delicious rum-based drinks which seem so innocuous but which have a mule-kick in their fruity depths. One of my favourites became a Missionary's Downfall, which I strove not to make my own undoing.

At midnight we got back to the hotel, exhausted and slightly tiddly. What a day it had been!

Before I climbed into the gigantic king-sized bed I dutifully sat down to write the first commissioned pages of *My Hollywood Diary*, which I was to dispatch weekly to *Picturegoer Magazine,* Britain's most popular weekly film fan journal. Every day henceforth I had this task to complete.

The next day I again visited the studio and had a snack lunch in the large general dining-room, which was called the commisary. I looked at the menu, and decided that I would simply have ham with a fried egg. My waitress, a toothsome blonde typical of the legion of aspiring starlets who waited for the big break as they worked in drug-stores, restaurants and shops all over Hollywood smiled invitingly and said, 'How d'you like it – straight up or over easy?'

I'd had a few direct approaches in my time, but this one was totally unexpected.

Seeing my startled look, she rescued me. 'The egg – d'you want it fried both sides or just one?'

I said I would like it straight up, please. But I'm not sure I wasn't a little disappointed.

That evening we were summoned to Hedda Hopper's house for drinks and an interview. It seemed that the two rival columnist queens of Hollywood, Hopper and Louella Parsons, only gave audiences in their own homes and heaven help the unfortunate who did not immediately respond to the invitation. In those days the power and the spite of the gossip writers could be frightening, and I had been warned to try to keep in their good books.

This was something that scared me about Hollywood: there was no privacy and very little respect for the personal feelings of those who had to swim in the film colony's goldfish bowl.

We found Miss Hopper quite pleasant, handsome and forthright.

I still had no idea what sort of film I was going to be making, but I suspected that Warners had probably dug up some subject from their script archives and were rushing to cash in on the success of *The Hasty Heart*. I was not unduly worried; I reckoned I was lucky to be in Hollywood at all.

The following morning we were both asked to be at the studio to meet Henry Blanke, the producer, and the great old King Vidor, who was going to direct the picture. They were both extremely nice, especially King Vidor, who was a quiet-spoken, rugged man with a nice twinkle of humour.

They told me that the film was to be *Lightning Strikes Twice*, with a story set in cattle-ranching country, and I was to be a rancher. They assured me that the script was being adapted for me to explain my English background, and would be ready in a few days. Thank God I could at least ride a horse!

My co-star was to be Ruth Roman and the other leading players were to be Mercedes McCambridge and Zachary Scott. So we would have a pretty strong line-up – but what sort of script, I wondered?

We lunched later with a journalist from *Life* magazine.

That evening, our third in Hollywood, we had our first experience of a big 'professional' private party. It was, in a sense, our unveiling to a large gathering of local notables, and I had never met so many famous people in the space of a couple of hours. Amongst those we talked with were James Mason, Cecil B. de Mille, Reginald Gardner, Lauren Bacall, Sir Charles Mendl, David Niven, Joan Crawford, Loretta Young, Caesar Romero, Clifton Webb, Jeanne Craine, Humphrey Bogart, Ronald Colman and James Stewart. We would certainly be able to do some name-dropping when we returned home!

That was the special peculiarity of Hollywood: it was a close-knit colony where everybody knew everybody else (and supposedly everything about them, too) and were all involved in some way in the same industry. In London you could live for years without meeting many fellow actors except those that you actually worked with.

On the Friday I was again at the studio for a lunch-time interview with a fan magazine journalist, and in the evening Kitty and I went to Louella Parsons' house for the obligatory session with Hedda Hopper's great rival. We had already met in a way through the interview I had recorded for her on the train and she was apparently very pleased that she had had first bite at the cherry. She could not have been more friendly, and finished up by presenting me with a splendid gold Baume and Mercier watch which I used for years.

On Saturday we had lunch at Romanoff's with Felix Ferry, who, with Milton Pickman, was Al Parker's associate in California. Ferry and Pickman, a small agency, was to represent me in Hollywood and handle any professional problems I might have there.

'Fefe' Ferry, of mid-European origin, was a delightful man with an abundance of social graces. Amusing and witty, he was much sought-after as a guest in the leading power-houses of the colony and was on very friendly terms with most of the moguls, especially Darryl Zanuck. His chief contribution to the Ferry and Pickman partnership derived mainly from his contacts, but I was soon to find that Milton Pickman was the brains and the negotiator of the duo, with his enormous knowledge of the movie business and his keen intelligence.

That afternoon we moved to the Beverly Hills Hotel, with its palm-filled gardens, tennis courts, huge pool, most likeable staff and its famed Polo Lounge.

We had dinner with Jennings Lang, an agent working with the Jaffé Agency, one of the largest. He was a persuasive and well-informed talker and soon had me worrying about my professional set-up. He was also a very smooth and liberal host. He convinced me that I needed top-class advice and representation here, and was most disparaging about Ferry and Pickman, whom he dismissed as being a small, ineffectual and unprestigious partnership. His own agency, Jaffé, was the sort that could really handle my burgeoning career. I was destined for big things in Hollywood, of that he was sure. Furthermore, he was certain that I should stay in America, and that a number of the major production companies would be interested in buying my contract from Associated British and offering me long-term deals in Hollywood.

This was a suggestion that I was to hear many times, and if I had been a bit more worldly-wise I would perhaps have given it more thought. But two considerations were always obstacles to any such decision: first, Associated British had given me my first chance and deserved my loyalty (what I didn't realise was that if ABPC had been paid enough compensation they would probably have been happy to show an instant profit), and, secondly, I was very British in my outlook and way of life, and could not imagine living happily anywhere else.

I was pretty naive and unenterprising in my thinking, as events subsequently proved. But I don't complain.

Nevertheless, I did decide that I should write to Robert Clark and Al Parker voicing my misgivings.

When Jennings Lang had left us I was glad to join Ronald Reagan and a friend of his for coffee, and talk of less worrisome things till a very late hour. Ronald was his old, bantering, amusing self, and cheered us up considerably.

Monday saw the start of another pretty active week. The morning began with an early phone call from Logan Gourlay of the British *Sunday Express*, then continued at the Burbank studio where I had a photo session and a guitar lesson. The latter was directed towards a song I was to deliver in the film. Little did they know! We eventually shot the scene, but it was wisely cut out of the finished picture. I still have a recording of my ditty, and it can be guaranteed to bring mirth to the most sober gathering.

I lunched with one of Warners' publicity chiefs, and we spent all afternoon at Ace Hudkin's ranch. Ace Hudkin provided horses for films, all kinds of horses and all trained for Hollywood's particular requirements. Coach horses, cavalry horses, Indian cayuses, cattle ponies, English saddle horses: they had them all. Kicking horses, rearing horses,

biting horses, falling horses: they had them, too. With so
many Wild West and American historical epics being produced in those days there was a big market for the right
horses, unlike in England, where I was once provided with
a weedy animal who had to have a false tail strapped on
because he only had a moth-eaten stump covering his backside. He had been chosen because he could be guaranteed
to stand still during takes and not flinch at the clappers. The
problem was to keep him awake and open-eyed during
scenes.

The ranch gave me Reno, a pretty little black cow-pony
with white socks and blaze, to practise Western-style riding
and to use throughout the film.

I had a fascinating afternoon learning to 'sit-in' to the
high-pommelled Western saddle and long stirrup leathers
and how to 'bend' my horse at full gallop by just neck-reining
and weight transference; how also to gallop up to a hitching
post and get off at the crucial moment before the horse
actually stopped. Those cattle ponies are trained to slam on
the brakes and come to a sliding halt as soon as the rider's
right leg begins to swing across their backs; the rider's own
momentum completes the dismount.

The pattern of press interviews, horse and guitar sessions
and social events continued throughout our second week.
The whole of Wednesday was taken up with photo sessions,
for *Vogue* first and then six hours of photography for *Life*.
And that evening we attended our first and most unforget-
table private dinner party.

Our hostess was Joan Crawford. We arrived at her imposing house and were announced by a manservant from the
drawing-room door as we entered. Miss Crawford herself,
resplendent in a silver creation and a very elaborate hair-do,
introduced us to her collection of famous guests, and was
absolutely charming.

The pre-dinner cocktail period was in full and chatty swing
when Miss Crawford's two adopted children were brought
in. A silence fell as the boy and girl were required by their
mother to go round bowing and curtsying to each individual
in turn – a curious over-emphasis on formality, I thought at
the time, and patently embarrassing for the children.

However the atmosphere soon eased once we were at table and the excellent food and wines were circulated.

I was seated opposite Miss Crawford at the table, a large intervening candelabrum making a certain amount of dodging necessary during conversation. On my right was George Cukor, the director. He was very affable and seemingly interested in my film career – all eighteen months of it. His spectacles bore the thickest pebble lenses I had ever seen, and he suffered from Hollywood's occupational disease: ulcers. He was not served food like the rest of us, but as each course arrived so he helped himself to the contents of some mysterious little china pots that had been placed beside him on a small wine table.

As the splendid meal continued, Miss Crawford clearly became slightly tiddly. At one point, peering round the candelabrum as she talked to me, she was bothered by a strand of the elaborate coiffure that had fallen down over her face. Hardly pausing for breath, she tugged out the offending hair-piece, muttered 'Aw, shit!' and draped it over the arm of the candle-holder.

After dinner we all repaired to the pool-room, a very large, comfortable place complete with bar and cinema projection-room. To my amazement and some embarrassment we were then subjected to a full screening of *The Hasty Heart*. Miss Crawford had seen the picture, liked it, and was kindly making sure that it should be seen as widely as possible.

My first meeting with my leading lady, Ruth Roman, took place on the following Monday at the studio, where we both lunched with Gerry Ascher. I found her to be an extremely attractive, dark-eyed beauty with a figure as alluring as her face.

I think she found me a bit stuffy. Until, that is, talking about tennis, I said I'd love to have a knock-up with her sometime.

Her startled look told me that I had said something amiss, but after Gerry hurriedly explained the difference between the English and the American meanings for the expression, her giggle helped to break the ice, and we discovered that we were going to enjoy working together.

That week I also read the first half of the script of *Lightning*

Strikes Twice and did not much like it. It seemed to me contrived and heavy, with hammy dialogue. I felt depressed about it. Here was I, on the threshold of a potentially international screen career, and here was the clumsy, soggy vehicle that I and my fellow actors were being offered.

On Friday I had my most significant meeting of all when we dined with Milton Pickman, my agent. For the next ten years or so, until he left the agency business for other advisory and administrative posts, Milton was to be my mentor and counsellor, and the most creative and imaginative adviser I would ever know. Quiet-spoken, dark-suited and humorous, with an encyclopaedic knowledge of all that went on in the film industry (and of those who made it all happen), he was to have a wise and helpful influence over my career.

A few days later I had a long meeting with King Vidor about the script, and found that we were broadly in agreement about its shortcomings. Otherwise the time was taken up with the usual pattern of guitar lessons, riding, wardrobe fittings, and a series of sessions with the *Life* magazine journalist who also covered a luncheon ceremony where I had to receive a Motion Picture Council award for *The Hasty Heart*. And then, on the Thursday, we dined at King Vidor's house, high above Hollywood and with staggering views across the city and out to sea.

Our arrival there was ignominious. I stopped in the road by the gates, but could find no way of opening them. There were no bolts or handles or latches visible on the outside. When I shinned up to look inside, I stared down at two snarling guard dogs. I tried shouting, but the only response was from the dogs. I went back to the car and just when Kitty and I were about to turn back and look for a public phone-box, luckily another car drove up. In it was Roger Furze, the British designer, who was better accustomed than we to the wonders of American technology. 'Just drive up to them,' he said, 'and they'll open automatically.' This we did and all was well – at least it was until after dinner. When we came to leave, the battery of my car was flat because I had apparently failed to switch off the radio or something. King himself came to the rescue by helping to push us out onto the hill where we got a running start.

Next morning I took the car to the studio garage and asked them to change or charge the battery. That afternoon I drove away in a new car. Obviously that was easier than messing about with the battery.

During that day I had a long session with King modifying the script, and later we dined, again at Romanoff's, with Milton, Fefe Ferry and Lew Schreiber, the head of 20th Century Fox Studios. After dinner Milton drove us for the weekend at Palm Springs, over one hundred miles away, where we stayed at the Racquet Club, a famous sports and social centre run then by Charles Farrell, a former screen star.

The weekend had been King Vidor's idea, partly so that we could work together and partly so that we could see another aspect of Hollywood life: weekends in the desert resorts. We didn't do much work, but I certainly saw other aspects of Hollywood life.

When we arrived the bar was thronged. One of the first people I bumped into was Jennings Lang, who, to my amazement, greeted Milton with a bear-hug and great friendliness. Remembering his disparagement of Milton a few days previously, I found the situation embarrassing, and as soon as I could, I told Milton what Lang had been saying about him. He was hugely amused. 'I'd have done the same,' he chuckled, 'if you had been *his* client. It's the way we deal here.'

I had a lot to learn.

Our bungalow at the club was very comfortable, but we didn't spend much time in it, except to sleep. On Saturday morning Milton drove us around Palm Springs, showing us the smart homes of the Hollywood hierarchy; then I spent the afternoon with King, with whom I had formed a real rapport as we revised the *Lightning Strikes Twice* script. In the evening we joined in a dinner-dance at the club, and around midnight were whisked by car over the encircling hills to the Double 'O' Ranch, a gambling centre, which we did not greatly enjoy. Neither of us was particularly enthusiastic about craps or poker, and we had already drunk enough for one day. We stuck it out and were glad to crawl into bed at about 4 a.m.

On Sunday we both felt pretty awful. For a while we
watched Big Bill Tilden, the club professional, play tennis
and then I did some more work with King. Milton drove us
back to the Beverly Hills, dined with us at La Rue, and left
at 10.30 p.m.

On the Monday and Tuesday Ruth Roman and I had script
readings and rehearsals on the set and on Wednesday, 1
February, I did my first shots in a Hollywood movie. The
studio atmosphere was pretty well what I had been used to,
and the entire crew were friendly and helpful. I enjoyed
working with Ruth Roman, and we got along well together.
Altogether, the film had started nicely and the rushes were
excellent.

But the week was clouded by the fact that Kitty felt unwell
and finally needed to call a doctor. It was a couple of weeks
before she was her real self again.

During that week I also had various meetings with Milton
Pickman, who had been testing the Hollywood market for
me. He was quite definite in his opinion that I should allow
my ABPC contract to be bought out by one of the American
companies interested in me, and that I should settle in
California. I was equally adamant that I wouldn't do anything
to upset Associated British, to whom I owed my film career
anyway, and that I preferred to be based in Britain. During
all the ensuing weeks in America these discussions continued,
and to this day I am not certain that I made the right
decisions. Almost certainly I didn't financially, but I have
always managed to flounder along, and have almost all that
I could wish for. I thank God for what I have, and sometimes
ask Him if I could have a bit more.

On the Friday I had dinner at Romanoff's with Nat
Bronsten, a British film producer, and Frederick Weil, whom
I had met casually at the hotel. Freddie Weil, a tall, lean,
most charming man, was to become one of my closest and
dearest friends. That evening we found we had a lot in
common to talk about, including films, in several of which
he had a financial interest. He was a man of considerable
wealth who had sold his main business and was semi-retired,
devoting most of his time to his stud farm and racing stables
in Berkshire.

The first two weeks of filming were going well and towards the end of the second week I had a free day, so we lunched with Milton Pickman in the Polo Lounge at the Beverly Hills Hotel. It was during the two-hour session with delectable tossed salads with Roquefort dressing that I had my first experience of what a really creative and aggressive agent can do.

Milton had asked me what we would do when the filming was finished and had suggested that we should spend a week or so in New York. I had replied that we could not possibly afford that. 'Sure you can,' said Milton, 'I'll fix it.'

He then asked for a telephone to be brought to the table, called a New York number and spoke to some contact of his there. With the time difference between the East and West Coasts it would have been mid-morning there.

He explained that I would be in New York for a week or two in April and would be available to do a radio play. He put the phone down and grinned at me. 'Just hang on,' he said, 'they'll jump at it.'

Within minutes the phone rang. The New Yorker said it so happened that a leading radio producer had been putting together a major production of *Great Expectations* and my dates would be just perfect for it. Leave it to him, Milton's contact said, and he would see what he could set up. Milton said he could only give him half-an-hour as I needed to finalise my plans.

Within thirty minutes New York rang back again. Yes, they had a sponsor – The American Steel Corporation – and how about doing the broadcast with Joan Fontaine and a top cast? They offered fifteen hundred dollars. Overhearing this, I reckoned that would do nicely, but Milton slammed the phone down, saying they must have been joking. 'Don't worry. They'll be back,' he assured me. In seconds, they were indeed back. How about two thousand dollars? Milton said he couldn't even mention such a derisory figure to me. If they offered three thousand he could put the proposition to me, but didn't think that I would go for it. They agreed, so he said he would talk to me.

By now I was almost gibbering with anxiety, but he calmed

me down. 'They want you for this show, and they'll pay for you,' he said.

Finally he rang New York and said he had talked to me. He said the least I would contemplate accepting would be four thousand dollars, but he had an idea: as we were theatre buffs, if they would guarantee two house seats for any plays of our choice every evening in New York, he thought I might just be persuaded to accept three thousand five hundred. They agreed, so Milton had a further break for consultation with me. When he rang them back, the deal was completed.

Three and a half thousand dollars – that was a lot of money in 1950! Kitty was still pretty tired, but cheered up a lot when I bought her her first mink cape.

The next ten days were to be spent on location at Victorville, in the Mojave Desert. It was here that Reno and I would be able to show off our cowboy training.

Kitty and I stayed at, and I was filming around, a working ranch called North Verde, owned by the Kemper-Campbell family. The ranch-house itself was a very beautiful old Spanish-style adobe building with a first-floor gallery and lots of exposed timbers.

The area round about Victorville – a real Wild West town, complete with swing-doored saloon – abounded in small dude ranches which herded nothing more bovine than tourists and townie cowboys hobbling painfully in their high-heeled boots, but North Verde ran a large herd of cattle and had a fine Palomino stud. The ranch-hands were friendly and let me join them on Reno for some of their cattle drives and singling exercises, where certain cattle had to be separated from the main herd. Reno knew exactly what to do and all I had to do was to hang on as he twisted and turned. One evening a few of the lads took me for a long ride, fording a river, and we had a delicious barbecue supper over a brush-wood fire. I did some filming as well, of course, but that Victorville location was more like a very pleasant holiday.

I suppose the biggest moment for me came one evening when Jack Warner himself telephoned with the news that I had been nominated for the Best Actor award at the forthcoming Motion Picture Academy Oscar ceremony for my work in *The Hasty Heart*. He congratulated me warmly.

Back in Hollywood, on the Tuesday, we saw a preview of *Stage Fright*, together with Marlene Dietrich. It was not a vintage Hitchcock film, I'm afraid. I found it slow, over-theatrical and nowhere near as gripping as most of his films. At supper afterwards at Romanoff's with Marlene and Milton and Stewart Granger, we all shared the same dismal reaction.

That week I took possession of my first acting award. I had been voted Best Newcomer Actor by the Hollywood Foreign Correspondents Association and was presented with the Golden Globe, along with other recipients in the various categories, at a dinner where the awards were handed over by Olivia de Haviland and Gene Kelly.

That week I also received my first lesson in the need to be wary of the Hollywood gossip-column press – the very next day after the Golden Globe presentation, in fact.

I had left early in the morning with the rest of the unit and Ruth Roman for a day's location shooting in the Hollywood Hills. We expected to shoot until the light failed in the early evening, and I planned to get back to the hotel for a late dinner with Kitty, probably at about nine or ten o'clock. As it happened, though, we moved quicker than the schedule had allowed, and were back in the studio at Burbank by the early afternoon, where most of us headed for cold drinks at a nearby bar, celebrating an unexpectedly short day's work. On my way to pick up my car I began to have qualms about the drive back over the hills to the hotel, and decided that maybe I had better wait a while. Ruth came to my rescue, suggesting that I should stop off for coffee at her house, which was on my way. Nothing loath, I followed her.

Meanwhile, Milton Pickman had lunched with Kitty and at about three o'clock he rang the Warner studio to ask when they expected my unit back from location. He was told that we had already returned and that I had, in fact, set off for home a while ago. Alarm bells began to ring in various quarters, whilst I was seated happily in Ruth Roman's house, drinking coffee and feeling much more stable.

I was horrified when the studio phoned Ruth to ask if I was with her, as there was concern over my whereabouts. I don't think Ruth was too pleased either. I hurriedly thanked her, apologised for the embarrassment, and sped off.

When I arrived at the hotel it was still only late afternoon, but a very worried Kitty and Milton were relieved to see me. What a storm in a coffee cup!

It was the next morning that the full impact of my stupidity hit us. There it was: an exclusive in the Florabel Muir gossip column. Photographs of myself and Ruth Roman were captioned 'visitor' and 'visited', and the accompanying article was riddled with explicit innuendo.

My first reaction was to phone Muir herself. I was staggered by her answer. 'What's the matter? Don't you like it? Look, Dick, you've got the Oscars coming up soon. You need publicity.' She really seemed to think that she had done me a favour.

I phoned Pickman, who told me to forget the whole thing. 'Treat it as a comedy of errors, and never, *never* start a press feud. They will always find something about you that you wouldn't want to have published, and they'll get you in the end.'

It was an upsetting episode for us and must have been equally unpleasant for Ruth. I tried to phone her, but she was kept incommunicado by Warners for a couple of days.

The salacious interest of the press in the private lives of members of the film colony was the single most unpleasant aspect of Hollywood in those days. But I suppose it was only to be expected. Wasn't it President Truman who said, 'If you can't stand the heat, get out of the kitchen'?

Fortunately, on this occasion we had the weekend to recover our wind.

Our routine from then on remained fairly unvaried: filming continued, and Milton never ceased to work on projects for me and to try to persuade me to stay on in California. One break, however, was a radio play which I rehearsed and broadcast locally, sponsored by Hallmark Greetings Cards. In those pre-TV days radio shows had a big audience and, of course, were choppped into quarter-hour segments by commercials.

All went well with the broadcast and Hallmark Greetings Cards were duly plugged in the little pauses. The next pro-gramme was to be sponsored by a well-known brand of deodorant soap, and the announcer achieved his link by thanking me and Hallmark Greetings Cards for a very entertaining play and, without pause for breath, going on to enjoin me not to forget, Richard Todd, that Dial Deodorant Soap is the one for you. I had never publicly been told so clearly by a stranger what even my best friends could not tell me.

On 23 March Kitty and I attended the Motion Picture Academy Award (Oscar) presentation ceremony. It was then at Grauman's Chinese Theatre – a conventional cinema, I hasten to add, but with a vaguely Oriental design – with a good deal of public interest, though inevitably not on today's world-wide scale.

There were five nominees for each category, such as mine for Best Actor, and we were all allotted seats convenient to the centre aisle.

I had been warned not to expect to win the award in my category, as it had been gained the previous year, 1949, by Laurence Olivier for his epic *Hamlet*, and was unlikely to go abroad for a second consecutive time. Also, a couple of extremely popular American actors who had given years of fine service were contenders, and were bound to be viewed sympathetically by the Academy voters. As with all awards there were many factors, commercial and emotional, which affected the judging. I was to be a recipient several times in the future, but I have no illusions as to my comparative merit. Awards are nice publicity razzamatazz for the film and theatre industries and the nominees and productions concerned, but are objectively pretty meaningless. The only award I shall ever truly deserve is a long service medal – when, in the near future, I have completed fifty years in the business.

So on this particular occasion I was able to take a very relaxed view of the proceedings.

Afterwards we joined Stewart Granger, Deborah Kerr and Ruth Roman at Romanoff's for a dinner-dance, and had a very enjoyable evening, getting home in the small hours. Not surprisingly, Ruth Roman and I were not at our best at the studios the next day.

Lightning Strikes Twice was by now nearly completed, and the last two weeks entailed doing bits and pieces of pick-up shots, extra scenes, re-takes and hours of sound-dubbing from the location sequences.

Meanwhile, poor Kitty too found herself in a gossip column. She had been at the hotel pool one afternoon and had briefly talked with a man who had just returned from London and who professed to be an admirer of mine, having seen *The Hasty Heart*. He was apparently in the legal profession.

Next day Hedda Hopper had a paragraph in her column saying how sad it was that my bride of only a few months was already considering divorce proceedings and had been seen in deep discussion with one of Hollywood's leading divorce lawyers. When I got home that evening Kitty was in tears, having been unable to contact me all day as I was on location.

I managed to convince her of the wisdom of Pickman's advice to forget it. We were both learning the hard way.

On my last day at the studio I handed back my studio Mercury and in the evening I gave a farewell party to as many of our friends as I could muster, and Milton had arranged a private room at the Beachcomber, whose Hawaiian food and rum-based, fruity drinks we loved.

On Tuesday, 11 April, we were seen off for New York at LA Airport by Carl Schaeffer and the usual bunch of photographers, for whose benefit I was presented with a pair of Western boots as I mounted the gangway, this presumably to encourage my cowboy image in *Lightning Strikes Twice*.

That day in her column Hedda Hopper mentioned our departure, said we had been very popular and rejoiced in the solidity of our marriage by writing, 'And I am happy to say that Kitty is no longer contemplating divorce.' That was nice of her . . .

The next morning, in New York, I started rehearsals for *Great Expectations*, with, amongst others, Joan Fontaine, Francis L. Sullivan, Denis Hoey and Bill Owen. On the following Sunday we were on the air as part of the 'Theatre Guild of the Air' series, and our radio show went very well.

Our days in New York were pretty active. After the broadcast we stayed on for a final week of theatre-going, window-shopping, sightseeing and lunches and dinners with friends.

Our last day in New York was made especially exciting for me when I received a cable from London telling me that I had won the *Daily Mail* National Film Award as Best Actor for my part in *The Hasty Heart*. This particular prize was then Britain's premier screen award. With all my reservations about the awards system, I still have to admit that it is gratifying to gain one. I could not have hoped for a better send-off from New York.

My first stay in America, every week of the fifteen I had spent there, had been significant for me both personally and professionally. I had met several important people who would later influence my film career and I had made some lasting friendships, not least with Milton Pickman, who remained for years my adviser even when no longer an agent.

I had learned a bit about the dangers and delights of the Hollywood scene. Success meant a pampered existence; failure could be devastating and pathetic. The in-betweens just swam for their lives. I had seen examples of each type, and thanked God that I, at least temporarily, seemed to be in the upper bracket.

The competition at all levels in that community was fierce, and the pressures ever-present. No wonder marriages were under strain when so many actors and actresses were by trade professional charmers often thrown together in distant places and in emotional, intimate scenes.

I had also come to know, respect and enormously like Americans. Their open-hearted generosity and hospitality were almost embarrassing, especially when one had no means of returning it. One trait of theirs that I especially admired was their tremendous patriotism; even quite recent immigrants seemed to be imbued with fervent loyalty to the Stars and Stripes. Another was their admiration for success, and their lack of envy of those who had attained it or were on their way to it.

All these thoughts must have passed through my mind as we sailed eastwards from New York. It had been an incredible twelve months for me: marriage, the blossoming of my film career, a benevolent Providence and experiences far beyond my imagining had all been there to look back on. *The Hasty Heart* had put me into a stellar orbit, and my stay and acceptance in Hollywood had confirmed a degree of international status, whatever the outcome of *Lightning Strikes Twice*. I could scarce believe my good fortune. It all seemed so far away from the Workman's Hall in Ebbw Vale or a slit trench in Normandy.

And to look forward to? Well, there would be Wendy the corgi waiting for us at the flat, and the Railton to receive the new clutch assembly that I had bought at the Hudson Motors factory in Los Angeles.

And more films and visits to America, I hoped.

Quite a lot, in fact.

19

I SHOT AN ARROW IN THE AIR

It was love at first sight for both of us. I have to confess that the moment those gorgeous amber-brown eyes met mine I was without thought for the consequences. However much my conscience reminded me that I had other responsibilities, the youthful legginess, the immature shape that promised so much, the silky touch and warm scent, were more than I could resist. I was besotted.

Fortunately, Kitty was too.

So Baron von Grossewasser, a black great dane puppy descended from Christof, a very famous German dog, joined our household, and became my most devoted friend, my black shadow.

His first few months with us were not ideal. We lived in a flat on the fourth floor of a liftless block, and as climbing stairs tends to throw young Danes' 'elbows' out and spoil their shoulders, at least five times a day I carried him – an ever-increasing weight – up and down for 'walkies'. Danes have a large intake capacity and their output is commensurate. No matter what time we came home – frequently in the small hours – the dogs were always walked.

Baron was kept in the bathroom as this was the only part of the flat with a tiled floor. He soon learned his house manners, perhaps because, for obvious reasons, I put him through something of a crash course. One day, as I chastised him with a rolled-up newspaper, he curled back his lips and bared his teeth at me, dazzling white fangs in that coal-black face.

Then the penny dropped in my heated mind: he didn't growl at all, and it was then that I became aware of his most endearing mannerism: he was a compulsive grinner. He would curl his lips back, wrinkle his nose and hiss and sneeze convulsively at certain moments, such as when he was frightened, or felt guilty or was really pleased. If another dog made a mistake in the house, it was poor Baron who leered guiltily, so that it was only by the size of the error that one could tell that he was not the culprit. If one came into a room and found him on a chair, for example, he would sidle off, grinning and sneezing violently. He also grinned, I swear, when he saw the funny side of things.

He was a noble, gentle giant of a dog, hence the aristocratic, if descriptive, name I chose for him. And his bonhomie was infectious.

Wendy and he were splendid together, except when she bossed him about with little nips to put him in his place if he crowded her out of some cosy situation. In Hyde Park she took charge, taking his lead in her mouth and trotting along busily, while he dutifully plodded after her.

Indeed, they became a well-known duo in Park Lane and the Park itself, especially to the resident ladies of the night (and day). These friendly souls always greeted us warmly as we traversed their beats. 'Hello, Mr Todd. Hello, Wendy, hello, Baron,' would be the daily chorus. Two of them were especially incensed one day when we entered the Park by our usual route, passed by them with our customary greetings and were then propositioned by a third who was obviously new to the area or the job. As we walked on into the Park I could see the original pair berating the unfortunate newcomer, and as we returned one of them said, 'We're awfully sorry, Mr Todd. But that common woman won't bother you again.'

He joined us about a month after our return from California. They had been weeks of rapid adjustment. Four or five months before, we had left England for America, an impecunious, rather bewildered pair. Now, in May 1950, we were still fairly impecunious, but a lot had happened to my status. The Oscar nomination and four major awards for *The Hasty Heart*, plus the mere cachet of starring in a film in Hollywood, had shifted me into the international screen world. And I must admit I liked my new standing and enjoyed the attention that went with it. I was not greatly concerned that I didn't know what my next job would be; I was cocooned by a long-term contract that brought with it a weekly stipend more than adequate for our immediate needs. I just sat back and let things come to me: my failing always. Certainly it was not due to any efforts of mine that things did come to me over the years.

After our arrival at Southampton, for the next month or so I seemed to spend most of my time being chauffeured around to a series of meetings in expensive restaurants or to Elstree Studios for discussions with Fritz Gotfurt, the head of the scenario department. Various scripts and story lines were put forward, but nothing caught my fancy.

I had by now engaged a part-time secretary and had also had the good fortune to acquire an accountant, Basil Stebbings, who was to be my friend, adviser and tax consultant for many years, perhaps the kindest, most shrewd professional adviser that I have ever had. Today, nearly four decades on, he still takes care of my problems for me.

I soon regained the Railton, complete with its new clutch assembly from Hollywood, and, although restricted by petrol rationing, we started to drive into the country for our weekends, looking at houses and cottages. By now we were set on moving out of London. Baron was getting very heavy to cart up and down stairs!

On the second of these trips we spotted our dream-house: a half-timbered old place, Wayside House, with a pool, tennis court and pretty garden all set in hundreds of acres of National Trust woodland and grassland at Pinkneys Green, near Maidenhead, and only a couple of miles from our favourite hostelry, the Old Bell at Hurley, where we had spent our brief honeymoon. We had been entranced by it then but, sadly, even if it had been for sale, it was obviously far beyond our means.

Towards the end of May I received the British National Film Award for my part in *The Hasty Heart* in a ceremony at the Dorchester Hotel, where Jean Simmons won the Best Actress award. My prize was a silver lady holding aloft a star. We christened her Matilda, and she has lived in a bank ever since, where she is kept company by the fine Georgian

silver tea service I chose as my prize for the *Daily Express*
Tribunal award, which I shared with Alec Guinness for his
marvellous performance in *Kind Hearts and Coronets*, and
by the Hollywood Golden Globe and a splendid silver-gilt
urn for the *Picturegoer* award.

A couple of days later, on 26 May, petrol rationing ended.
Incredible now to think that, so long after the war, we were
still short of certain things! The rationing of sweets was to
continue for a year or more.

The day before had seen the première of *Stage Fright*, the
Hitchcock film. It got a mixed press and was not one of
Hitchcock's best but the less-than-enthusiastic notices I personally received did not disturb me – I had always thought I
had become a big name under false pretences.

In some ways at that time (and ever since) I suffered from
being a sort of Jack of all trades and probably master of
none. I had not been endowed with film-star good looks and
neither I nor those seeking to find subjects for me had quite
categorised me into the type of role I was best suited for.
The film world liked their actors to be predictable, and to
play themselves with only the dialogue and the stories to be
varied. And yet so far in my short screen career I had played
a broken-down, vengeful little ex-convict; an irascible, lonely
Scottish war casualty; a conniving lover and deceitful husband; a psychopathic killer; and, finally, a well-meaning but
misunderstood rancher. What next? we all wondered.

Meanwhile, during May and June I ploughed through a
variety of scripts. In nearly every case, either I didn't like
them or the producers were having finance problems. In my
theatre days I had played every conceivable type of role,
with perhaps best effect in light comedy parts, but nobody
now seemed to consider this suitable for me. Still, I was in
no hurry, with my nice cosy contract keeping the home fires
burning.

One of the most persistent producers trying to persuade
me to do a film for him was Gaby Pascal, a larger-than-life,
middle-European who came nearest to my picture of the
flamboyant movie-maker. He was setting up a production of
Androcles and the Lion, and wanted me to play the captain.
I didn't see myself as a Roman gladiator, but Gaby did his

best to persuade me – God knows why. Amidst a plethora
of cigars, caviar and champagne, he promised in his fractured
English, 'First, I send you to my villa in Capri. For weeks
you lie on the beach and get tanned, so you will wear no
make-up. Then I ask Noel Langley, the writer, to work on
your part so it fit you like a glove. It will be *von*-derful for
you.'

Fortunately, my boss, Robert Clark, agreed that I should
not do the picture if I didn't want to.

We spent the last ten days of June on a very wet holiday
in Scotland with Kitty's parents. The big, powerful Railton
ploughed through the rain, canvas hood and flapping side-
screens spraying us with constant trickles of water, and we
stopped the night at the Olde Bell Hotel at Barnby Moor in
Yorkshire, where the dogs were welcome in our room.
Thereafter I made a rule never to stop at a hotel where I
could not bring the dogs.

I had taken with me a script given me by Anatole de
Grunewald, one of Britain's leading independent producers,
and a charming erudite man of Russian origin. It was *Flesh
and Blood*, a story based on James Bridie's *The Sleeping
Clergyman*, and scripted by Tolly himself.

I loved it when I read it, and immediately phoned Mr
Clark to tell him.

So my next film was at last agreed. I was to play a tubercular
doctor engaged in laboratory experiments. It was a good,
dramatic part and, even if I was a very well-fleshed consump-
tive, at least after a few days' filming I started a nasty cold
which led to a realistic hacking cough.

I enjoyed working for Tolly de Grunewald and found a
special rapport with the director, Anthony Kimmins, a large,
bluff ex-Fleet Air Arm pilot who had apparently been the
first Briton to fly a plane off an aircraft carrier.

We filmed at Teddington Studios, a small, pleasant complex near the River Thames and easily reached from London.
Work started on 17 July. Baron now went everywhere with
me and spent his days either in my dressing-room or on the
set. An old duffle coat was his talisman, and wherever that
was laid was his place.

My two leading ladies were Glynis Johns and Joan Greenwood, at that time probably the most sought-after English film actresses, and the main supporting roles were played by Ursula Howells, André Morell, Freda Jackson and Michael Hordern. It was a very strong cast, and we all got on extremely well together.

So, altogether I was a most happy fellah. I even managed to extract a loan from ABPC against my *Flesh and Blood* earnings to enable me to buy a Bentley car that I had seen and coveted – a beautiful hand-built pre-war sedanca-coupé that had been stored for years and had done very little mileage.

The bank holiday at the beginning of August saw us still scouring round in our glossy new acquisition looking for country properties, and spending the Sunday and Monday with Freddie and Ann Weil in their dog-filled house at Maidenhead Thicket. On the Monday morning we went round his stables and stud farm at Knowl Hill, a couple of miles away. More than ever Kitty and I hoped to find somewhere to live in that area.

On the following Saturday, 12 August, we celebrated our wedding anniversary. It was our lucky weekend. On the Sunday we had decided to drive down to Hurley for supper at the Old Bell, and had stopped at Pinkneys Green to let the dogs have a run in the woodland there while we gazed covetously at our dream-house, Wayside.

While we looked, a bent old figure, almost a caricature of Old Father Time, even to the scythe he carried, came shuffling by on the open grass space opposite the house. He was clad in black trousers, long black coat, and high-crowned bowler hat that I had not seen since the days of Mr Prout, our gardener at Holsworthy in my childhood.

As he drew level with us he touched his hat and gave us a gummy smile. 'Nice house, that,' he said.

'Lovely,' I said. 'Do you know anything about it?'

'Oh, ar,' he replied. 'When I were a boy it were the Shoulder of Mutton Inn. Very old. Dick Turpin, the highwayman, used to stay there.'

'Really? Gosh!'

'Ar. This grass ride were the old main road from London to Bath. Very dangerous for robbers. Jack Scott, the highwayman, were taken in the Shoulder of Mutton and hanged at Tyburn. That big bit at the side were the barn. Dick Turpin's Black Bess would have been stabled there.'

If we had thought it charming before, now it positively entranced us. 'It certainly is lovely,' I said.

'Ar,' said he. 'Pity they've got to go.'

'You mean the people are leaving it? Is it for sale?'

'I shouldn' wonder.'

I got the name of the owners – Harrison – and determined to phone them. At least we could look inside the house, something we had always wanted to do.

When I rang the next day, Mr Harrison told me that the house was indeed for sale, though not yet advertised, as they had only recently decided to go to live in Canada. He gave me the name of his London estate agents.

I immediately phoned them, and they quoted a price which I could not possibly afford. However, I still made an appointment to view the house, which we did a couple of weeks later.

Meanwhile I was filming busily at Teddington, mostly with Glynis Johns. And when the Sunday came to view Wayside House, we found the place enchanting: lots of wood panelling, a fine drawing-room and dining-room, morning-room, eight bedrooms, four bathrooms, two staff bedrooms and an intriguing cellar entered by a concealed trap door in the hall. Too much for us, but very desirable!

My conscience did prick me when I confessed to the Harrisons that I couldn't nearly afford it. They had been very hospitable, and I felt we had misled them by asking to view. But two days later, their estate agent phoned us to say that Mr Harrison had decided to accept exactly what I had said I might be able to run to. Bless him! It was a huge reduction.

Now I really had to rush things . . . The figure I had mentioned was purely wishful thinking, based on a mortgage and a hypothetical deal with Associated British. If I could have the whole of my *Flesh and Blood* payment, instead of splitting it with them, and repay them over a period, only then could I buy Wayside.

Mercifully, the enigmatic and very Scottish Mr Clark fixed

it, drawing up an agreement granting me the whole of the proceeds from my work on *Flesh and Blood*, the Corporation's share to be repaid by me 'only if the Corporation should at any time require it'. I could have kissed him – Kitty and I spent sleepless nights working out our budget, and realised that our finances were strained almost to breaking point. In fact, the *Flesh and Blood* money covered the whole of the purchase price, so I only needed a mortgage sufficient to cover the costs of bare essential furnishing, carpeting and curtaining. Within a week I had signed a contract for Wayside, and at the end of September 1950, I became the proud owner of my first house.

Within a week we had also sold the lease of our Park Street flat. The proceeds were Kitty's, but she willingly put it into our new household needs.

A whole new way of life. I could scarcely believe my luck.

From the moment that Wayside became part of our existence the place exuded a happy atmosphere and our good fortune increased. In mid-September we finished *Flesh and Blood* and Kitty and I embarked on a mad spree of antique furniture-buying. We even daringly engaged an interior decorator and adviser.

I was, of course, still reading scripts, including one for a French film and one from Tolly de Grunewald based on part of Shakespeare's life. The latter I particularly liked, and hoped that he could get it set up.

Every day that we had to spare Kitty and I were down at Wayside House, apprehensively trying to curb the ever-mounting costs. We ourselves spent hours on the panelling, feeding and polishing it with a mixture of linseed oil and vinegar. We had decided not to use the drawing-room as we simply could not afford to decorate it. Eventually, we polished the floor, put some deck chairs in there, and jokingly called it the ballroom.

While all this was going on I was rehearsing with Glynis Johns, Michael Wilding, Margaret Lockwood and others, a perfectly awful Floradora dance routine for the annual Royal Film Performance. We must have been the most expensive and inept chorus line ever put together.

I had also accepted an invitation to fly to Dublin to make

a personal appearance at the Adelphi Cinema there and to address the Trinity College Philosophical Society the day after. God knows what I talked about or why I had been invited to this august gathering.

A few days before the Royal Film Performance Milton Pickman phoned from Hollywood. He wanted to know if I could fly out to California to do a radio broadcast of *Great Expectations* with Jean Simmons on 5 November, immediately after Dublin. Readily I agreed, subject to Associated British permission, which I got at once.

Somehow, I reckoned, I could just about last the pace! Not since Normandy had I had such an action-packed schedule.

All weekend we rehearsed the dreadful song-and-dance routine, which we performed at the Royal Film Performance on the Monday. This was followed by a party at the Savoy from which we returned to the flat at 3.30 a.m., just in time to take the dogs for a much-needed walk.

I was up at 8.30 a.m. to rush to meet Kitty's mother at Euston, arrived to help Kitty move into Wayside – a traumatic chore I had unwittingly but thankfully avoided by going to Dublin and then America!

At 5.30 that afternoon I took off from Northolt for Dublin, where I was met by one Bill Ryan and taken to my hotel. After the cinema 'personal' I was joined for dinner by David Lean and his then wife, Ann Todd, and also by Uncle Fintan and Aunt Eileen FitzPatrick – and, of course, by Bill Ryan, who had organised the evening and who kept me up until 3 a.m., drinking and chatting – not against my will, I must admit.

One of my projects in Dublin had been to purchase a load of china and glass, these being much cheaper and more readily available there than in London. 'No problem,' said the resourceful Mr Ryan, and told me which shop to go to.

Next morning I was up early doing press interviews and photo sessions, then met Aunt Eileen at the china shop. In the afternoon I went out to visit my dear old Granny Todd, now very frail, but as sweet as ever, in her retirement home. That evening, after my speech at Trinity College, I had dinner with Bill Ryan (who else?) and again we talked until the not-so-small hours. And the following morning I just

made it to my 10.30 flight at the airport, driven there by
(who else?) Mr Ryan.

In London I had a quick lunch, collected some US dollars
at the bank, and set off for my new home at Pinkneys Green.
Now that the move-in had been organised by Kitty and her
mother, it was gorgeous! I was thrilled beyond words. All
my life, since my family home and Brecart had gone, I had
wanted my own home in the country, and now I had it.

We had a lovely quiet weekend. There was only one phone
call – from Tolly de Grunewald reporting progress on the
Shakespeare story, and asking me if I could get Jean Simmons
interested in the project.

On the Sunday evening I left Northolt Airport at 8 p.m.,
and flew to Shannon Airport in Ireland, where I boarded a
plane for my first trans-Atlantic flight.

As so often happened in those piston-engined days, on the
East-West crossing we met headwinds and had to put down
at Gander, Newfoundland, to refuel. After a miserable hour
in a wooden hut on that storm-lashed base, we flew on to
New York, hours late. There was just time at La Guardia
Airport to catch my flight to Los Angeles, where I arrived
at 10.30 p.m.

To me this was about 6.30 the next morning. I had already
lost two nights' sleep, and I was just about cross-eyed with
weariness. Milton was at the airport to meet me and, after
dropping off my bags at the Beverly Hills Hotel, took me to
dine at Romanof's. Although this was an early breakfast for
me I revived (I must have been very fit then) and we talked
till late.

I suppose because I had not adjusted to Pacific time, I
awoke early and read the broadcast script, then spent the
afternoon at Hollywood Park races. That evening we went
to an election-day party and finished up at the Mocambo,
ending the revelry at about 5 a.m.

Somewhere amongst all this activity I managed to rehearse
and record the broadcast before the week's end.

I also had another taste of the gossip-writers' fertile
imagination when I lunched one day with Patricia Neal. She
was wearing a tartan outfit, and one columnist managed to
suggest that we were a woosome twosome and that she had

dressed to please her Scottish hero, despite the fact that Fefe Ferry was with us.

I spent the weekend at Palm Springs with Milton and Fefe and was present at a very illuminating Hollywood scene.

We had been invited to spend the afternoon at the weekend home of Darryl Zanuck, the legendary boss of 20th Century Fox, and when we arrived Zanuck was playing croquet, one of his regular pastimes. He was playing a foursome game, and every shot of his, good or indifferent, was greeted with lyrical applause by the circle of onlooking guests. 'Oh, great shot!' was the chorus. Mr Zanuck, of course, won the match.

Mrs Zanuck was very sweet to me, and when, in answer to her query, I said I had played a little croquet at various vicarage tea-parties, she insisted that her husband should give me a game. He shot me a 'Who-the-hell-is-this-guy?' look and said, 'OK. You play with John Hodiak and I'll take Fefe,' and marched back to the lawn.

John was no expert at the game, and I could barely remember the rules, but what we lacked in skill, we made up for with enthusiastic beef. I managed to hit some real flukes and several times croqueted the irate Mr Zanuck almost out of sight, totally unaware that an unforgivable social gaffe in these parts was to trounce the redoubtable tycoon at one of his favourite games. His cigar was becoming clamped at an ever more aggressive angle, and I was beginning to enjoy whacking the balls around. At least I didn't ram my mallet up his backside, as it seems David Niven had done to his horse in a polo match.

Eventually, to an appalled silence from the gallery, we ran out the winners. I don't remember Mr Zanuck speaking to me for the rest of the afternoon.

The following Monday I went to Burbank to meet the most legendary of all the movie-world figures, Walt Disney. I don't remember whether the idea had come from Disney himself, or whether Milton Pickman had suggested it, but Walt was planning a film about Robin Hood, and wanted me to play the English folk-hero.

The atmosphere in the Walt Disney Studios was quite different from any I had so far experienced in the film factories. Walt first of all took me on a brief tour of his empire, going round acres of sound-stages and rows of drawing offices, where animators were busy sketching. And everywhere he went he was greeted with 'Hi, Walt,' and he replied, 'Hi! Jack – or Fred – or Art – or Lou.' He seemed to know every single one of the workforce.

Eventually, we arrived in his office, a large, panelled, comfy room with a bar at one end. Before we settled down to talk, Walt proudly showed me how, at the touch of a button, the bar became a soda-fountain for youngsters. He adored children, and delighted in surprising them.

We were joined by Perce Pearce, his senior live-action producer, a jolly, rubicund Pickwickian figure, who was going to take charge of the Robin Hood project, and Walt then outlined his ideas for the planned film. With images of Douglas Fairbanks and Errol Flynn in my mind, I simply could not see it as a vehicle for me. I was not physically built to play a larger-than-life swashbuckler, and I could not see myself swinging from the same Sherwood family tree as the mighty Flynn.

Above all, I considered myself an *actor*; not for me the Lincoln-green equivalent of Tarzan.

Walt was very persuasive. He described his idea of Robin Hood as a quick-thinking welter-weight, not a ponderous heavyweight. But even so, much as I liked and admired him, I felt I could not abandon all my thespian principles for a child's play romp in the forest. I must have been taking myself very seriously at that time.

And it never occurred to me that it might be a darned sight more difficult to make a fantasy character believable than to play some of the straight conventional parts that I had already done.

Having spoken to Jean Simmons about Tolly's Shakespeare film project, and learning that she was not at that time interested in returning to London to work, I left next day for England.

During the flight, and for days afterwards, I had one big question on my mind: should I not have agreed to do Robin Hood? Pickman had been beside himself with incredulity that I had not jumped at the chance. But perhaps his attitude, understandably, was typically movie-world: never mind the quality – feel the width.

I managed to quell my rising doubts and to convince myself that I had been right, and a busy few weeks before Christmas, coupled with domestic problems, took my mind off my questionable decision.

And I *did* have problems! First of all, the couple we had engaged as cook and houseman proved useless, and left, leaving Kitty to do the cooking and housework while I stoked the boilers, cleaned the cars, attempted to tidy the garden and generally tried to be useful during a period when I had lots of meetings in London, did a BBC broadcast, and flew to Scotland and back in twenty-four hours for the annual Travel Ball in Glasgow.

Kitty was none too well, and I think the task of moving home, running the house and facing a Christmas which involved having guests and a good deal of entertaining without any help had taxed her.

However, fortune was again with us. Within days we interviewed and engaged a couple, Mr and Mrs Rutland, who moved in straight away with their two children; I found an excellent local gardener and a handyman; and even came up with Peggy and another local daily lady to do the house.

Until Rutland arrived that bloody boiler had been the bane of my existence. It was a very antiquated, solid fuel engine of war, which glowed red-hot, belched acrid fumes and clouds of soot, clanked and shuddered when the coke-box was opened, made alarming gurgling noises, and altogether frightened the life out of me.

It was housed in a small concrete pit in a little courtyard in the middle of the house, where the stack of coke was dumped. First, I had to clear out the clinker before feeding the monster. To do this I had to don an old overcoat, a pair of Wellington boots, a cap pulled down to my ears, and a muffler to keep the soot from my collar.

Twice a day I performed this feat. Oh, the joys of a ramshackle country life! I could well see why our original couple had been quite glad to leave – although it was apparently her cooking rather than his coking that had caused the breach.

I still managed to drive up to London almost daily well-washed and cleanly clad.

I also had a couple of agonised phone calls from Milton Pickman in California. He pleaded with me to do Disney's Robin Hood picture. His main arguments were that it was, firstly, a very big international movie, and, secondly, that it would pull in a huge world-wide audience of youngsters, probably seeing their first screen programme, to whom Robin Hood would be a hero for ever. He was absolutely right, I realised, and to give myself time I said I would read the new script as soon as it was ready and meanwhile hoped that Tolly's Shakespeare picture might come to my rescue.

Near the end of the month, with Kitty now much better, after a day's script talks in London, we had dinner with a well-known agent, Bill O'Brien, and his sweet actress wife, Liz Allen. After a pretty bibulous evening I drove carefully home (no breathalisers in those days), both of us wondering why we had a little bundle of pot-bellied puppy swaddled in an old blanket on Kitty's lap. In a weak moment we seemed to have been unable to resist the cross-eyed charms of a baby bull terrier, just weaned, one of a litter that the O'Briens' bitch had produced. So Sally bull terrier joined the family.

Christmas came that year in the perfect seasonal surroundings of pretty old Wayside House in its pastoral setting of grassland and woods, and was a very convivial occasion for us in our first country home. Even our bare, unfurnished drawing-room was put to good and energetic use. The festive season became a series of parties at Wayside and the Old Bell at Hurley, where the latter, with its blackened old beams and great open log fires provided the ideal atmosphere for Yuletide revelry. The only thing lacking was the snow, and that arrived in abundance a few days later.

It was at the Old Bell that Kitty and I saw the New Year in. Last year we had been on a train crossing the United States: next year – where? I wondered.

On the first day of 1951 I crawled out of bed, shuffled into my bathroom, wiped the condensation from the window – and beheld a snow-white world. The outlook from Wayside was pretty enough at any time but the woodland round about was quite enchanting under snow. I was more than ever thrilled with our home and my good fortune.

But I had forgotten the drawbacks of rural life in winter: shovelling snow from the paths and doors, digging out the car, and slithering off to reach the hard-packed main road to London.

Since Christmas I had read the latest version of the Robin Hood script, and liked it. Also, I was beginning to enjoy the thought of larking about in the forest with a band of merrie outlaws – subject to one proviso: that I should not be doubled by a stunt-man in any of the action scenes. I felt that if I could do the stunts myself, however clumsily, then they would be that much more believable. Besides, although perhaps not a very practical attitude for a professional actor, it was a small matter of pride – what would my ex-Airborne friends think if they knew that I had been standing around watching somebody else do the dirty work!

Perce Pearce arrived in London in mid-January and I met him in his suite at the Dorchester Hotel. With him was Maud Spector, the leading British independent casting director, who was to find the actors for all the leading roles.

That afternoon I agreed to play Robin Hood, and we spent several hours going through lists of candidates for parts in the film. My only contribution was to suggest James Robertson Justice as Little John, and this turned out to be a good idea.

Perce, however, was less enthusiastic about my request for a special doubling clause in my contract. It might entail an insurance problem, and would certainly need to be agreed by Disney himself. I decided not to press too hard at this stage.

Now that I had finally made up my mind, I was thrilled at the prospect of working for the great Disney organisation. Milton had been right to badger me, and I was already impatient to start learning some arrow-slinging.

My only regret was that I felt that I had let Tolly de Grunewald down, and he was obviously upset when I phoned him that evening. Still, we hoped that this would mean only a postponement of his Shakespeare film, and I persuaded him to join me next day for lunch with Perce Pearce, after which he ran a screening of *Flesh and Blood* for us. The film was good; it had real quality and some terrific performances, especially from André Morell and George Cole. Perce was very complimentary about it, which delighted Tolly.

We were due to start filming *Robin Hood* on 30 April and for the next three months I learned about the meticulous planning and preparations that went into a Walt Disney 'live action' film.

A gymnasium was set up for me at Pinewood Studios, and here, under the watchful and energetic tutelage of Paddy Ryan, the doyen of British stunt men, I worked out almost daily, and practised back-flips and tumbles that I hadn't tried since my early army days. Rupert Evans, a former Champion at Arms of the British Army, coached me in sword-play, and he and Paddy worked with me throughout the picture. In addition, I had hours of tuition in archery and practice on horseback, with and without bows and arrows. I may not have been the greatest celluloid Robin Hood, but I was certainly going to be the fittest!

Nothing was left to chance by Perce Pearce and his production team. For weeks there were planning meetings. I sat in on many of these, and was fascinated by the attention to detail. At each of them a sketch artist was present, and as each camera set-up was worked out and agreed, he produced a pencil-and-wash picture of exactly what would be in the camera lens. These sketches were photo-copied and bound into folders, and all of us at these meetings were eventually issued with the bound volumes, showing every single shot. Never was a piece of studio set built but not used, and never was time lost looking for a suitable camera position, even on exterior location shots, which were carefully scouted.

This pictorial presentation may have stemmed from the Walt Disney Organisation's cartoon-based experience, but it was a practice which could have benefited several time- and money-wasting productions that I have since witnessed, where I have sat around for ages whilst director and crew frantically tried to decide what to do and where to go next.

Nor did the director need to feel constrained by this forward-planning: variations and additional shots were, of course, from time to time found necessary.

On 31 January, Perce Pearce officially announced the

forthcoming film and my part in it at a press reception at the
Dorchester Hotel, and afterwards he and I and Maud Spector
went through the cast-list again. Joan Rice was chosen to
play Maid Marion, whilst Peter Finch and James Hayter were
confirmed in their roles as the Sheriff of Nottingham and
Friar Tuck respectively. James Robertson Justice was also
signed to play Little John.

Soon after, *Flesh and Blood* opened and got a good reception. That was quite a day for me, because a script from
RKO Pictures had arrived for me to do with Jane Wyman.
The money offered was terrific, but the dates could not be
arranged. That seemed to be the pattern for me for years:
either I had more offers than I could cope with, or anxious
months went by when I wondered if I would ever work again.

During all the excitement of those weeks one depressing
incident made me realise how lucky I had been. In mid-March
I flew to Belfast for some civic function at the City Hall, and
drove out to Toome. This was the first time I had been back
there since childhood, and I was not sure what to expect.
The scene at Brecart was devastating.

The great iron gates and railings at the main entrance were
gone – probably for war-time scrap – and the gate lodge was
empty and dilapidated. One gate pillar had been knocked
askew and the park on either side of the drive was covered
with concrete hard-standings and corrugated huts.

Worst of all, around the house hardly a tree had been left
standing: the majestic line of limes bordering the river had
disappeared and the woods leading to the back of the house
had all gone. We didn't drive all the way up to the house;
from half-way along the drive I could see that the place
looked dreadful: forlorn, peeling and derelict.

The Brecart curse had taken its impoverishing toll. What,
I wondered, had happened to Uncle Jimmy? And I thought
of my Aunts Amy and Dolly, who were in Australia. Did
they know what had happened?

I felt sick.

Back in London, Perce Pearce had at last received approval
from Disney for my special doubling clause, and my contract
was drawn up and signed.

I had meantime arranged for Kitty and me to have a

holiday in France, our first real break away from it all since our marriage. I could not have chosen a worse time, weather-wise, for motor touring, but that was partly why our expedition was so enjoyable. The whole of eastern France was hit by particularly heavy snow falls, and we had some pretty exciting drives.

We spent our first couple of days in Normandy at the Hotel Chez Mahu, near Deauville, and I drove around the Normandy battlefields reviving wartime memories, especially at Ranville and at Pegasus Bridge, where the charming Gondrée family made us greatly welcome to Pegasus Café for lunch, and where I signed the visitors' book reserved for ex-members of 6th Airborne Division. Many well-remembered names had been entered before mine.

One evening at dinner, whilst we waded through the lengthy menu I asked for two gins and tonic. Evidently Schweppes' famous product had not yet caught on in France, but when I pronounced the word as *tonique*, then the waiter got the message: '*Ah, oui!* Sheep's water,' he beamed.

I was amazed at the speed and efficiency with which this part of France had recovered from its war devastation. There were hardly any signs of ruination, and Caen, which I had last seen as a stinking mound of rubble, was almost totally rebuilt.

From Normandy we drove via Le Mans and Tours through the most beautiful and rugged countryside of the mountainous Haute Loire region to join the main Paris–Marseille route. Kitty was a splendid navigator as we ploughed through the virgin snow scarcely ever seeing another vehicle on the tricky mountain roads. The Bentley never hesitated as we slithered and bulldozed our way along. Amazed locals looked in wonder at the folly of the English, and we loved every moment of our adventure.

On the third day we came into the sunshine as we met the main road at Valence, had a gorgeous meal there, and then drove very fast down to our charming waterside hotel, where we spent the next week.

Our last night in Cannes was spent at a cheerful bistro with paper-topped tables and walls totally obscured by photographs and autographs of celebrities. The gravelly voiced *patron* noted your order by sketching it on the table top, tearing off the drawings, and handing it to a waitress. A hilarious evening, finishing at a night-club, left us only a couple of hours in bed before we set off for Paris, where we arrived after a fast and gruelling drive, both of us dead weary.

Four days in Paris, then another fast drive to the Dunkerque Ferry, and we got home to Pinkneys Green late one evening. My diary for the day notes, 'Dogs in great form.'

Which is more than we were.

But three weeks of hard training and riding at Pinewood soon made up for our excesses. I got on especially well with the massive James Robertson Justice, who joined me in my gym to practise the quarterstaff fight that we were to have in the film. And when I wasn't at the studio training, testing horses or working with the production team on the preparations, I was at Wayside gardening and mowing lawns, even the rough grass of the common around the house, with an old push mower, which was a fairly sweaty activity.

And at last the great day came: Monday, 30 April 1951, the first day of shooting on *Robin Hood*.

I was up soon after dawn, determined to drive to the studios at Denham with plenty of time to spare. I parted the curtains to see how the weather was – and it was snowing heavily! And we were scheduled to film exterior scenes that day . . .

Even Perce's schedule had not allowed for this kind of setback. Rain we could cope with, but a mantle of snow covering Sherwood Forest supposedly in mid-summer would look incongruous, to say the least. But the British weather gods had served stern warning to the sun-soaked Californians, and from that day on, 'cover' scenes were always on stand-by.

Next day the snow had given way to intermittent chilly rain, and the rest of the week was spent shuttling back and forth between Burnham Beeches, a few miles away, and Denham Studios.

Clad only in our skimpy Lincoln Green, Robin Hood and

his band of outlaws presented a less-than-merrie sight as we huddled dejectedly waiting for the clouds to pass, and for close-up shots we actually had difficulty controlling our shivers and chattering teeth. No doubt Errol Flynn and Douglas Fairbanks had been made of sterner stuff.

Even Baron, who went with me every day to Denham, was glad to clamber into the back of my car and slumber on his duffle coat.

On the first Saturday of *Robin Hood* I borrowed one of Freddie Weil's stable of five cars to go on a very wet location session at Burnham Beeches. Kitty, driven by Rutland, who also doubled as our part-time chauffeur, had gone to London in my Bentley to pick up Milton Pickman at Claridges. He was on a visit to England, and was coming down to Wayside for the weekend with us. Milton was to have his first experience of the hazards of staying in an English country house.

As he arrived in the hall of the house, which was dark-panelled and rather gloomy in the dim evening light, his first shock was to be greeted by the black and almost invisible shape of the now-enormous Baron, whom I had left at home that day. Baron welcomed him warmly by rearing up, putting his paws on Milton's shoulders, and giving him a sloppy kiss on his forehead. Milt, who was not a doggy type, stood rigid with fright until Kitty called him off. His courage fortified by a large Scotch on the rocks, our Californian friend eventually got over his nervous reaction to our three canine pets, and by the time I got home he was happily sharing the extra-large sofa which I had had specially made to accommodate them.

But worse was to follow for the hapless Pickman . . .

We were joined for a late dinner by the Weils and Maggie Hall-Caine, and after a pleasant, chatty evening, Milton, well-oiled, retired to bed. As he slid under the covers in his raftered and beamed old room, his feet came to rest on something warm and squashy. Horrified at what might be occupying his bed, he leaped out and threw back the sheets and blankets, and his eyes lit on what was, to him, an unfamiliar sight – a hot water bottle that somebody had thoughtfully provided for him.

Nor was that all . . .

By now convinced that the place was haunted, Milton finally fell into an uneasy sleep, only to be wakened by a sense of suffocation as something enveloped his face. With a terrified screech, he again shot upright, felt for the light switch, certain that something ghostly had tried to smother him, and was just in time to see our tabby cat, Winnie, scoot out through the open window. Winnie, who had started life being called Churchill because of a 'V' shape in the markings on her head, but had to be renamed when we discovered our sexing error, had hopped from the porch roof below on to the windowsill and decided to spend a cosy night on Milton's pillow.

Eventually, worn out, he got to sleep again, only to awake late next morning to feel Baron's wet and cold nose nudging him as the great dog proceeded to climb into bed with him. He had got in through the open door of the adjoining dressing-room.

Bed-sharing was a bad habit of Baron's. Officially he slept on a blanket in my dressing-room, but frequently he would glide silently to my side of our bed and lean against it. Because he was so tall he could quietly hitch himself onto the side of the bed, and from there it only needed a few crafty wiggles for him to lie full-length beside me. As the night wore on he managed to take up more and more space, as I in my sleep gave way to him, unconsciously pushing Kitty to the very edge. More than once I and my black friend were belaboured by a furious Kitty with a slipper as she climbed back in.

The bleary-eyed Milton had a late Sunday breakfast, called with us on the Weils for drinks and then had lunch with us at the Old Bell. We spent the rest of the day showing him round the lovely Thames Valley countryside of Henley and Marlow, before finally dropping him back at Claridges, after a weekend that he never quite forgot.

The following week, mercifully, we were doing interior scenes in Robin Hood's camp, so we had no weather problems.

All through May and June the film progressed on schedule, and I thoroughly enjoyed working on it. We were a very

happy cast and unit, and the results which I saw at the
rushes were fine, especially Geoffrey Unsworth's beautiful
photography. When he died some years later, still quite
young, it was a tragic loss to British cinematography.

My only bad moments were with the horses and some of the
fight scenes that I had insisted on doing myself. Sometimes,
bruised and stiff, or waterlogged after hours immersed in the
studio tank, I felt that I had been a bit of an idiot to take on
something best done by the trained experts.

This was especially so when in June I had to drop from
the branch of a tree onto the back of a cantering horse. God
knows how many times we repeated the action, trying to
get it right. The trouble was that, after the first couple of
rehearsals, the bloody horse, Jacko, got wise to what was
going to happen, so that as he was given a whack and
sent careering off towards my tree, he either stopped dead,
swerved, or accelerated, with the result that I thumped down
on his head, or in front of him, or beside him, or onto his
bouncing backside. And if I actually hit the saddle, more
often than not it was the high wooden pommel of the
medieval saddle that banged into my tender parts.

Even my hands were suffering, the palms and fingers
becoming raw from the scraping of the tree-bark, so we
wrapped a binding round the branch.

By the time we got everything co-ordinated – horse, rider
and camera – I was glad to hobble away, stiff, sore and
spraddle-legged. All this for a few seconds' screen-time!

On the anniversary of D – Day (only seven years ago!) we
first used the swimming pool at Wayside, after many hours
of scraping, cleaning and painting by Kitty and me. I had
also spent much of my spare time on days off at Freddie
Weil's stud farm and racing stable, and was becoming more
and more interested in registering my colours and running
some horses myself, as Freddie suggested.

Our nearest neighbours, the Husseys (he was PA to the
American Ambassador) were keen tennis players and had a
flock of children, so our court and pool got a lot of use. And,
to our pride and delight, our restored and replanted garden
was beginning to burgeon and look really pretty.

My thirty-second birthday found me shooting the quarterstaff scene with Jimmy Justice, and this entailed several days of battering and falling into the studio water tank. Fortunately, the water was heated and the sustaining nips of brandy plentiful.

Walt Disney himself came over to London near the end of June, and spent some time with us. He seemed thoroughly pleased with the way things were going, and I found the great man always warm and easy to get on with. Like Perce Pearce, he was a great chuckler, and we three had some hilarious moments together. He was genuinely concerned about my riding mishaps but fortunately there were no sticky moments while he was there.

Soon after his departure, however, I had to work with an absolute brute of an animal. His name was Star, a misnomer if ever there was one. He was only used in a couple of scenes where I had to back a horse that would rear up on his hind legs. Unlike the horses in Hollywood, who would stand up for ages pawing the air so that non-riding cowboys like Sonny Tufts could be pictured atop them, gaily waving their stetsons, Star had never been trained to rear – he just went up out of sheer evil temper if you dug him sharply enough with your heels and gave a sharp tug on the bridle.

A few days after Walt had left London I had a particularly bad day. Of my three unlovely nags, Star, Nellie Dean and Jacko, Nellie's misdemeanours were quite benevolent. She simply kept dozing off, and whenever I gave her a mild jog to wake her up, she invariably took this as a signal to get moving, and lunged forward no matter what was in her path, camera, technicians or crowd artistes.

Jacko was more spirited, but again took exception to me jumping onto his back as he cantered by riderless while I launched myself into the saddle, this time from a stall in the set-up for Nottingham Market.

To finish my day of painful woes, a Saturday, Star then performed the ultimate in back flips and came right over backwards on me. Fortunately I was more or less ready, and as he passed the vertical I managed to get my feet clear of the irons, pulled his head to the right and shoved myself off to the left, so that I fell beside him but clear of his weight, then rolled and scrambled out of the way of his flailing hooves. All I suffered was a bruised ankle and a severely damaged ego. But never again would I knowingly climb onto a horse with a tendency to rear.

Work packed up for the day then and I got home early and went straight to bed, even though Kitty's parents were with us for the weekend. For weeks now word had got amongst the youngsters of Maidenhead and Pinkneys Green that I was playing the legendary Robin Hood in a film and on my way home I had run my customary gauntlet of grinning little archers who sprang from the trees along the road – thankfully not actually loosing their arrows at me – as I neared Wayside.

My worries that month were not confined to recalcitrant horses, because gentle little Wendy Corgi also gave us a few sleepless nights. She had been mated in April and was due to whelp in early July, but she was obviously having great trouble and got very agitated in her labour. Eventually the vet performed a Caesarian operation, which produced three enormous stillborn pups.

Fortunately, Cadno Kennels were able to let us have a tiny corgi puppy which we introduced to her in the evening. By 3 a.m. we decided to go to bed. When we awoke for our early call, she was washing it, and all was well. And so Tinkerbell Corgi joined the family circle.

By now the major work on *Robin Hood* was nearing completion, but we still had to film Robin's capture and imprisonment in Nottingham Castle, and his subsequent escape by scaling the fast-closing drawbridge, dropping into the moat, and swimming to safety, an exercise that nearly ended in disaster.

As I floundered across the moat a group of expert archers were lining the battlements above and plopping their arrows into the water all around me. The most proficient of these bowmen had been provided with a special target bow and some very light metal arrows rather shorter than normal. His task was to actually hit me in the back as I swam, for which I had been provided with a safety shield in the form of a steel plate, about ten inches square, strapped to my back under my heavy clothing, and to the outside of this was stuck a further shield of cork, about two inches thick. The idea was that when one of the light metal arrows struck, it would stick into the cork and remain there, as though lodged in my back.

The trouble was that, never at my best when out of my depth in water, and encumbered with leather boots, thick woollen tunic and a wide leather belt, I was intent only on getting to the opposite bank before I sank. So I threshed away wildly, quite unaware of arrows or anything else, even a pricking sensation in my lower back.

I could not understand why half the crew, led by Peter Bolton, our amicable and super-efficient first assistant director, had rushed to the bank to haul me out, their faces full of concern. The reason for this became apparent as Peter pulled the arrow from my back – not from the reinforced cork pad, but from my flesh, fractionally lower. Luckily its barb had just slightly nicked me, no harm had been done, and the scene was very effective.

Towards the end of July I was approached by Ivan Foxwell, a successful independent British film producer, and presented by him with a script based on *Twenty-Four Hours of a Woman's Life*, a book by Stefan Zweig. The film, all set in Monte Carlo, was to star Merle Oberon and be directed by Victor Savill, and would start in time for me to finish *Robin Hood*.

Here was a tempting offer! The right director, the beautiful Merle and weeks in Monte Carlo – what a combination! I *wanted* to like the script even before I read it. And I did . . .

So whilst we were finishing off all the final bits and pieces on *Robin Hood*, arrangements and negotiations were worked out between Associated British and Ivan Foxwell, and I had various meetings in London with him and Victor Savill, and a series of wardrobe fittings. And that is how things often were in a busy screen actor's life in those days of a vibrant industry: the film is dead, long live the film! Even before shooting ceased on a picture, no matter how much one had enjoyed making it, one's thoughts were on the next project, and one was eager to start on it.

The last few days on a happy picture are always a bit scrappy and nostalgic, as one by one the members of the cast and unit come to say goodbye, and *Robin Hood* was no exception. But my last day at Denham Studios was a particularly sad time. Ours was the last film to be made there, ever, as the Rank Organisation who owned it had decided to close film operations there, and had let it go to be used as a supply depot for the US Army. Walking about in the empty corridors and echoing sound stages was a lonely experience, indicative, perhaps, of the decline of film-making in England. Much of the cinematic activity in Britain had been kept going by American productions using up frozen sterling earnings, and for that bridging operation many of our actors and technicians had reason to be grateful.

I was at Denham on that final day to film in the afternoon the Associated British trailer for the forthcoming annual Royal Film Performance, and Perce Pearce had arranged a splendid luncheon party for me and the few remaining people still there.

It really was a celebratory farewell 'do', as he had just seen a rough-cut of the whole film and was delighted with it. The restaurant staff excelled their best efforts that day, and we feasted luxuriously at a meal accompanied by unlimited champagne and liqueurs.

I had quite overlooked the constraints of my after-lunch chore, however. Just *you* try saying crisply, 'And Her Majesty the Queen has graciously consented to be present' when you're having considerable difficulty with your diction!

Playing Robin Hood in a major world-targeted movie had been a most enjoyable experience for me, even though it was a considerable departure from any role I had ever imagined myself attempting. Whether I would be accepted as a mini-swashbuckler remained to be seen. I would never have cast myself in the part. I had shot an arrow in the air – it would fall to earth I knew not where. I could only hope that Milton Pickman had been right and that Walt Disney's faith would be justified.

Looking back, I realise that I had been blessed and most fortunate to survive so far. It had been a tumultuous life, from Lough Beg to Lincoln Green.

INDEX

Compiled by Gordon Robinson

Unsworth, Geoffrey, 288

Valence, 284
Verity, Terence, 234
Victorville, 260
Vidor, King, 251, 256, 257, 258

Walker, Lieutenant-Colonel J.
    F., 129–30, 137, 138
Walsh, Kay, 239
Walt Disney Productions, work
    for
    Robin Hood, 277–9, 280,
    281–3, 285–92
Warner, Jack L., 248, 249, 260
Warner Brothers, work for,
    245, 247, 248, 251, 261, 262
    Lightning Strikes Twice, 251,
    255–64
Warspite, HMS, 161, 173, 177
Wayside House, Pinkneys
    Green, 269, 272–4, 275,
    276, 279, 280–1, 285, 286,
    288, 290
Webb, Clifton, 251
Weil, Ann, 272, 286, 287
Weil, Frederick, 258, 272, 286,
    287, 288
Welsh Players repertory

company, 83–90
Welwyn Garden City film
    studios, 224, 226, 229
West Moors, Dorset, 48–57, 59
Western Gazette, 63
Whatmore, Whatty, 215,
    216–17, 218, 221, 223
Wilding, Michael, 238, 239,
    242, 274
Wilmot, Chester, 174, 179
Wilson, Sergeant, 112–13
Windsor, Duchess of, 246
Windsor, Duke of (earlier
    Prince Edward), 47, 246
*With the 6th Airborne Division
    in Normandy*, 145–6
Wood, Hon. Richard, 100, 101
Woodgate, Leslie, 72
World War II, 93–204
Wyman, Jane, 235, 239, 242–3,
    283

YMCA Club, London Central,
    75
Young, Loretta, 251

Zanuck, Darryl, 252, 277
Zanuck, Mrs Darryl, 277
Zweig, Stefan, 291